D1022016

The New American Politician

THE NEW AMERICAN POLITICIAN

Ambition, Entrepreneurship, and the Changing Face of Political Life

BURDETT LOOMIS

Basic Books, Inc., Publishers *New York*

Library of Congress Cataloging-in-Publication Data

Loomis, Burdett A., 1945–
The new American politician.

Includes index.
1. United States. Congress. 2. Legislators—United States. 3. Politicians—United States. 4. United States—Politics and government—1977– I. Title.
JK1051.L76 1988 328.73'073 88–47672
ISBN 0–465–04997–4

Printed in the United States of America
Designed by Vincent Torre
88 89 90 91 HC 9 8 7 6 5 4 3 2 1

For my parents

Mary Anderson Loomis

and Butler Ives Loomis

CONTENTS

PREFACE

AS WITH many research efforts, this one began by accident. In November 1975, as an American Political Science Association Congressional Fellow, I was looking for an office where I could fruitfully spend my fellowship period. I interviewed with a first-term House member, Max Baucus (D-Mont.), and noticed that Paul Simon's (D-Ill.) office was across the hall. I walked in and asked if they might be able to use my services for the next few months. Simon was interested, largely because he was embarking on an effort to draft Hubert Humphrey for president. He needed help, and I was a likely candidate. So, as a Congressional Fellow, I became part of a presidential campaign. When the Humphrey efforts fizzled in June 1976, Congressman Simon graciously allowed me to do some purely scholarly work on the large number of freshmen House members elected in the post-Watergate election of 1974.

Working with the New Members Caucus staff, Professor Jeff Fishel and I conducted a thorough survey of the class, as well as interviewing a considerable number of the freshmen. In 1976, all but two of the class retained their House seats, and it dawned on me that this large class represented a unique opportunity—to study the careers of a *generation* of politicians. This book is not a complete report on that research project; there may well be a monograph in the future that provides exhaustive detail about career choices over, say, a twenty-year period. Rather, I have used my research on the class of '74 from 1976 through 1987 to provide a base for understanding a new breed of national politician—many of whom entered the Congress between 1974 and 1982, a period when membership turnover was consistently high.

This research includes a second survey of the class of '74, conducted in 1980, and dozens of interviews with congressmen, senators, and staff members. In addition, as director of the Congressional Management Project (in 1984), I had the opportunity to supervise the interviewing of most of the members of the class of '82, many of whom saw the "Watergate babies" as models for their own behavior.

Much of the evidence reported here comes from interviews with members of the House and Senate, staff aides, and Capitol Hill journalists. I found the legislators most willing to speak on the record, and a complete list of these interviews can be found at the start of the notes section. Staff members, on the other hand, were granted confidentiality in their interviews. They spoke candidly, but with the guarantee that they would not be identified. Virtually all the interviews were conducted in Washington, D.C. I did not use a tape recorder, although most of the interviewees would have allowed me to do so. Rather, I took notes and wrote up an extensive transcript immediately after each interview.

Substantively, this book focuses on the interrelated notions of policy entrepreneurship and individual enterprise. Most members of Congress can act as entrepreneurs in pushing their favored policies, and the legislators possess adequate resources within their enterprises to move these initiatives along.

The individual politician's ambition holds together a host of entrepreneurial activities and enterprise components. With the decline of the traditional seniority system, the demise of apprenticeship, and the proliferation of party and committee positions, the structure of opportunities after the mid-1970s became much more open. Couple these changes with the new generation's willingness to seek publicity, and what emerges is a context that allows a Richard Gephardt (D-Mo.) to choose between running for House Democratic whip, senator, or president—a set of options that would have been unthinkable before 1974.

What difference does this all make? The basic outlines of our political system—two contentious legislative chambers, partisan position-taking, the sharing of powers between the president and Congress, and an independent judiciary—remain. Congressional backbenchers may be able to make some waves, but their ultimate ability to influence major policy decisions is questionable. Legislators thus tend to focus on proximate goals such as building their enterprises and obtaining publicity. In turn, these activities often serve the cause of individual advancement rather than policy making. The question becomes whether the generation that burst into national politics in the turbulent 1970s can engineer a new set of arrangements that serves the nation's needs as effectively as it serves their particular desires. For example, the same institutions and individuals that reached agreement on immigration and tax reform in 1986 have failed repeatedly to resolve budget deficit and clean air issues.

This book will not fully answer such questions, but it should provide an understanding of the generation of politicians who will wrestle with these and other issues in the years to come.

ACKNOWLEDGMENTS

IN REVIEWING a project that has taken more than a decade to complete, I find myself understanding how award recipients sometimes feel compelled to thank everyone who ever offered them a kind word—from a kindergarten teacher on. Still, there are a lot of folks who have helped me understand what I was doing.

Jeff Fishel provided good advice and helpful insights in the initial work on the class of '74, and he was instrumental in my spending a year in Washington. Likewise, Tom Mann and the American Political Science Association's Congressional Fellowship program were invaluable in providing the opportunity for me to set an interesting research agenda. Paul Peterson and the Brookings Institution gave me a home and an intellectual environment to think through how political careers have changed in recent years.

It was my good fortune to spend a year on the staff of then-Congressman Paul Simon, who offered me the opportunity to examine at first hand how a policy entrepreneur operates. Simon staff members Al Cissell and Terry Michael, among others, demonstrated how a congressional enterprise could prosper over the years. Susan Annable and Joe Crapa, directors of the class of '74's New Members Caucus, were never too busy to provide information about their work and the activities of the class.

Serving as director of the Congressional Management Project (CMP) allowed me to study at first hand the organization of congressional offices and put me in contact with Ira Chaleff and Gary Serota of the Congressional Management Foundation.

Their annual salary surveys, other publications, and general insights have proven consistently beneficial in putting together the picture of new political styles. In addition, Deborah Szekeley provided the crucial financial assistance and original idea that began the CMP.

The financial support of the Dirksen Center for Research on Congressional Leadership and the University of Kansas's Graduate Research Fund is gratefully acknowledged. And the Dirksen Center's Frank Mackamann (now with the Gerald Ford Presidential Library) has been a great friend of congressional scholarship for a decade.

Many political scientists and journalists have made useful comments on my work, demonstrating time and time again the collegiality of those who study the Congress. Any list will be incomplete, but among those who provided useful observations are: Ross Baker, Richard Cohen, Tim Cook, Roger Davidson, Chris Deering, Larry Dodd, Steve Fehr, Irwin Gertzog, George Kundanis, Paul Light, Michael Malbin, Walter Oleszek, Glenn Parker, Pat Patterson, Ken Shepsle, Barbara Sinclair, Steve Smith, Jim Thurber, Charlie Tidmarch, Eric Uslaner, and David Vogler.

My largest debt is, however, to the members of the class of '74, their staff, and their congressional colleagues. Dozens of interviews and two waves of surveys were endured, usually with good humor and cooperation. Almost without exception, my conversations and interviews with these congressmen and staffers have been enjoyable and enlightening.

Also, this book would not have been published without the continued interest and encouragement of Martin Kessler of Basic Books over a six-year period. I am most grateful for his commitment and nourishing comments. Paul Golob has served as a most supportive and generous project editor.

Finally, whether in Washington or Lawrence, Kansas, Michel and Dakota have given me a lot of "up" times to balance off the inevitable "downs" of putting a book together. They have made the whole experience a pleasant one.

The New American Politician

1

Politics and Politicians in a New Era

FROM the *New York Times,* August 8, 1986:

> Campaigns for six Democrats running for the Senate stand to profit considerably from a $1 million Hollywood fund-raising party next month starring Barbra Streisand, who has not sung in public for six years, and Robin Williams, the television and film comedian. Tickets, available by invitation only, will cost $5000 a couple, for a limit of 400 people. Candidates sharing in the proceeds include . . . Bob Edgar of Pennsylvania and Tim Wirth of Colorado.[1]

How time flies when you're having fun. Scarcely a decade earlier Bob Edgar (D-Pa.) and Tim Wirth (D-Colo.) would have welcomed a five-dollar contribution. Fifty bucks would have been a windfall and five hundred dollars almost beyond hope. In 1974 Edgar won a seat in the U.S. House of Representatives for the bargain-basement price of $38,819. Wirth, an effective fund-raiser ever since his initial 1974 campaign, spent all of $134,000 to join him. In 1986 Edgar raised and spent more than one hundred times as much—$3,905,186—in his losing bid for one of Pennsylvania's two Senate seats. Running in Colorado, a state with a third of Pennsylvania's population, Wirth matched Edgar's funding, spending $3.8 million in his successful 1986 Senate race.[2]

Still in their forties, Edgar, Wirth, and a horde of other national politicians have shaped a new era in American political life. Weaned on the Kennedy presidency, the civil rights movement, Earth Day, Vietnam, and Watergate, this cohort has produced a new style of policy-based activism that emphasizes both a serious consideration of issues and a fresh approach to the traditional rules of the game. Publicity-oriented and independent, the post-Watergate political generation has restructured both the process and the results of American politics. By the same token, years of working on Capitol Hill have affected the "Watergate babies" as they have matured and risen to influential positions.

Writing in 1987, Chris Matthews, former press secretary to Speaker of the House Tip O'Neill (D-Mass.), concluded that

> the American electorate sent a "new breed" of legislator to Washington [in 1974]: young, brash, independent of its elders and their system. It was the year of Watergate. . . . Rejecting cronyism and parochialism, [voters] elected a slate of freshman candidates pledged to a new order of ethics and independence. . . . More than a decade later, those who campaigned against Watergate in 1974 and 1976 remain the new kids on the political block.[3]

However oversimplified Matthews's assessment may be, the results of the 1974 election continue to define—inside and outside the Congress—a break point in American politics.

Matthews and other pundits are instrumental in keeping these ideas—of a new era and a new breed—alive. In 1984

Congressional Quarterly devoted eight pages to the Watergate babies—the House class of '74.[4] The *Wall Street Journal* offered a similar front-page article, commemorating the tenth anniversary of this group. When a Tim Wirth or a Tom Harkin (D-Iowa) wins a Senate seat in the mid-1980s, the press reminds its readers of the senator-elect's post-Watergate lineage. Even after losing a Senate race and moving into arms-control lobbying, Bob Edgar is still, according to a 1987 *National Journal* headline, a "Watergate Baby."[5] No other contemporary group of legislators has received this kind of continuing attention. The congressional class of '74 remains distinct, well over a decade after its arrival on Capitol Hill.

Although scholars continue to debate the overall impact of Watergate on the 1974 electoral results,[6] members of Congress, the media, and the Washington community view that election as a dividing line in national politics. Not only did the members of the heavily Democratic House "freshman class" serve immediate notice that they were a force to be reckoned with, but they also demonstrated the skills that allowed them to take advantage of the great opportunities that the decentralized Congress and high levels of membership turnover afforded them, both in the aftermath of the 1974 elections and throughout the 1970s.

The impact of this group, for the most part, has been due to the emergence of effective individual politicians, like a Senator Chris Dodd (D-Conn.) or a Congressman Henry Waxman (D-Calif.), who have sought creative ways to gain major policy-making roles. As one Democratic leadership aide notes, "Every time we want something done, we go to one of these guys. It's like the teacher always knows the kids with the right answers and they're the same kids every time." The *New York Times*'s Martin Tolchin observes that the "new leaders are less patient, more pragmatic, and take greater risks than their counterparts of a decade or two ago," and they have moved into positions of power "by doing the heavy legislative lifting, tackling the onerous, time-consuming tasks."[7]

In brief, this post-Watergate off-year election resulted in a Democratic landslide that was to alter the composition of the Congress and introduce to the public a new generation of attractive, impatient, and issue-oriented national politicians. These individuals moved almost immediately to center stage in our continuing political drama and have remained there ever since.

Thus, John Glenn (D-Ohio) and Gary Hart (D-Colo.) first won their Senate seats in 1974, as did Dale Bumpers (D-Ark.) and Patrick Leahy (D-Vt.); current Senators Charles Grassley (R-Iowa), Paul Simon (D-Ill.), Chris Dodd, Max Baucus (D-Mont.), Larry Pressler (R-S.D.), Paul Tsongas (D-Mass.), and Robert Kasten (D-Wisc.) all entered the House of Representatives that year, on their way up the political ladder; so did the popular two-term Democratic governor of Michigan, James Blanchard. The House found in its ranks a host of issue activists whose interests ranged from the environment (Henry Waxman), to foreign policy (Stephen Solarz [D-N.Y.]) to abortion policy (Henry Hyde [R-Ill.]). As part of the Democratic majority, Waxman and Solarz, together with most of their party colleagues, would soon—through good fortune and substantial political skills—chair subcommittees and thus enter the increasingly important "middle management" that is central to running the contemporary Congress.

The Class of 1974: Movers and Models

Political observers, whether in journalism, academia, or government, are all too apt to label unusual events as watersheds of historic proportions. Within the Congress this is especially true, given the glacial pace of most legislative change. Nevertheless, the Congress does undergo an occasional fundamental transformation, which profoundly alters both its internal power structure and its external relationships (such as with the president and with home constituencies).

Although the 1970s produced no single confrontation as dramatic as the 1910 insurrection that removed Speaker Joseph Cannon and ushered in the era of a dominant seniority system, they did result in changes that profoundly transformed the politics of Congress and its members. Indeed, the abrupt ousting of three senior committee chairmen in January 1975 may well rival the successful challenge to Speaker Cannon's authority. As Tip O'Neill notes, "In all my years in the House, this was one of the few times when I was genuinely caught by surprise."[8]

With the 1974 election and the subsequent organization of the 94th Congress, the three key elements of Watergate-era changes—fresh personnel, the outside environment, and the internal distribution of power on Capitol Hill—came together to fashion a qualitatively different legislature and an altered set of career choices for legislators.

The class of '74 has made its mark in two related ways. First, the class itself, with 103 newcomers in 1974, has been a real force. Its size, long-term electoral success, and talents have ensured that many of its members have become important national political figures. Second, and perhaps as significant, is the impact of these politicians as models for succeeding congressional cohorts.

With only a few exceptions, the class of '74 was young. In a House where the mean age in 1974 was over fifty-three, the members first elected in 1974 were thirteen years younger. This striking youth has had a continuing impact within the House; as of 1986, the thirty remaining members of the 1974 group had an average age of forty-nine, as compared to the representatives first elected in 1986, whose mean age was forty-six. With youth came inexperience; considerably fewer than half of the 1974 class had any legislative experience, the lowest percentage in more than twenty-five years. As former Congressman Toby Moffett (D-Conn.) observes, "We were different . . . not only much younger for the most part, but much *newer* to politics."

In addition, as Kevin Phillips and Tom Edsall have argued, the 1974 elections solidified the Democratic hold on the House of Representatives, perhaps aborting a nascent pro-Republican realignment.[9] Of special importance were the inroads that Democrats made in previously solid GOP territory—winning forty-nine previously Republican seats, often in suburban districts like those captured by Tim Wirth and Bob Edgar.

The arrival of large numbers of newcomers with little legislative experience allowed societal forces to exert great influence on the Congress. Not only did the class of '74 hold together as a group when voting on major reform issues, but its unified presence stood as strong testimony to the perceived need for institutional change. The newcomers created neither the agenda for reform nor the outside pressures for change. Rather, they served as messengers from the public to the Congress about how far reform might be pushed. More than a decade after their arrival, members of the class of '74 retain an identity with the institutional reforms that fundamentally altered the rules of the policy game. Lobbyist Daniel Dutko noted in 1987 that the 1974 entrants "had a charter to see to it that Congress didn't get run by muscle. . . . That started a move toward a development of a new way of doing things."[10]

The conditions behind political change and the nature of that change itself are significant only if its impact is substantial and long lived. The important effects of the class of '74 fall into these categories. First of all, the Watergate babies have survived impressively, in both their initial reelection bids (almost unanimously) and their subsequent electoral challenges. For all their reformist origins, the 1974 entrants have acted pragmatically in shoring up their local political bases. In fact, they discovered that their office resources could serve them both as policy activists and sensitive representatives of their districts.[11] To this end, many 1974 newcomers found that developing sophisticated local political enterprises could give them a great deal of flexibility in pursuing their policy goals on Capitol Hill.

No matter how large and cohesive a single entering legislative cohort may be, its members can have little lasting impact unless they profoundly affect their colleagues and the entire context of national policy making. The class of '74 meets these criteria. Its members have helped to alter radically the role of the rank-and-file legislator and have contributed to the public style of policy articulation, which emphasizes the importance of agenda setting to the point that the notion has become a cliché. House majority whip Tony Coelho (D-Calif.), perhaps the most effective contemporary practitioner of internal congressional politics, concludes that the class of '74 "set an example for other classes, by striking out as individuals and developing their own power centers. They became independent and they didn't become beholden to the leadership."[12]

At the same time, they emphasized issues and understood them with a speed that impressed and puzzled their senior colleagues. Former Congressman Richard Bolling (D-Mo.), another keen observer of congressional talent, notes, "These guys understand the complex. They're comfortable with it. With computers, technology, and all that. They're a different breed of cat."

Bolling was right, and so were the legislators and pundits who saw the class as different in its approach to the media and in its formative experiences. More than any other political figure, John Kennedy dominated their political consciousness. As then Congressman Tim Wirth concluded in 1984,

> We were the children of Vietnam, not children of World War II. We were products of television, not of print. We

> were products of computer politics, not courthouse politics. And we were the reflections of JFK as president, not FDR. We were the first class that was like that, and now the whole place is.[13]

With such a talent for providing a summarizing set of quotes, it is no wonder that Wirth obtained a lot of press attention and eventually won a Senate seat. And there is a lot of truth in Wirth's assessment. Nevertheless, it misses the sense of change within the class, and the way Congress molds its members, rather than the reverse. Congressman Tom Foley (D-Wash.), first elected to the House in the Johnson landslide of 1964, places the class in a somewhat different perspective. Sympathetically, yet with an unmistakable edge, Foley commented in 1982 that a lot of class of '74 members

> see themselves as the "new model" member of Congress—the first with style, with tailoring, with media awareness. The first who knew what an i.c. [integrated circuit] is. They see themselves as qualitatively removed from those who came before. We [in 1964] came in thinking we were building a new model too.

For the "middle management" members of the House and the Senate, most of whom arrived on Capitol Hill in the 1970s, the very predominance of this independent, policy-activist style causes continuing difficulties, as Foley points out: "At worst, these guys say in effect, 'It doesn't matter. I am my own party,' [and] they emphasize their personal qualities." Although the Congress is a permeable institution that responds to societal changes, it is also a mediating body that seasons the raw talents attracted to national politics. The real capacities of the Watergate generation can scarcely be questioned. Its members have generally survived and prospered, often against long odds. The outstanding problem for this group is whether its members can help the Congress overcome the independence that they have practiced and encouraged in others. As David Broder concedes, a "New Breed, they are. But there's still the old need . . . to find enough followers to allow anyone to lead."[14]

Entrepreneurs, Enterprises, and Ambition

On December 1, 1975, my first day at work on Capitol Hill, I quickly discovered how contemporary politicians operate at the national level. There I sat, in the overcrowded office of Congressman Paul Simon (D-Ill.), then a first-term member of Congress, drafting a letter to the newly created Federal Election Commission (FEC). My task was simple: to request an FEC opinion on the guidelines and limitations that applied to Simon's efforts to establish a "Draft Hubert Humphrey for President" committee.

Like a good staffer I "plowed right ahead" (to borrow one of Simon's favorite phrases), never really questioning what business a freshman congressman had in organizing an attempt to piece together a presidential draft. Rather, I wrote the letter, followed it up, and for four months served as the coordinator of a murky, ill-defined "Draft Humphrey" effort that collapsed mercifully after Jimmy Carter wrapped up the nomination in the last big set of June primaries.

Only upon reflection did the significance of this work dawn upon me. Simon was exhibiting key characteristics of a new political style that he and his colleagues have developed since the mid-1970s. First, he did not wait to be invited into the higher reaches of presidential politics. Rather, he acted as an entrepreneur to press his interests, which encompassed both candidate preferences and policy goals. Second, Simon understood that entrepreneurs need resources. Eager, optimistic, and enthusiastic, I represented a politically useful resource. Equally important, my modest stipends came from an American Political Science Association fellowship, not from federal funds, thus freeing me to work openly on partisan politics. So it was that I became part of the Simon "enterprise," which comprised his office staff, his campaign organization, and a host of former staff members and confederates.[15] Transcending any formal organization, it revolved totally around the person and the unfolding political career of Congressman Simon.

Ten years after entering the House of Representatives, Simon won a Senate seat. By then, Simon's enterprise had grown so large that his Washington, D.C., victory party occupied a large private club and spilled over onto the street outside, where legions of his supporters (many from Illinois) waited in long lines to congratulate the senator-elect. Scarcely missing a beat, Simon declared his candidacy for president in 1987, only three years after reaching the Senate, and his enterprise grew exponentially, if temporarily, through the presidential campaign season. In addition, three members of the class of '74—former Congressmen Berkely Bedell (D-Iowa), Bob Edgar, and Floyd Fithian (D-Ind.)—became prominent aides in the Simon presidential organization.

Despite being somewhat older and considerably more experienced than most recent entrants into the Congress, Paul Simon nevertheless embodies many of the central characteristics of a "new style" of national politician. Simon has consistently cared a great deal about a wide range of issues, from enforcing the Helsinki accords to obtaining black lung benefits for coal miners. Just as consistently, Simon, a former newspaper publisher, has sought publicity to promote both his favored issues and his involvement with them. In addition, he has grasped the importance of resources—of staff, funds, position, and information—that are essential for allowing him independence to pursue his own agenda, which may or may not mesh with the preferences of party or committee leaders. Finally, and of great importance, Simon's substantial (but not atypical) ambition, both for higher office and for policy influence, has provided the glue to bind together the disparate elements of his personal style.

POLICY ENTREPRENEURS: ADVOCATES AND BROKERS

More than any other single metaphor, that of the politician as entrepreneur captures the essence of how most top-level officials operate today, in or out of the Congress. Secretary of Education William Bennett is no less a policy entrepreneur than is Senator Bill Bradley (D-N.J.). What has changed within the Congress is a context that fosters more entrepreneurial behavior from more legislators than ever before.

Relatively few politicians have succeeded at both issue advocacy, the public side of entrepreneurial activity, and its more private face of brokerage among interests.[16] Few push for the acceptance of a truly new idea. Rather, they tend to endorse, repackage, or resurrect concepts and ideas that either come from the outside (for example, academia) or have previously circulated within the Congress. Policy entrepreneurs are often both patient and persistent as they reshape policy solutions to fit emerging political conditions. Again, Paul Simon offers an apt illustration.

In the late 1970s, then Congressman Simon became alarmed by the declining status of foreign language education in the United States. This problem affected both elites—such as foreign service officers, who often could not speak the language of the country where they were stationed—and the public at large, which was faced with severe reductions in language training in high schools and colleges. Simon was convinced that as a nation the United States was paying a growing price in trade, security, and culture for its increasingly monolingual approach to the rest of the world.

Ever the entrepreneur, Simon moved beyond the House of Representatives to publicize the issue. He successfully urged

Jimmy Carter to appoint a presidential commission to study the question. With Simon as a member, the commission undertook more than a year of research and made its report in October 1979. In and of itself, establishing a commission meant little. "[On] Capitol Hill . . . most members of the House and Senate yawned," Simon notes. "[The report's] ultimate impact will not be clear for several years as its recommendations are analyzed, refined, debated, and—I hope—confronted."[17]

Not content to let one more presidential commission's recommendations sit on the shelf, Simon persisted in campaigning for major foreign language reforms. Drawing on commission findings and his own research, Simon wrote a book that put forth the case for revitalized language training and awareness. That effort, *The Tongue-Tied American,* was well received within the educational community. It received especially positive comments in the national press, often getting better play on the editorial page than in the book review section.

Inside the Congress, Simon kept a watchful eye for a legislative opening to enact at least some of the commission's recommendations. That window of opportunity appeared in early 1983, as national concern grew over a crisis in science and math education. As he attached foreign language provisions to a "can't miss" set of science and math proposals, Simon's role shifted from advocate to broker. From his strategic vantage point as a subcommittee chair on the Education and Labor Committee, Simon could help ensure that this package held together.

Although Simon has always kept his share of policy irons in the fire, the five-year campaign for foreign language policy change absorbed a great deal of his attention and effort. Sheer persistence is a crucial part of much entrepreneurial achievement.[18] Simon's efforts were notable in their almost complete success, but they differed only in degree from the activities of many, if not most, other legislators. Increasingly, individual members of Congress have developed the capacity to place their favored issues on the legislative agenda. With almost half the

House Democrats chairing a committee or subcommittee and with virtually all majority-party senators occupying similar slots, even reluctant legislators have the opportunity to act as entrepreneurs. In turn, this limits the influence of committee chairs. Within the Senate today, for example, such a position confers essentially "positive control" over items that chairs wish to place on the agenda, not the ability to obstruct their colleagues' major initiatives.[19]

LEGISLATORS AS ENTERPRISES

Whether for a fledgling congressman or a hardened veteran, the enterprise concept captures the mix of personal goals, substantive issues, and structure that grows up around almost all national politicians. Policy entrepreneurs need vehicles and resources to promote their activities. From one point of view, legislative activists can usefully be depicted as independent operators who attempt to affect agendas or bring coalitions together. To a certain extent this is true; a Richard Gephardt (D-Mo.), a Bill Bradley, or a Phil Gramm (R-Tex.) does act on his own, expecting to receive personal credit for his entrepreneurial work. Nevertheless, even the least staff-dependent policy entrepreneurs must rely on their legislative assistants and committee personnel for a wide range of information and services.

Once again, it is the Congress of the mid-1970s that serves as the cutting point between legislative eras. The growth of staffs and other congressional resources in the approximate 1960–75 period permits the consideration of all members of Congress, and especially policy entrepreneurs, as "the head of an enterprise—an organization consisting of anywhere between eight or ten to well over one hundred subordinates."[20] The great usefulness of this "enterprise" notion arises from its capacity to encompass the individual member of Congress and his or her staff (see figure 1.1). There is no need to determine where a member's own activities end and those of the staff begin.

FIGURE 1.1

The Congressional Enterprise

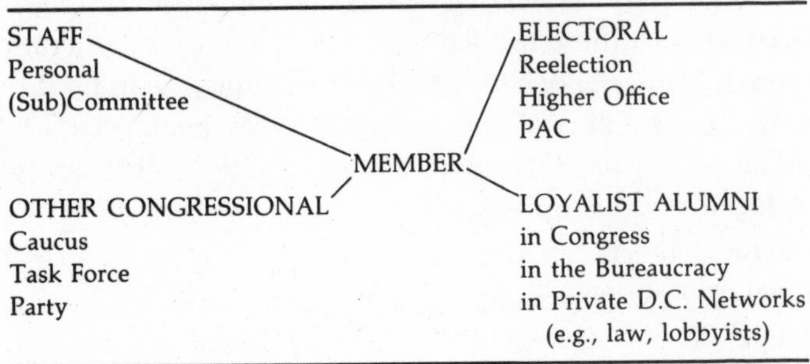

Rather, given the requirements of personal loyalty and staff subordination, the legislators and their aides can be viewed as single units, however complex (or confused) their operations.

Although legislative operations have many facets, "the core of any congressional enterprise," observe Robert Salisbury and Kenneth Shepsle,

> is the *personal staff.* This is so in part because the personal staff is unequivocally and entirely dependent on the member for hiring and promotion. Its explicit responsibility is to serve the member's needs and interests, and its primary normative commitment is loyalty to the member.[21]

For a few senior legislators, the personal office may lose its primacy within the enterprise, but for the vast majority it is central to almost everything that they hope to accomplish.

Beyond the base of a personal office, there are great variations in congressional enterprises. Senator Robert Dole (R-Kans.), for example, can rely on resources from his position as minority leader, from his senior rank on the Agriculture and Finance committees, and from his own large political action committee (PAC), Campaign America. In addition, his almost thirty years in Congress, three national campaigns, and a stint as chair of the Republican National Committee provide him with a wide network of alumni within the Washington community. Conversely, most low-seniority members of the House can count on little more than their personal office resources, although many junior legislators have become major figures in the growing number of informal caucuses organized since the mid-1970s.

Legislative enterprises extend well beyond Capitol Hill in three related ways. First, increasing numbers of staffers serve in district or state offices. Second, many incumbents' campaigns exist as ongoing organizations. As one electoral consultant puts it, "Whether or not you have an opponent . . . your campaign strategy is in place. Now, essentially, it is a full-time operation."[22] Third, to sustain such organizations, both senators and representatives have begun to accumulate large campaign war chests. More than fifty House members, for example, had over $250,000 cash on hand *after* the 1986 elections.[23] In a related vein, growing numbers of legislators have formed their own PACs. As with excess campaign funds, much of the PAC money is directed toward the election efforts of others, including both other members of Congress and candidates for local office. PACs and "full-time" campaigns serve an important maintenance function for a congressional enterprise. With these repositories for funds, legislators can expand their staffs as well as provide avenues for continuing financial support from their allies.

In assessing congressional enterprises, it is important to bear in mind that they encourage—even demand—a good deal of shifting around among their separate parts. Personal office staff members often leave the official payroll for temporary campaign work. During 1987, for example, thirteen of Paul Simon's staffers split their positions between his official Senate payroll and his presidential campaign.[24] For better or worse, the enterprise revolves around its principal, and the resources serve the goals, ambitions, and—on occasion—whims of that individual.

THE GLUE OF AMBITION

Ambition is as American as apple pie, yet we distrust it profoundly. On the one hand, ambition is "the fuel of achievement" that usefully prods individuals into persistent attempts to gain their ends.[25] Thus, without ambition we would be a poorer society, in terms of artistic accomplishments, private institutions (from IBM to the NAACP), and public achievements (from the Constitution to the New Deal). At the same time, Joseph Epstein notes, "A person called ambitious is likely to arouse anxiety, for in our day anyone so called is thought to be threatening, possibly a trifle neurotic."[26] And dangerous, the Constitution's framers would add.

Politicians face a special set of problems here. Their ambitions are so public. At a minimum, they must continually seek approval from their constituents. To advance, they must impress new and wider audiences with their strength and competence. Always lurking on the other side of advancement is the real threat of failure—both political and personal. At the same time, most top-level elected officials are comfortable with their ambitions and those of their colleagues. As House majority leader Thomas Foley observes, "Most people who get into politics have great ego strength, to put it nicely."

Political institutions channel these ambitions by providing a "structure of opportunities" within which politicians operate.[27] From 1910 through 1970, the legislative structure of opportunities became increasingly restrictive, largely due to the Congress's strict adherence to the seniority system. Representatives either ran for the Senate within their first four or five terms or hunkered down for the long, predictable journey toward major positions of power in the House.[28] In addition, only senators could realistically hope to seek the presidency from Capitol Hill. Thus, Richard Nixon and John Kennedy, members of the House class of '46, soon abandoned the lower chamber for the "presidential incubator" of the Senate.[29]

The opportunity structure has become increasingly fluid, as witnessed by the serious presidential candidacies of House members Morris Udall (D-Ariz.), in 1976, Jack Kemp (R-N.Y.) in 1988, and Richard Gephardt in 1988. Both Kemp and Gephardt have passed up attractive (if difficult) Senate races to mount presidential bids. In a related vein, such House members as Paul Simon and Tim Wirth abandoned powerful subcommittee chairmanships to seek Senate seats. This exemplifies a kind of undifferentiated ambition that may steer a politician toward both insider openings, such as party and committee slots, and the obvious outside targets for advancement of the Senate and the presidency.

Political Change and National Institutions

At the heart of political change is a set of two to three thousand national politicians who must react to new technologies, altered power alignments, and shifting voting coalitions. Given the constitutional requirement that all House members and a third of the Senate must face the electorate every two years, the Congress is, almost by definition, especially responsive to changes in the society at large.[30] Such responsiveness does not always provide for happy or successful solutions to difficult policy problems, but few serious issues escape congressional scrutiny and action—regardless of how (or if) the legislature eventually chooses to act.

Within the complexity of the Congress and its political environment, the long-term impact of most off-year congressional elections—no matter how substantial the immediate results—is extremely limited. Even the 1946 Republican sweep was little more than a blip in the post-1933 congressional dominance by Democrats. The 1974 elections, however, constitute a major exception to this generalization.

The politics and results of the 1974 congressional elections represent the intersection of three major dimensions of political change. First were broad, secular trends that came to a head in the aftermath of the Vietnam War and Watergate. The political system had served the United States well neither internationally nor domestically, and although the sources of discontent ran deeper than just these two specific issues, the war and the ethical implications of the Watergate affair posed serious questions for all national politicians.[31] Questions about inflation, energy policy, the environment, and the overall role of government also demanded responses, regardless of who was elected in 1974. In addition, the public expressed very little faith in the ability of any political institution—particularly the Congress—to generate effective solutions to increasingly complex policy problems.[32]

Perhaps more immediately significant to members of Congress was the second dimension of change—the internal legislative developments of the 1969–75 period. The class of '74 entered a Congress dramatically different from the institution that a handful of senior party and committee leaders had dominated for the previous half century. Major procedural changes were in place by the mid-1970s entrance of the post-Watergate class.[33]

Finally, wholesale change rarely occurs in politics without substantial turnover—new faces who can infuse an institution with new ideas, different voting coalitions, and, in some cases, a profound sense of fear.[34] Many committed, careerist politicians, including veteran state legislators like California's Waxman and Illinois's Simon, first won national office in 1974, but such professionals were the exception, not the rule, among the newly elected officials. To the contrary, it was the large proportion of amateurs and reformers that best characterizes this group.[35] While a Waxman or a Simon could bring the perspective of considerable governmental experience to his new job, a majority of 1974 entrants possessed no such mediating background. For them, electoral and legislative politics required extensive on-the-job training. In fact, even after more than a decade of congressional service, many members of the class of '74 continue to reject the idea that they are "professional politicians."

THE CLIMATE OF NATIONAL POLITICS: BEYOND VIETNAM AND WATERGATE

Since the early 1970s, the seminal events of Vietnam and Watergate have profoundly affected the politics of the legislative branch and its relations with the executive.[36] Trying to disentangle the strands of influence of these national crises on the Congress is not productive, especially when it comes to explaining the evolution of political styles. Rather, of real importance are the broad effects that Watergate and Vietnam had in decreasing the public's general support for all political institutions, and the Congress in particular.

As the members of the legislative class of '74 laid out their plans in 1973 and began to campaign in the first months of 1974, the public's confidence in the Congress had fallen to historically low levels. Only about one person in four gave the Congress a positive rating in early 1974.[37] This contrasts dramatically with the extraordinarily high ratings (64 percent positive) accorded the institution in the salad days of the Great Society. Richard Fenno's dramatic findings of Congress-bashing by House members in their home districts testify eloquently to the growing willingness of many legislators to promote themselves at their institution's expense.[38] The public's low regard for the Congress does not, in itself, explain the rise of the entrepreneurial style among members, but it does provide one of the underlying conditions for individualistic behavior.

Coupled with the growing distrust of political institutions

in the 1970s was what Kevin Phillips has labeled the "Balkanization" of American society. Whatever the reasons behind this rise of particularism, specific segments of the Balkanized society—whether based on "ethnicity, regionalism, selfish economic interests, sects, [or] neighborhoods"[39]—have aggressively sought to win policy concessions from the very governmental institutions they distrust. In addition, societal fragmentation affects politicians through partisan dealignment and decomposition. Very few of those entering the Congress of the 1970s came from strong party backgrounds, and even the handful that did, such as Congressmen Marty Russo (D-Ill.) and the late Adam Benjamin (D-Ind.), and Senator Alfonse D'Amato (R-N.Y.), have adapted to the requirements of a Congress that rewards individualistic behavior as well as teamwork.

At the same time, the representation of diverse interests grew more professional and centralized in Washington.[40] Not only were increasing numbers of interests organized, but their focus sharpened on Washington, especially on gaining access to the permeable Congress (often by hiring an ex-legislator, whose numbers grew rapidly in the 1970s).

CHANGE WITHIN THE CONGRESS: THE RISE OF THE INDIVIDUAL

Much time and effort have gone into detailing the array of institutional changes that the Congress adopted during the 1970s. And rightly so. Cumulatively, the House, and to a lesser extent the Senate, changed more in this period than at any time since the 1910 revolt against Speaker Cannon and the 1913 adoption of the Seventeenth Amendment, mandating the popular election of senators. Formal regulations, informal rules of the game, and the distribution of resources all changed dramatically within the decade. In the end, these developments greatly advantaged individual legislators at the expense of the power of party leaders and, particularly, committee chairs.

In the late 1950s a member of Congress could assert, with little chance of contradiction, that: "All committee chairmen are despots. Some of them are benevolent despots . . . but in any case they are despotic. They can run their committees as they see fit, and they usually do."[41] The ability of strong committee chairs to dominate the House, and to a lesser extent the Senate, reflected a system that was internally undemocratic and fragmented only to the extent that a couple of dozen key committee "despots" ran their fiefdoms with a variety of personal styles. No contemporary committee leader can realistically hope to exert despotic power, although some, such as Energy and Commerce's Congressman John Dingell (D-Mich.), clearly covet the opportunity.

Democratization of the congressional committee structure would have had only a limited impact on political styles if legislators had not had the staff and resources necessary to take advantage of the many changes. This, however, was scarcely a problem, either in terms of personnel or many modern office amenities, such as WATS lines, computers, and automated communications. Congressional staffs expanded at record rates during the 1970s, both for committees and within the personal offices of individual legislators.[42] Although staffing grew throughout the Congress, House members have benefited the most. By 1980, each one could hire up to eighteen full-time personal staff members and four part-time workers. Compare this to Donald Matthews's 1960 description of staffing a typical Senate office, placed in its own historical perspective:

> Some of the fastest-growing "bureaucracies" in Washington are to be found in the Senate Office Building. Within the memory of Senate old-timers, a typical senator's office staff consisted of an executive secretary and a typist or two. The average postwar senator, with his vastly increased work load, has a staff of a dozen or so people squeezed into his three- or four-room office suite.[43]

As if the increase in resources and the democratization of the Congress were not enough, many House members and some senators developed a new legislative tool, which complemented both the committee system and the growth of staff. During the 1970s, dozens of unofficial caucuses were organized around such interests as race (Congressional Black Caucus), gender (Congressional Caucus on Women's Issues), region (Northeast-Midwest Congressional Coalition), industry (Auto Task Force), and issues (arms control). Although some congressional veterans do take part in the activities of these groups, relative newcomers have generally played the major leadership roles.

Junior legislators have also benefited from the changes in the unwritten norms, or "folkways," of Congress that took place in the 1960s and 1970s. All senators and representatives were affected, but younger House members were especially advantaged. By the mid-1970s, freshman legislators were encouraged, even expected, to participate actively within both Senate and House. With such expectations for activism and a loosening of the straitjacket of apprenticeship came increasingly diverse individual styles. Such stylistic variety has complemented the structural fragmentation of the Congress, thus opening up new career development possibilities for imaginative policy activists.

Since the 1970s, national politicians within the Congress, from top leaders to freshman backbenchers, have found themselves more on display than ever before. First, internal reforms required considerably increased congressional openness across the board. In the House, members could force recorded votes with relative ease, and from 1973 on, such tallies took much less time due to the introduction of "voting by electronic device." Although the smaller Senate did not bow to such alleged technological advances, its recorded votes also rose sharply during the 1970s. In short, the legislators opted to create a much more extended set of recorded positions on a wide array of issues.

Similar changes profoundly affected committee operations in both chambers, to the extent that well over 80 percent of all bill-writing (or markup) sessions were open to the public by 1975. For example, the House Appropriations Committee, which had allowed public scrutiny in none of its 1970 meetings, opened its 1975 proceedings 94 percent of the time.[44] Although subsequent Congresses have rediscovered the merits of privacy in some circumstances, the norm of openness remains firmly entrenched.

On a different front, the adoption of campaign reform legislation in 1971 and 1974 produced relatively stringent campaign-reporting requirements along with an independent agency, the Federal Election Commission (FEC), to monitor compliance. A candidate's expenditures and, especially, contribution patterns could become campaign issues. Similarly, the Congress adopted some reasonably specific financial disclosure requirements that gave openings to the press and potential opponents. Together, these reporting rules placed greater emphasis on the member of Congress as an individual, separate from the institution.

In sum, the Congress became a much more open place during the 1970s. Technology (television and electronic voting) and the currents of reform combined to create a legislative body in which many members—not just a few top leaders and potential presidential candidates—would regularly seek publicity as an important way of doing business. In addition, openness has meant that more individuals, whether inside or outside the Congress, have access to information—on policies, procedures, and bill status—that previous generations of congressional leaders could control. The number and variety of important legislative players has increased, as has the uncertainty of their game.

REPLACEMENT: HOW MUCH CHANGE IN CHANGING THE GUARD?

In 1980 David Broder published *Changing of the Guard: Power and Leadership in America,*[45] which lyrically described the rise of the next governing generation, including several activists of the class of '74. Broder was often prescient: the emerging leaders he identified are by and large the ones who have begun, a decade later, to hold the reins of power. At the same time, one wonders, How much change? As much as when the generation of post–World War II politicians came to power in the 1960s, replacing those whose formative experiences had been of World War I? As each Congress reorganizes itself, the guard changes, but the effects are typically at the margins. Not in the 1970s, however. Career legislators retired in droves, which provided an infusion of new blood to a Congress that was primed to offer real opportunities to its incoming members.

With high levels of turnover in the late 1970s, class of '74 entrants found themselves in a relatively short queue as they waited to ascend to positions of power. Indeed, of the 535 members of Congress who took their oath of office in 1981, only one in eight could claim to have served during both the Kennedy and Reagan presidencies. And more than 60 percent of the 535 had served for no more than six years.

During the 1970s the Congress became somewhat younger and considerably less experienced in governmental service (see table 1.1). However, even with wholesale replacements and the upsets of the 1974 elections, the average age of legislators did not fall all that drastically. Much more striking was their declining seniority—especially within the majority party in the Senate. In 1971 majority Democrats averaged twelve or more years of previous Senate service. Ten years later, Ronald Reagan began his administration with majority Republicans who averaged only slightly more than six years of Senate experience and whose median tenure was a truly remarkable three years. If the House Democratic queue was shrinking during the post-Watergate era, the waiting period for Republicans to achieve an influential position in the Senate was, as of the early 1980s, almost nonexistent.

These dual turnovers, of new members and partisan control (of the Senate), accelerated changes in congressional style.

TABLE 1.1

Members of Congress, Changes in Age and Tenure, 1971 and 1981

	Average Age		Median Years of Service		Careerists (10+ years)		Average Years of Service, Chairs	
Chamber	1971	1981	1971	1981	1971	1981	1971	1981
House								
All	51.9	48.4	8.0	6.0	35%	24%	26.4	20.6
Democrats			8.0	6.0	42	27		
Republicans			6.0	4.0	24	20		
Senate								
All	56.1	51.7	10.0	4.5	45	24	19.6	9.9
Democrats			12.0	7.0	54	35		
Republicans			6.5	3.0	33	15		

SOURCE: Compiled by author from *1971 CQ Almanac* and *1981 CQ Almanac* (Washington, D. C.: Congressional Quarterly Inc., 1971, 1981).

Beyond advancing quickly themselves, relatively junior members of the House and Senate became models for their even less senior colleagues. At the same time, both chambers lost a great deal of their informal institutional memory between 1974 and 1980. National Public Radio's Cokie Roberts makes the point that

> significantly, the class of 1974 [and subsequent new members] did not take part in the writing of the War Powers Act [1973] or . . . the Budget Reform Act, so they don't have any memory of the entire process of pulling influence back down to their end of Pennsylvania Avenue, and this is important later on. . . . That was my whole angle on Gramm-Rudman. That they weren't taking responsibility. Once I went to the Speaker and asked him why this was happening, and he said, "I don't understand it. . . . Don't they remember the War Powers Act? The Budget Act?"

Of course the newer members remembered the legislation, but they had stood on the outside as these laws were written. A decade later, they controlled many of the levers of power.

A New Political Style

Beginning with the class of '74, a new generation of leaders rushed to the fore of American politics and brought with them a new way of doing business. In the late 1980s these individuals have come to shape the political landscape, for better or worse. They have established an issue-oriented, publicity-conscious style that differs dramatically from that produced within the seniority-dominated Congress of the 1950s. This style encourages politicians to reach out to national constituencies from a succession of legislative positions that range from subcommittees to party leadership slots and informal caucus chairs. The central elements of this new style include expertise and the willingness to work hard, often at the expense of comity, collegiality, and compromise.[46]

These traits—expertise and hard work—allowed post-1974 legislators to pursue the key proximate goals of (1) obtaining publicity; (2) setting the policy agenda; (3) participating fully within the Congress; and (4) establishing large enterprises that move well beyond personal office staff. These goals can be achieved by virtually all members of Congress, and they can provide some sense of achievement even if full-blown legislative victories are not forthcoming. Indeed, these proximate goals relate directly to the overarching objectives of most members of Congress: advancement, good policy, internal power, and reelection.[47] Unfortunately, the goal of producing good policy often becomes an orphan on Capitol Hill. The proximate goals are more easily translated into advancement, power, and reelection than they are into policy achievements. The jury remains out on whether a Congress of policy entrepreneurs can temper its members' independence with enough teamwork to produce coherent policies. So far, the outlook is far from promising.

Whatever happens, the Watergate babies and their colleagues have stood center stage since the 1970s. Given their number, relative youth, and talents, they will continue to shape the nature of national politics well into the next century.

2

The Class of 1974: The First Hundred Days and Beyond

UNDERSTANDING the impact of the class of 1974 requires some attention to its earliest days, when its members discovered that the combination of raw numbers, rudimentary organization, and naive optimism could profoundly affect congressional structure and process—to say nothing of luck and the ability to take advantage of good fortune. As former Congressman Ned Pattison (D-N.Y.) reminisced:

> There were a series of lucky coincidences for us as a class. One thing built on another. It was just luck that the first [Democratic] Caucus vote was on Jimmy Malloy [as Doorkeeper of the House]. The class elected him. It was totally unsubstantative, but it showed that we had some power. . . . The press picked up on us as a good, upbeat story.

No one can deny the class of '74 has been, from its earliest days, a lucky group. Its members entered a Congress willing and able to use their talents. The congressmen rose to positions of power with dispatch, and they have survived at surprisingly high rates, especially in light of their highly competitive districts. For example, almost two-thirds of '74's freshman House Democrats (forty-nine of seventy-five), won seats held by Republicans in the previous Congress, and all but one of these "switched-seat" victors won reelection in 1976.[1] Such a record suggests that luck was but one element of the class's progress, which began even before its members took the oath of office.

Starting Out

Within a week after the November 1974 elections, newly elected members of Congress—mostly Democrats—began to filter into Washington. These individuals knew little about each other or about congressional procedures, and they were faced with a December 2 meeting of the House Democratic Caucus for the 94th Congress. The members-elect generally desired to push forward the reform process within the House, and they recognized that they possessed the crucial numbers—making up over one-fourth of the party's ranks in the chamber. But numbers alone were not enough; organization was essential. Setting a pattern that would repeat itself over the next few months (and years), the class responded to the severe pressures of time and a lack of information by developing and relying upon its own organization.

The Democratic Study Group (DSG) and the liberal National Committee for an Effective Congress (NCEC) welcomed the newly elected representatives, some of whom they had actively supported during the 1974 campaign. These groups did not, however, set out an all-encompassing set of reforms for the upcoming caucus. In fact, the DSG had seen most of its major reform proposals enacted over the previous five years. As DSG staff director Richard Conlon notes, "It was essentially the end of the reform era, [although] we did have a reform agenda at the time, which the new members helped us act on." The DSG and the NCEC focused attention on two important, but relatively obscure, issues: expanding the number of members on the Ways and Means Committee and transferring the committee appointment powers for Democrats from Ways and Means to the leadership-dominated Policy and Steering Committee. Ned Pattison, then a member-elect, wrote in his diary for November 13, 1974:

> There is a feeling of fatigue on the part of [reformist Congressman Donald] Fraser [D-Minn.] and [Brock] Adams [D-Wash.] and [DSG staff director Dick] Conlon. They have fought the reform fight for a long time and have made many changes in spite of great resistance. However the failure of the Bolling select committee on committees to get through many changes as a result of a coalition of senior Democrats and the Republicans was a major disappointment.[2]

The veterans' pessimism did not inhibit the energetic activism of the new members, whose self-appointed leaders set up a skeletal organizational structure and arranged for their own meeting to precede the Democratic Caucus. Almost by happenstance, Pattison, Gladys Spellman (D-Md.), Tim Wirth, Andy Maguire (D-N.J.), and returning member Richard Ottinger (D-N.Y.) established a base for a continuing freshman organization that would move far beyond the traditional new members' social grouping. Supported by $8000 in foundation grants and personal contributions solicited by Wirth, the freshmen hired two temporary staffers and set about systematically contacting all their newly elected colleagues. Thus, even before they had taken their seats, members of the class of '74 had organized an unofficial caucus of their own, which would help them to build upon the reformist foundations erected by the long-term efforts of their senior colleagues.

The freshman Democrats quickly concluded that the DSG's aims were too modest. The potential offered by the seventy-five new members, especially if they could be even minimally organized and informed on key issues, was enormous. Strangely enough, the class of '74's overall dearth of political experience was crucial to exercising its numerical advantage—less than half (49 percent) of the new Democrats had ever held any elective office.[3] Moreover, as Pattison noted upon later reflection, newcomers, armed with their vigor and naiveté, often are unrestrained by the memories of past defeats. "No doubt it frequently turns out that enthusiasm uninhibited by experience is not the wisest course. Occasionally, however, positive results can occur, and the ignorance of 'reality' can be a blessing."[4]

From November 30, 1974, through January 22, 1975, the freshmen combined their resources—their numbers and a modest organization—with a rejection of conventional political wisdom to provide the votes on a series of key issues that would change the distribution of power in the House. The Democratic Caucus, which controlled the chamber's operations, extended the reforms enacted by previous Congresses along several fronts. It stripped the Ways and Means Committee of its "committee on committees" responsibility, shifting this task to the leadership-dominated Steering and Policy unit, and increased Ways and Means seats from twenty-five to thirty-seven; it made automatic the requirement that committee chairs be subject to secret-ballot election and further mandated that Appropriations subcommittee chairs be treated in a like manner; it allowed the Speaker to appoint Rules Committee members, given caucus approval; it gave the authority to subcommittee chairs and ranking members to hire staff; and it recommended that the House rules be changed to require open conference committee meetings. In addition, the Democrats decreed that subcommittee membership be democratized, with every committee member receiving one subcommittee assignment before anyone else obtained a second slot.[5]

For any other Congress, changes of this magnitude would have been regarded as historic modifications of a tradition-bound institution. In 1974–75, however, these decisions, while significant, served as preludes to the key personnel votes taken by the caucus. As the DSG's Conlon points out, requiring committee chairs to be ratified by the caucus represented the centerpiece of reform. Altering procedures was one thing; overturning a powerful chairman was a profound, personal action that sent direct messages to every would-be autocrat in the House.

After supporting the winning candidates in the December votes on the positions of Doorkeeper and, more important, caucus chair (Philip Burton [D-Calif.]), the freshmen felt sufficiently assertive to invite committee chairs to appear before the class as a whole.

The press played up these dramatic appearances by the chairs, and Pattison observes that "this new demand was viewed as being revolutionary, and described as 'audacious' and 'unthinkable.'"[6] The threats implied by such invitations were palpable, in that the large class was increasingly perceived as confident and well-organized. Such self-assurance derived from both the class's early successes and the newcomers' sense that they owed very little to any of the established congressional powers. Many freshmen discovered they had run similar, underfinanced campaigns that attracted only the most modest support from the major Democratic centers of power. Floyd Fithian noted, "We didn't owe anything to any ward heelers. . . . We were pretty brash, not scared. We didn't know that we shouldn't take on a [committee] chairman. I didn't know [Armed Services Chair] Eddie Hebert [D-La.] from a hole in the ground."

Behind everything was the strength of the group's numbers. Congressman Norman Mineta (D-Calif.), an early class leader, observed during the first term that

> when we've acted together, it's made a difference. Take the chairmanship thing. We first sent a letter to each chairman asking that they come to one of our meetings and talk a little about their committee. To a person we got back polite notes saying "No." So we then sent a second letter saying we were going to vote en masse against any chairman who didn't come. They all came. Even Hebert, who showed up the day before the Super Bowl in New Orleans.

The freshman bloc posed a very real danger to the incumbent chairs. Between January 15 and January 22, 1975, in a complicated series of votes, the Steering and Policy Committee and the caucus decided to oust three sitting chairs—Hebert, Agriculture's W. R. Poage (D-Tex.), and Banking's Wright Patman (D-Tex.)—and barely retained another, House Administration's contentious chairman Wayne Hays (D-Ohio). Hays actively responded to the new member-liberal coalition with his singular capacity to control official perquisites (through House Administration) and campaign resources (through the Democratic Congressional Campaign Committee chairmanship). Pattison concluded that Hays had "convinced the freshmen that he had the intestinal fortitude to provide the members with the tools of incumbency that they needed but were politically unable to vote themselves."[7]

The politics behind the caucus actions, especially by the new members, reflected a idiosyncratic mix of ideology, evaluations of competence, and pragmatic, even cynical, calculations of electoral survival. In the end, the reformist thrust was directed at chairmen who were autocratic, incompetent, or both. One veteran reformer commented that he "had a genuine affection for Patman, but he was much too old and cranky to have an unassailable position like that." The caucus actions demonstrated that chairmanships were no longer sacrosanct and reforms could make House leaders more responsive.[8]

Could the class of '74 legitimately claim credit for overthrowing the three senior chairmen? For better or worse, the clear answer is yes. The *CQ Almanac* flatly states that "various reasons were given for the defeats, but there was little doubt that the three had been poorly received by the 75 freshman Democrats who had interviewed committee chairmen . . . in order to decide whom they would support."[9] As Congressman William Hughes (D-N.J.) explained, the class had "numbers and solidarity [and] really stuck together to change the way things are done around here."

LIMITATIONS OF THE FRESHMAN ACTIONS

Of course, there was plenty of criticism. With its characteristic restraint, the *Wall Street Journal* editorialized that "long-sitting committee chairmen, not sufficiently in step with the post-Watergate cadence, were purged by the Democratic Caucus," which helped create a confused and unstructured legislative body. Thus, "the reformers of 1975 tore down the congressional leadership, but put none in its place."[10] Careful review of the House actions offers little support for such a conclusion.

First, the reform process was drawing to an end in the 94th Congress. The DSG's Conlon, long a reform leader, notes, "One of the banes of my existence is the notion—widely accepted—that the Class of 1974 came in and reformed things around here. That's the myth of the Class of 1974." Rather, the class took full advantage of the previously enacted reforms and its own considerable numbers.

Second, and of greater importance, the new members did not categorically reject strong direction, especially from top party leadership as opposed to the committee chairs. Indeed, many reform efforts sought to strengthen the party leaders—by giving them more control over committee assignments, by allowing the Speaker to make appointments to the powerful Rules Committee, and by rejecting a proposal to elect the whip.

In addition, the reelection of Wayne Hays, the very antithesis of reform, as chairman of the House Administration Committee, demonstrated that the new members would participate in traditional political horse-trading. Former Congressman Toby Moffett recalls that when the class held a retreat in Virginia after a few months in office, one key agenda item was campaign reform. "What actually resulted," Moffett notes,

> was an exchange of ideas on ways to become more visible in one's district. Members told of . . . holding office hours in public places . . . and sponsoring "congressional town meetings." . . . Such innovations might come under the category of better representation, but they were clearly intended to enhance our prospects for re-election.[11]

Even as they voted for various institutional reforms and against the unresponsive committee chairs, the newly elected members grasped that unity on procedural matters would not easily translate into clout on substantive issues. The new members soon recognized that with class size came great diversity—based on differences in region, experience, ideology, and electoral circumstance. Moreover, as Congressman Hughes insightfully observed, "you only have a chance to change the organization in the first one or two months." At the six-month mark, Congressman Mineta noted that the class had initially raised expectations, only to have "the system swallow us up."[12] With the passage of time, of necessity, there was a shift from procedures to substance as committee business and constituency issues came to dominate the schedules of the new members. But these reformers, unlike most of their predecessors, did not retreat quietly to play the traditional roles of backbenchers and supernumeraries.

THE FIRST TERM

However much their successes of the first 100 days meant to both the class of '74 members and the House as a whole, the most important decisions for the individual freshmen were not made in the caucus but within the Steering and Policy body, where committee assignments were hammered out. Although the class of '74 had requested and received a slot on Steering and Policy, senior party leaders, as always, dominated the assignment process.

Committees. Here again, the class of '74 was fortunate. First, they had provided many of the votes that had placed the power in the hands of Steering and Policy to assign committee seats. Second, the Democrats had achieved a net gain of forty-three seats in the 1974 congressional elections, thus virtually assuring more Democrats on all committees. Consequently, Steering and Policy was under pressure to award the new members good committee assignments, and the two-to-one Democratic ratio in the House permitted this with relatively little pain.

Although two bastions of inside power, the Rules and House Administration committees, received no Democratic freshmen, new members did win seats on all other panels, including four on the expanded Ways and Means Committee and three on Appropriations.[13] More telling in the short run, perhaps, was the composition of those major committees where first-termers comprised a near-majority of panel membership. The Agriculture and Banking committees each had large freshman contingents (thirteen of twenty-nine Democrats). But the Interstate and Foreign Commerce Committee (subsequently relabeled Energy and Commerce) presented the most interesting opportunities for its twelve new Democratic members (see chapter 7).

Commerce has historically been an attractive committee because it deals with large numbers of difficult, important issues, ranging from transportation to health and communications. From 1973 through the early 1980s, however, the committee's energy responsibilities took center stage. No other set of issues provided such great entrepreneurial opportunities during the 1970s, as Congress struggled to formulate policies in the context of OPEC (Organization of Petroleum Exporting Countries) actions, presidential initiatives, and the contradictory demands of producers and consumers. Matched with these opportunities was a set of new Democratic members who were both talented and impatient; they included first-termers Tim Wirth, Henry Waxman, Robert Krueger (D-Tex.), James Florio (D-N.J.), Toby Moffett, Bill Hefner (D-N.C.), Andy Maguire, Phil Sharp (D-Ind.), Bill Brodhead (D-Mich.), and Jim Santini (D-Nev.), as well as James Scheurer (D-N.Y.) and Richard Ottinger, who returned to the House in 1974. All twelve demonstrated real abilities in understanding the committee's complex political and policy contexts. In addition, this group has proven to be an inordinately ambitious lot; seven have run for higher office at one time or another. It is no overstatement to conclude that since 1974 Energy and Commerce has demonstrated many of the individual opportunities and institutional frustrations that help to define the contemporary Congress.

Energy Activism: Robert Krueger. Although class of '74 members came to chair most Energy and Commerce subcommittees during the 1980s, their influence was felt much more quickly as they helped fashion major congressional responses to the complex and politically difficult energy problems of the 1970s. Ironically, the most prominent and promising member of the group in this period was Robert Krueger, a Shakespearean scholar and Texan (via Oxford and Duke universities), whose political career, by the mid-1980s, had probably reached a dead end.

During the 94th Congress, Krueger exemplified how influential a freshman member of the House could be—educating both his junior and senior colleagues in the process. Krueger recognized that the decentralized congressional system would reward the combination of hard work and expertise when applied to specific problems, such as the proposed decontrol first of domestic oil (July 1975) and then of onshore natural gas (January 1976). Krueger played no major role in the early, reformist activism of the new members' caucus. Instead, the Texan hired a Harvard graduate who had written a senior thesis on oil and gas legislation to help him become as knowledgeable as possible on the intricacies of energy policies.[14]

After six months of diligent work, Krueger came within a whisker of winning the deregulation of domestic oil prices, having put together his own coalition of producer-state members and other decontrol advocates. Despite losing close votes on the House floor in both his decontrol/deregulation attempts, he won widespread admiration for his legislative skill and policy knowledge.[15]

Krueger's energy policy initiatives served directly to expand his overall congressional enterprise. His "efforts on behalf of oil and gas interests," reported David Rosenbaum in the *New York Times,*

> have not gone unrecognized by the beneficiaries. He has received more than $50,000 in campaign contributions from those interests—more than most of his colleagues received from all sources combined—and the bulk of the

TABLE 2.1

New Members' Legislative Activism: 94th, 91st, and 89th Congresses

	New Members Participating (percentages)		
Activity	94th Congress[a]	91st Congress[b]	89th Congress[a]
Floor manager of major bill or amendment	37	—	0
Offered floor amendments	86	40	12
Floor amendments accepted	68	—	—
Committee amendments offered	96	—	24
Committee amendments accepted	91	—	—
Subcommittee amendments offered	98	—	—
Subcommittee amendments accepted	93	—	—
Served on conference committee	69	17	6
Made "major" floor speech*	72	—	30

SOURCES: a. Burdett Loomis and Jeff Fishel, "New Members in a Changing Congress: Norms, Actions, and Satisfaction," *Congressional Studies* 9 (Spring 1981): 81–94. b. Herbert B. Asher, "The Learning of Legislative Norms," *American Political Science Review* 67 (June 1973): 499–513.
*self-defined

> money, used to pay off a large debt from his 1974 campaign, was donated after he became prominent last July.[16]

Not only did Krueger become the most prominent legislative force among the first-term members, he also spent the most money ($359,000) to reach the House and accumulated the largest debt ($200,000) in winning his seat. His colleagues were slower to understand (or risk) such enterprise building, but they were not far behind when it came to legislative activism (see table 2.1).

Moreover, Krueger became one of the first of his cohort to run for higher office—barely losing a 1978 Senate race (he was defeated again, in 1984, in an extremely tight Democratic Senate primary). With the Senate's great tolerance for individual action and bipartisan coalition building, Krueger might well have emerged as a major national politician by the early 1980s.

The Class of 1974: Activism and Attitudes. In historical terms, Robert Krueger's fast start was nothing if not exceptional. Guiding important amendments through difficult subcommittee and committee votes and then serving as floor manager for proposals that would drastically change the direction of national energy policy were not traditional activities for freshman representatives. Among the ranks of the class of '74, however, Krueger was not atypical (see table 2.1). More than a third of the Democratic new members took on similar—if less dramatic—floor manager duties at least once during their first term, and almost all of them participated actively at each stage of the legislative process—from subcommittees to conference committees. The attention given Krueger and a few of his most prominent colleagues overshadowed the fact that the Congress had become truly open to serious participation by all its members.[17]

Changes in behavior went hand in hand with changes in attitudes. The class of '74's actions marked the end of House Speaker Sam Rayburn's (D-Tex.) era of apprenticeship—of passive learning and almost complete deference by junior members.[18] In its place the congressional classes of the 1970s established an "active apprenticeship," which virtually mandated a good deal of legislative responsibility.[19]

Not only was the process open, but the new members expressed satisfaction with their roles in the 94th Congress (1975–76), especially at the committee level. In addition to being pleased with their committee assignments (71 percent were "highly satisfied"), the first-termers were generally satisfied with their ability to participate in committee and subcommittee deliberations.[20] Despite some isolated sniping, the freshmen did not act like "bomb throwers" when it came to committee activities. Rather, like Krueger, they concluded almost unanimously that hard work and expertise were essential to influencing the decentralized policy process, and they put together personal styles and enterprises reflecting this.

On the other hand, relations between these new members and the senior leadership were often strained. In general the class of '74 (unlike the one that followed) approached the party leadership with suspicion, if not downright hostility. Congressman Robert Carr (D-Mich.), at one extreme, called for Speaker Carl Albert's (D-Okla.) resignation, and a group of freshmen did meet with Albert to iron out their differences. Little was accomplished, and the new members continued to express marked dissatisfaction with their leaders; in 1976, more than six in ten reported that they were at least somewhat dissatisfied with the "organization and functioning of the Democratic leadership"—a far cry from their general satisfaction with the committee system they had helped to reshape.[21]

Many new members articulated a need for greater consultation, which helped to define the general notion of "inclusive" leadership that Tip O'Neill and his lieutenants implemented during the ten years (1977–87) of his speakership.[22] Early on, Congressman Pattison echoed the sentiments of many junior members and presaged the development of the inclusive style:

> I'm not saying I won't accept leadership, but what we need is consultation first, then leadership. If I've had my say, I'll go along with those I've disagreed with. . . . One of the problems around here is that people think of leadership in hierarchical terms. We need more consultative leadership. . . . A person in the middle levels knows as much about a problem as one at the top. They're dealing with new problems, not something you learned on the way up through the hierarchy.

Consultation with the leadership began with the ad hoc maneuvers that commenced before the class members took their seats. In December 1974, Congressman Bill Brodhead helped to convince the leadership that a freshman should sit on the party's newly strengthened Steering and Policy Committee. This seat, which would later be seen as a real plum, subsequently fell into Brodhead's lap. He recounts that

> during the [class] meeting someone said that we didn't really know each other very well and that we ought to draw the name out of a hat. . . . Since the Michigan House was out of session, I had nothing to do and since it was random, I threw my name in. . . . There were only four or five of us that did. And my name was drawn. A month later we had an election, and I won.

Over the next decade, the Democrats would formalize such freshman representation, along with more important measures to expand the whip system and institutionalize the appointment of task forces. All in all, the new members' vision of a consultative leadership became a reality by the early 1980s.

The Other New Members: Republicans and Senators. The Democratic class of '74 was news, and this obscured the arrival of a handful of strong GOP House members, as well as eleven new senators, including future national leaders John Glenn, Gary

Hart, and Paul Laxalt (R-Nev.). There were few post-Watergate analyses of these personnel changes, largely because the Senate allowed for much of the individualism that House members sought. Senate rules underwent some revisions, but nothing like the wholesale alterations within the House. More important, Senate Democrats did not oust any senior leaders from key positions. Hart, Glenn, Laxalt, and their colleagues went about their entrepreneurial business, pushing their favored issues, agenda items, and eventually themselves as possible presidential candidates.

Still, within the 94th Congress, the new House Republicans and even the senators of both parties served as extras, while the main actors, the rambunctious class of '74 House Democrats, held center stage. Congressman Richard Ottinger commented, without malice, in 1984: "I don't know who [the Republicans of 1974] are to this day. I may know them as individuals, but not as a group. We didn't have any contact with them."[23] Congressman Henry Hyde, who relishes the spotlight, observed with only a trace of regret that "we Republicans were relegated to holding spears. We were props, part of the set, rather than part of the action."[24]

THE 94TH CONGRESS IN RETROSPECT

Within a half-year of entering the Congress and engineering the ouster of three committee chairmen, the new House Democrats found themselves in disarray. Predictably, their unity on procedural issues had crumbled when substantive policy decisions (for example, Krueger's amendment to decontrol natural gas prices) came to the fore.

The class of '74 quickly discovered that the pulls of constituency, committee, and ideology were ordinarily more powerful than the accident of cohort. Nevertheless, while recognizing their diversity, the new members established both formal and informal ties that stood for years. Indeed, a reliance on organizational skills continues as a hallmark of this group, as witnessed by their strong individual offices, reelection operations, and participation in informal caucuses.

The Democratic freshmen institutionalized the informal grouping they had developed in the wake of their election. The New Members Caucus (NMC) received office space from the leadership and obtained staff from members' regular clerk-hire funds. It sponsored weekly forums where members could hear prominent speakers (such as Energy Secretary James Schlesinger) and exchange information on both the issues and politics of reelection. In subsequent interviews, one after another of the freshmen observed that they had "learned a lot" from their colleagues in these sessions. Some benefits were less tangible. Congressman Phil Sharp concluded that the caucus's "primary purpose, and its best contribution, was simply to give us psychological security and reinforcement."

Such contact not only allowed class members to learn whom to rely upon on policy matters but also enabled them to develop overlapping friendship networks based on a series of common experiences. Many of these members' friendships have remained intact, more than a decade after the class entered the Congress. Especially for some of the younger members, such as New York's Tom Downey, California's George Miller, and Illinois's Marty Russo, a kind of fraternity "pledge class" aura hovers over ties that transcend issues, interests, and ideology. Indeed, Miller and Russo, along with Leon Panetta (D-Calif., '76) and Charles Schumer (D-N.Y., '80) share a Capitol Hill townhouse, while maintaining permanent residences in their districts.[25]

Nonetheless, strong friendships do not develop easily.[26] Russo argues that "close friendships around here are tough to come by." His strong ties to Miller, he points out, developed only after they began sharing their Washington residence, more than eight years after first entering Congress.

Once formed, friendships can have substantive implications, as when Congressman Schumer became a key immigration player after discussing the issue with his housemates

Miller and Panetta. More generally, Congressman Carroll Hubbard (D-Ky.), hardly an ideological bedfellow of most of his activist classmates, noted in 1984,

> when I'm on the floor and a bill is being handled by Tim Wirth or George Miller or Bill Hughes, I'm somewhat anxious to see them win. There have been times, in a close call, when I've voted for amendments of the 94th class that I might not have voted for otherwise.[27]

Beyond the First Term

The class of '74 was, is, and will continue to be a lucky group, and the Democrats were especially fortunate. They ran in a Democratic year, and they almost unanimously won their initial bids for reelection, often in very difficult districts. They entered the Congress in an era of substantial turnover and unprecedented democratization. Thus, they advanced quickly to positions of real power. By 1981, for example, only three of the forty-four remaining 1974 House Democrats neither chaired a subcommittee nor sat on one of the chamber's "power" committees—Rules, Appropriations, and Ways and Means. Many of the class, Republicans as well as Democrats, ran for the Senate, and nine have won (in fact, of the one hundred sitting senators in 1988, thirteen were first elected to Congress in November 1974). Although a handful of the 1974 entrants have retired, most of the remaining members seem poised to stay in the Congress for another decade or longer.

Winning election to the Congress, however, is not like winning the lottery; a legislative seat provides only an opportunity for politicians to act and advance. The 1974 entrants took full advantage of their opportunities. It is difficult to compare generations of politicians, but without question the new members set high standards for hard work and activism. In addition, many of these representatives felt real pressures to make a legislative impact within the postreform Congress. As Marty Russo observes, "In the 70s there was a proliferation of subcommittee chairs, and a lot of them had to prove that they could get something done."

Their prevailing legislative philosophy emphasized problem solving by individual legislators, often at the expense of the Congress as a whole. Political scientist Eric Uslaner argues persuasively that comity on Capitol Hill waned noticeably during the late 1970s, and he sees the new members of this era as a major factor.[28] As their congressional careers progressed in the 1970s, members of the class of '74 were less committed than previous generations to core legislative values such as compromise and civility (see table 2.2).

In the House, comity may have reached its nadir in the early days of the Reagan administration, when Speaker Tip O'Neill, the ranking national Democratic leader, served as the major target of attacks, both policy based and personal, of conservatives like Newt Gingrich (R-Ga.) and John LeBoutiller (R-N.Y.), respectively. These well-publicized thrusts eventually proved counterproductive, as LeBoutiller lost his seat and Gingrich's caucus, the Conservative Opportunity Society, was increasingly discounted. More important, O'Neill made a remarkable political recovery, both on Capitol Hill and nationally. Within the House his inclusive philosophy brought large numbers of junior members into the ranks of the leadership.[29]

The Senate, however, has shown few signs of growing more civil or cordial. With tough-minded individuals like Jesse Helms (R-N.C.), Phil Gramm, and Howard Metzenbaum (D-Ohio) operating in a body that allows a single legislator great obstructionist powers, the Senate continues a policy-based decline in comity. To the extent that a senator rejects the need for

TABLE 2.2

Support for Informal Rules of the Game Within the Class of 1974: 1976 and 1980 Responses

How important are the following to your long-term success and effectiveness in the House?	Very Important (percentage responding)		Somewhat or Not at All Important (percentage responding)	
	1976	1980	1976	1980
Subject-matter expertise	77	72	22	28
Legislative specialization	54	44	46	46
Seniority	21	26	79	75
Legislative apprenticeship	19	8	81	92
Ability to compromise	50	49	50	51
Personality cordiality	63	37	38	63
Hard work	—	74	—	26
Institutional loyalty	—	5	—	95

SOURCE: Burdett A. Loomis, "Congressional Careers and Party Leadership in the Contemporary House of Representatives," *American Journal of Political Science* 28 (February 1984): 195.

popularity, he can have wide-ranging impact. Gramm optimistically notes that the unwillingness of many legislators to confront difficult issues works to his advantage; "If you're willing to tackle tough issues like the budget deficit, you don't have to worry about stepping on people's toes. They're going to step out of the way and shove you to the front."[30] Perhaps. But Gramm's partners in the deficit-reduction legislation paint a different picture. In 1987 Senator Warren Rudman (R-N.H.) concluded that "Phil is going to stonewall it up to the end. . . . I don't play it that way because I don't think it works." Senator Ernest Hollings (D-S.C.) is more blunt: "[Gramm] loves guerrilla warfare and he loves to lose. He's my heaviest burden."[31]

Although none of these senators came to Capitol Hill in 1974, all entered the Congress during the 1970s and currently benefit from the Senate's almost limitless tolerance for the actions of individual policy entrepreneurs. In contrast, their Senate colleagues from the class of '74 have carried forward their own relatively conventional activist agendas (for example, Dodd on Latin America, Simon on public jobs, Grassley on military waste). As senators, a Tom Harkin and a Tim Wirth have increased visibility and responsibilities, but their activities are essentially the same as they were in the House. They need strive not quite as much for publicity or attention, but most of their efforts resemble their previous House activities.

Given their favored place in the congressional queue, members of the class of '74 continually find themselves in a position to define the nature of politics in the postreform Congress. This role was most obvious in the ousting of the committee chairs, but any number of other, less dramatic, examples also exist. For instance, in 1979 Congressmen Henry Waxman and Toby Moffett successfully challenged more senior colleagues in straightforward contests for subcommittee chairmanships that hinged on political skills, not ideology or senility. With this sink-or-swim philosophy, the surprise is that so many of this group have stayed afloat, although for every Downey or Simon there is a Krueger or a Moffett, whose aggressiveness in approaching political life ultimately ushered him out of the congressional arena.

The Class of 1974 and Middle Management

"Even ten years later," notes Congressman Butler Derrick (D-S.C.), "I go to my buddies in the class of '74. We've now moved up to middle management. Tom Downey, George Miller, Tim Wirth still bring a fresh perspective to policies, to problems." Widely accepted by most midcareer members, the "middle management" label reflects an accurate assessment of the progress of these new politicians through a changing Congress. This notion is significant for at least four reasons. First, it acknowledges an increasingly important layer in congressional politics, especially within the House. Middle managers occupy some readily identifiable positions—important subcommittee chairs, deputy whip posts, power committee memberships, key caucus chairs.

Second, the concept recognizes the organizational necessities of the contemporary Congress and a continuing need for communication between rank-and-file members and top leaders. Beginning in 1969 with the initial stirrings of the Democratic Caucus and running through the 1980s, the trend has been to expand opportunities for participation and communication, even when, as with Les Aspin (D-Wisc.) and the Armed Services Committee chairmanship contests in 1985 and 1987, that process is wrenching. For the most part, the middle management framework allows members to stay abreast of ongoing developments and take their turn as leaders on given policies.

Third, middle management in the Congress is a state of mind. Within a few years of their entrance into the House (and virtually upon entering the Senate), legislators can feel, and rightfully so, that they have both the ability and the regular opportunity to affect the policy-making process and its results, on a range of subjects.

Finally, most middle managers control large and growing political enterprises that often extend beyond the Congress. For example, in 1986 Congressman Stephen Solarz had a campaign surplus of $812,000, sponsored his own political action committee, spent more than $200,000 on a noncompetitive campaign, employed a full complement of personal staff, and controlled the resources of a Foreign Affairs subcommittee.[32] Making effective use of these diverse assets requires remarkable managerial talent from an administrative aide, if not from the congressman himself.

The entrepreneurial style, with its emphasis on agenda

setting, flexibility, and ad hoc coalitions, stands in apparent contradiction to the managerial necessities demanded by most institutions—even the Congress. For the most part, these middle managers have reconciled the potential contradictions, largely because management in the contemporary Congress includes a great deal of creative activity. Leaders do not manage coalitions, they build them, usually around policies or proposals. The Watergate babies, as they reach political maturity, have shaped the current institutional arrangements, which reward the very attributes—independence, policy expertise, and hard work—they value most.

3

Issues: The Currency of Political Life

As THEY ENTERED public life in the 1970s, the Watergate babies and their colleagues encountered few of the intractable institutional barriers that their predecessors had faced. House members found a weakened seniority system, and a "new apprenticeship,"[1] which virtually required them to become actively involved in the legislative process. Young senators found no restrictive, exclusive "inner club."[2] Instead, 1974 entrants Gary Hart and Patrick Leahy, as freshmen senators in their thirties, discovered a thoroughly individualistic body, which allowed for the almost immediate testing of newcomers' talents. What to do? The new pols by and large developed into policy entrepreneurs who hooked their careers to ideas, issues, and problems—and prospective solutions. This does not mean that they all acted alike. Rather, they became "players"—individuals who had to be taken into account, who could compete in the arena of national policy making.

As a group, the insurgents' 1975 success in overthrowing three senior, unresponsive House committee chairs put the entire body on notice that many of the old rules of "going along" or "being seen and not heard" no longer applied. Still, the opportunity to participate was only that—an opportunity to play the congressional game. Like a salesman, once their foot was figuratively in the door, these newcomers had to sell their wares—by demonstrating competence on the issues. Congressman Marty Russo points out, "If you screw up, you're no longer a player," and Congressman George Miller, laughing, adds, "It's like being a trial lawyer, only it's worse. If you're a lawyer, at least it's your client who goes to jail."

Demonstrating Substance: Readin', 'Ritin', and 'Rithmetic

To enter the national policy-making debate requires credentials and, usually, position. Only a few positions provide enough leverage to assure that one's views are taken seriously, at least for a while, and even a Senate seat does not automatically qualify its incumbent. California's former Republican senators George Murphy and S. I. Hayakawa, for example, were almost totally discounted during their congressional tenures. Legislators and other policy activists must provide evidence that they can both understand and contribute to the policy debate—by manipulating ideas, theories, and data. As former Congressman Floyd Fithian, now a top aide to 1974 classmate Senator Paul Simon, observes, "Reporters and other members clearly relate to members in terms of their *skills and abilities.* The leadership certainly does. Folks like [Class of 1974 members] Wirth, Hyde, Downey, [Matt] McHugh [D-N.Y.] will find a way to affect the debate and have an impact" (emphasis added).

READIN': THE NEOTRADITIONAL MODEL

The traditional road to acceptance within the ranks of serious issue activists is to master a policy domain thoroughly in order to participate intelligently in sophisticated discussions.[3] This is, of course, the path trod by generations of House members as they served apprenticeships, accumulated seniority, and waited patiently to become the lords of their particular, specialized committee domains.[4] Older congressional hands saw this on-the-job training as essential for junior members to compete effectively with an expert and politically savvy bureaucracy.

Former Congressman Barber Conable (R-N.Y.), a widely acknowledged tax expert when he retired from Congress in 1984 who later became World Bank director, commented upon his entrance to the House in 1965 that "the main thing that I've told [Minority Leader] Gerry Ford is that I want to go on a working committee where I can learn the business of legislation."[5] Implicit in Conable's statement was the conclusion that long hours of committee and subcommittee work were essential to gain the knowledge for effective participation in policy debate. Specialization on committee work would lead eventually to policy expertise.

The new generation of politicians thoroughly endorses the idea that expertise is essential for entering the national policy debate (see table 2.1). What differs has been their unwillingness to wait, to sit through interminable committee sessions, dominated by their senior colleagues. As one Pennsylvania House member commented, in evaluating his state's younger legislators, they represent a new style—"the 'issues model.' . . . The [Peter] Kostmayers, [Bob] Edgars, and [William] Grays gained influence by trying to make sure that they had more knowledge than anybody else on their issues; by articulating the issues, they'd be able to get things done."[6]

This stands in stark contrast to Congress as recently as the mid-1960s. As Majority Leader Tom Foley recounts, Agriculture Committee chair Harold Cooley (D-N.C.), an old-fashioned Southern oligarch, lectured his panel that he "hated and detested" questions from uninformed sources such as junior members. If they would just stay quiet and wait patiently, their senior colleagues "would ask all the questions worth asking." Foley and Conable, two highly intelligent freshmen, held their peace, but they and many other entrants of the 1958–64 era understood that Congress needed the talents of all its members, not just a select few. The generation of the 1970s has understood the importance of expertise, but as well-educated products of an information age, they often learned their lessons outside the committee classrooms. Ironically, the most notable congressional example of this development was not a member of the House, that traditional bastion of specialized expertise, but a junior senator, Georgia's Sam Nunn, who steadily gained influence in the 1970s because of his reputation as a diligent student of national defense policies.

'RITIN': THE ENTREPRENEUR AS AUTHOR

National politicians have often surfaced as authors, and in the English tradition of Winston Churchill and Benjamin Disraeli, talented writers have also emerged as skilled leaders. Sometimes, as with President James Madison, the written work has far surpassed the formal leadership. Although the Congress of the 1950s and 1960s did produce some member-authors, with the exception of Congressman Richard Bolling[7] and, to a lesser extent, Senator Joseph Clark (D-Pa.),[8] these officials did not seek to advance the policy debate or establish intellectual credentials through their writing. In fact, Bolling and Clark wrote in frustration; as veteran reformers, they could not obtain an adequate hearing for their concerns on Capitol Hill in the 1960s. Neither did they gain much immediate internal stature from their publishing ventures.

What distinguishes the new politicians from their predecessors is their use of writing to establish credentials as intellectuals and as serious participants in national policy debates. Given that the class of '74 included in its ranks several Ph.D.s and college professors (even a dean in Robert Krueger), this comes as no surprise.

Among contemporary legislative authors, Senator Paul Simon has written the most books[9] and Senator Daniel Patrick Moynihan (D-N.Y.) has had the most profound effect on policy, but among the 1974 newcomers Gary Hart is the archetype of this approach to gaining credibility. Although Hart's works include a couple of adventure novels, his coauthored (with William Lynn) defense tract, *America Can Win,* is the more conventional effort to gain issue-based status. Unlike Simon, whose writing is often tied directly to specific legislative initiatives, Hart's policy books emphasize the broad "new ideas" motif that has served as the intellectual basis for his forays into presidential politics. This is similar to former Senator Paul Tsongas's attempt to recast liberalism for the eighties in his 1982 volume, *The Road from Here.*[10] Although Tsongas's book won mixed reviews at best, he did take issues seriously and received credit for the effort, if not for the prescriptions. In the end, the Hart and Tsongas books have lent more weight to their participation in policy debates than to their successes on any specific policy issues.

However many volumes politicians may write, this form of gaining credence remains the exception. Most activists have neither the time nor the inclination to discover whether they have the talent to write a book. Ghost writers do offer an attractive alternative, especially for would-be presidential candidates,[11] but few legislators go to such lengths.

Party commissions and task forces have given many political newcomers a chance to demonstrate their policy competence beyond the confines of the Capitol. The Democratic Policy Commission, an official arm of the party's national committee, appointed three task forces that issued separate reports as well as a comprehensive document, "New Choices for a Changing America," which sought to outline broadly acceptable party policies. Composed of leading academics, legislators, and former executive-branch officials, each task force was headed by a class of '74 Congressman: New York's Steve Solarz (Foreign Policy); Washington's Don Bonker (International Trade and Competitiveness), and New Jersey's Jim Florio (Environment). That a middle management House member, like Bonker, was tapped for such a chore signifies his acceptance as a major player in trade policy, with the potential for influence far beyond the confines of his House Foreign Affairs subcommittee.

The abundance of party factions and groupings has allowed many activists to make their mark as authors of key reports or sets of findings. Tim Wirth's Democratic Caucus task force issued a well-publicized appraisal of long-term economic policy (dubbed the "yellow book" for its distinct cover). Wirth took his job and the issues seriously, but a year or two after the report was published, his role in hammering out the document remained a more visible and concrete achievement than any of its recommendations.

Finally, the most prominent (if short-lived) writing is found on the op-ed pages of leading national newspapers. Several decent pieces over a year or two can label almost any legislator as a thoughtful contributor to one or more policy debates, even if the articles are ghost-written by congressional staff.

'RITHMETIC: DAVID STOCKMAN AND OTHER CALCULATING POLITICIANS

The congressional budget process has helped to produce a new type of policy expertise. Manipulating figures and, equally important, explaining their implications, have become important talents inside the Congress. Almost without exception the Congress has turned to middle management to handle related chores of budget and macroeconomic policies.[12] Elected in the same year the Congress adopted budget reform, the class of '74 has remained integrally involved in this process, with fifteen of its number having served on the House Budget Committee.

Even though many Democrats have exhibited considerable skills here—Congressmen Leon Panetta and Buddy McKay (D-Fla.) among others—two Republicans have gotten the most policy mileage from their budgetary roles. In 1979–80, as junior congressmen, David Stockman (R-Mich.) and Phil Gramm, using their familiarity with the budget and macroeconomics, put together a bipartisan budget package that included a large tax cut. Even though this proposal went nowhere, the two entrepreneurs learned an important lesson as they talked with their colleagues and the press. Stockman recounts that "even the appearance of being an expert is self-validating. I didn't know much about budgets, but I knew more than the rest."[13] To the extent that $600 billion budget reconciliation packages and complex tax negotiations remain central to the congressional policy process, understanding, manipulating, and explaining figures continue to serve as keys to demonstrating legislative competence.

Issue Credibility in a New Era: The Bill Bradley Model

Senator Bill Bradley embodies the "Three R's" approach to establishing credibility in the Congress. For example, Reagan aide Michael Horowitz observed that "the only Democratic think tank in [Washington] is in Bill Bradley's head."[14] Even before his tax reform proposals had won congressional approval, Bradley had received great credit for pushing the idea to the point of serious consideration. The enactment of tax reform propelled Bradley to the front ranks of national policy entrepreneurs (and highly touted presidential contenders). "Taxes intrigued me conceptually," he notes, "because it's a closed body of knowledge you can come close to mastering with some certainty."[15] That Bradley could regard tax matters as "closed" provides a real insight into how far he will extend himself to understand an issue.

There is, however, a touch of naiveté that differentiates Bradley from his fellow student of policy, Senator Sam Nunn. Nunn sees the great complexities of defense policies and immerses himself in the sea of debate, confident that he is the most powerful swimmer. Bradley, perhaps equally knowledgeable, used his expertise to build an overall vision of tax reform that many politicians applauded, but few thought politically realistic.

Even before tax overhaul moved center stage, Bradley's studious style had an impact within the Senate. For example, after Congressman Paul Simon won a much-publicized Senate race over incumbent Charles Percy (R-Ill.), he could have opted immediately to become a highly visible, big-state legislator. After all, one of Simon's major reasons for seeking higher office had been to obtain more attention for his policy initiatives. Simon and his staff chose, however, to project the lower profile of a congressional workhorse, to focus on a small number of issues and to "do things that were substantive, not flash-in-the-pan things that give you today's headline."[16] Despite the fact that in the 1950s, while Simon was writing legislation in the Illinois House, Bradley was honing his jump shot as a junior high school student, it was the younger man who provided the veteran with a model of effectiveness in the contemporary Senate.

Whether for Bradley, Simon, Nunn, Gramm, or any of a hundred other legislative players, the links between policies and personalities have grown stronger within a Congress that allows a first-term congressman (for example, Robert Krueger) or a renegade Democrat (Phil Gramm) to shape the legislative agenda. This linkage between activists and their policies is central to understanding the importance of the entrepreneurial style.

Individuals and Issues

Issues have become increasingly important to the unfolding of entrepreneurs' careers. As Senator Bob Packwood (R-Oreg.) observes, "The fact that an idea is floating in a vacuum doesn't make any difference unless someone grabs it, hones it, and pushes it."[17] Early in their terms, members of the class of '74 demonstrated that issues could provide the base for an effective political style. Many of these legislators entered the Congress as naifs, "who came," notes McHugh, "feeling very strongly on issues. We got involved in politics initially because of reform or issues. We've carried that through to the present. . . . If we didn't feel we were making progress, we wouldn't want to remain." In the intervening years, almost all remaining members of the class have become identified with at least one major issue or policy area, while developing into increasingly sophisticated policy entrepreneurs. As the *New York Times*'s Martin Tolchin notes, the issue-oriented neophytes of the 1970s have cultivated new skills, while not sacrificing their initial drive.

> Something outside Congress sparks their interest, and then they run with it. At the same time, they're professionals. There are some boundaries, but not many. You're limited by your professionalism. Someone who's not a professional probably won't stay around very long.

Policy entrepreneurs and their policies are judged together; consequently they must continually assess for themselves where the boundaries lie. A few would-be players are totally discounted. The publicity-conscious Congressman Robert Dornan (R-Calif.) is accorded little respect from any quarter, and former Senator Mike Gravel (D-Alaska) lost prestige, if possible, during his single term in office.

More important, especially in an era of great change, are the politicians who force their peers and their institutions to reconsider what is appropriate behavior. The current informal congressional "rules of the game" for example, allow, even encourage, a lot more publicity seeking than was considered appropriate around 1970. As long as serious issues are at the core of media coverage, entrepreneurs will not be ostracized. Congressman Jim Florio points out that "it's not direct one-to-one communication any more. You've got to get the attention of others. You're looking for allies, and you need to affect public opinion. And you need the press to do that."

Even a publicity hound like Congressman Steve Solarz can command the attention and grudging respect of his colleagues because of his foreign policy expertise (see chapter 4). Still, his effectiveness does suffer. As one veteran congressional aide observes, "You've got to consider what the primary motivation for publicity is. . . . Hell, everyone's ambitious around here. It's the visibility and obviousness of Solarz's ambition that is so grating." As a result, Solarz does pay a price for his style. In 1987, along with seven freshman Democrats, he requested a seat on the Science and Technology Committee. Had he not withdrawn the request, a senior party aide reports, the party's Steering and Policy would have rejected it. While of no great consequence to Solarz, such a failure illustrates both the costs of his public style and the fact that party leaders do hold some crucial resources as they seek to rein in an independent operator. In short, Solarz's expertise on foreign policy does not enhance his overall effectiveness.

POLICY REPUTATION

Few legislators illustrate the positive impact of policy reputation better than Illinois Congressman Henry Hyde, one of the few remaining House Republicans from the class of '74. Hyde's initial legislative successes came with a series of politically motivated, tactically astute amendments that cut off much federal funding for abortions, but in the 1980s he has emerged as an articulate GOP spokesman for a wide range of foreign and defense policies. As the Iran-Contra hearings have demonstrated, Hyde is no shrinking violet, but both smart and funny—a corpulent Bob Dole, without the advantages of a major party leadership position. What comes through is an intelligent politician, who cares deeply about issues and who can be both persuaded (occasionally) and persuasive (regularly).

As he illustrated with his anti-abortion amendments, Hyde can seize political advantage, even when his actions are far from popular. At the same time, he has offered his fellow partisans "cover" in supporting the 1982 extension of the Voting Rights Bill. The best entrepreneurs can use their issue positions to bring people together as well as to set the policy agenda. Fellow GOP activist Congressman Dan Lungren (R-Calif.) notes:

> One of the ways you establish coalitions . . . is to show that coalitions are worth belonging to. You have to attract people not only because of the politics of the matter, but because of the force of the idea. . . . If you don't have a Henry Hyde articulating those views very forcefully, very well, and with intelligence behind them, it's hard to attract people to come over.[18]

The combination of rhetorical skill and policy substance is powerful, though not always irresistible. Still, entrepreneurs need tactical flexibility and require attention from the press. Hyde discounts this a bit, saying, "I think you earn your spurs with your colleagues not so much because the press quotes you a lot, but because you know what you're talking about."[19] But the media generally find Hyde a good source and an effective advocate. National Public Radio's Cokie Roberts, when asked about Congressman Hyde's entrepreneurial skills, responded, "What you've got to realize is that Henry Hyde is one of the smartest men who ever walked. So no matter what he has to do, he knows how to do it, how to get attention, how to use the media to have an effect."

Despite his status as a House minority member, Hyde begins any battle with a reputation that usually helps him. Without guaranteeing success, it provides him with a hard-earned edge, which he will exploit if possible. However strong their abilities and reputations, Republicans like Hyde and Barber Conable have found that life in the House consists of a series of partisan obstacles. As a result, given the truncated nature of their opportunities in a chamber that they have not controlled in over thirty years, almost no Republicans remain for an entire career. They often run for the Senate—successfully, like Iowa's Charles Grassley, or unsuccessfully, like Texan Tom Loeffler—at a relatively early stage in their careers, knowing that other, less frustrating possibilities await them, win or lose.

PLAYING AND WINNING

It is a simple fact of life, which virtually all members understand, that in the Congress most policy initiatives fail to become law. An earlier era might have produced a Wilbur Mills (D-Ark.), whose skills and position allowed him to avoid defeat in the House,[20] but the predominant theme of the 1970s and 1980s emphasizes participation—playing the game. As Congressman Henry Waxman, an archetypal entrepreneur, puts it, "If you don't try, you've lost already." At the same time, playing has its risks, especially in contemporary politics, when relative newcomers expect, and are expected, to contribute almost immediately to debates over policy. The old seniority system served to protect congressional newcomers from close scrutiny by their colleagues, and judgments were ordinarily withheld for a term or two. In a Congress where new members seek immediate influence and generous publicity, their peers render verdicts in a more timely fashion.

Winning Isn't Everything: The Degree of Difficulty. No member of the class of '74 has wrestled with more technically complex and politically problematic issues than did Senator Tim Wirth during his 1981–86 tenure as a subcommittee chair of the House Energy and Commerce panel. In these years, Wirth's plate was full of difficult subjects, such as the AT&T breakup, the regulation of the cable television industry, and the conduct of financial institutions. All of these required a great deal of knowledge and even more patience. The Wirth record on these thorny problems was decidedly mixed. As Congressional Quarterly's *Politics in America* concludes:

> The subcommittee's exhaustive investigations and innovative proposals have educated the country on a baffling and volatile set of issues. When it comes to getting bills passed, however, Wirth has had more than his share of failure.[21]

This summary rings true, yet Wirth did not suffer much from his indifferent record of legislative success. The failure to engineer political solutions to difficult policy problems is hardly fatal to an entrepreneur's reputation for expertise. Indeed, taking on formidable issues and powerful interests can win a politician the respect of his or her peers, even when no policy resolution materializes. Wirth's fellow legislators, almost without exception, expressed real admiration for the congressman's mastery of a wide array of technical issues. A veteran congressional and administration staff aide concluded that policy expertise was the least of Wirth's difficulties in the House, noting in 1984 that

> Wirth runs a hell of a good subcommittee. He understands the issues, even banking, and he knows cable and communications cold. . . . His colleagues respect him, but they don't completely trust him. They're a little afraid of him, I think. But they do trust him not to screw up the institution . . . because he is good on the issues and the politics.

Wirth's peers were not "a little afraid" of his competence, but of his ambition, which might have led to unnecessary confrontations on tough issues. In the end, however, when he ran for the Senate in 1986, Wirth benefited from his reputation as a knowledgeable legislator. With twelve years of environmental policy making on the House Energy and Commerce Committee and countless hours of briefings on high-tech communications issues, Wirth was more than comfortable in debating these concerns.

A variation on the "degree of difficulty" theme has been performed by Congressman Tom Downey, whose expertise includes both defense policy and tax issues confronting the Ways and Means Committee, where he moved from Armed Services in 1981. The oldest entering member of the class of '74, former Congressman Joe Fisher (D-Va.) notes that Downey's youth made his expertise both unexpected and all the more impressive: "Downey learned so much about the arms business so quickly. The combination of young age and expertise mystified me. I respected his views on a whole group of issues. . . . When he takes the floor, people listen." Although Downey has not won any major arms control victories during the 1980s, he and his House allies have helped to shape the debate throughout the Reagan administration.

Winning may be even less significant in the Senate, where senators often are satisfied to make a good showing and to articulate a key point.[22] One Senate aide notes that "we don't want to tilt at windmills all the time, but we will do that sometimes. . . . We'll sometimes get involved in something where we know we're going to lose, but maybe over time that will change the process a little."[23]

Helping to construct a winning coalition on a complex issue does wonders for one's perceived influence, as Bill Bradley discovered. The persistence and political skills he exhibited enhanced his overall reputation, but his policy competence had previously been established. Nor is the issue-based expertise of a Henry Waxman or a James Florio questioned if an acid rain coalition breaks down or a toxic waste vote goes the wrong way.

Some performances do have real costs, especially when they are subjected to scrutiny by the press, and participation in major policy issues is not an unmixed blessing for inexperienced national politicians. They can founder, like Reagan's Environmental Protection Agency (EPA) chief Anne Burford, or succeed, like a David Stockman or a Phil Gramm. Within the Congress, being pinned with a reputation as a lightweight or an incompetent means that a legislator faces, at best, years of work to gain credibility.

Actually, there are relatively few real incompetents within the Congress today. As the institution has distributed the power, the peer pressure to contribute has grown steadily. Logically, if unexpectedly, the House demands more of its members than does the Senate. As Paul Tsongas concluded, after serving in both bodies, "There are 435 people—a lot of very bright people [in the House], and the competition ironically is much tougher than [in the Senate]."[24]

Still, persistent negative assessments can destroy a legislator's ability to participate meaningfully in the policy game. When these judgments appear in print, the effects are all the worse. For example, after interviewing dozens of congressional insiders, *California Magazine* assessed the quality of the state's forty-five-member House delegation and published profiles of the best and worst five.[25] The latter group included junior Democrats Marty Martinez and Jim Bates, both of whom have some aspirations to play major policy roles. Martinez was rated simultaneously "lazy" and as the least intelligent among the entire delegation. Although Congressman Bates is perceived as neither stupid nor lazy, he receives low marks for having no policy focus and for being unable to build a stable or talented staff, two further indications of issue incompetence.

A few subcommittee chairs are given outright bad marks on their performance. Such evaluations make them losers, either within the Congress, or worse, with the electorate. The experience of former Congressman Daniel Albosta (D-Mich.) is noteworthy. In a highly publicized set of hearings Albosta attempted to investigate the alleged leak of the Carter "briefing book" during the 1980 presidential campaign. The result was that Albosta lost, in sequence, the confidence of his peers, the press, and, in 1984, his constituents. Entrepreneurs must often take real risks, although most verdicts are not so clear as those offered on Albosta. Nevertheless, the other players continually scrutinize the performances of their colleagues.

Within the class of '74, the careers of Congressmen Marty Russo and John LaFalce (D-N.Y.) illustrate the problems posed by reputation—although they face different predicaments. A protégé and top lieutenant of Ways and Means chair Dan Rostenkowski (D-Ill.), Russo, who sits on both the Budget and Ways and Means committees and serves as a party whip, has become an important House insider. Most notably, he helped pull together the House coalition on tax reform. A tireless worker, Russo acts in a policy broker role that is crucial to building bridges to various factions. Tax reform negotiations demonstrated Russo's skills, and a substantial number of House members appreciate these talents.[26]

Regardless, Russo must continually work to overcome a negative and parochial reputation acquired during his first few years in the House when he served as point man for legislation favoring the interests of funeral directors, hospitals, and commodities dealers. Russo claims that, as an "insider," his public reputation means little to him, in contrast to his standing with fellow members. The congressman forcefully states:

> I'm a workhorse. What I care about is how my peers see me, not the media, [which] view me through the hospital cost containment and the funeral legislation. It doesn't bother me, because my peers understand what I do. They come to see me when they want something done. They know I can get things done around here.

Unfortunately for Russo, much of what other House members know about him—as well as about most of their other fellow legislators—is learned through media reports. Drawing absolute distinctions between inside and outside perceptions may not make much sense. Indeed, even potential allies often view Russo with preconceived notions.

Congressman George Miller recounts that his fellow California Democrat, Congressman Howard Berman, had asked him to approach Russo for some assistance on arms control, an issue that the Illinois legislator has emphasized for some time. Miller observes, "Berman had a [party] task force on arms control—it was his only one, I think, and he didn't want to screw it up. Howard asked me if I thought Marty would help out." With his ties to Rostenkowski and other House leaders, Russo was an attractive potential ally, but Berman was still put off by his special-interest notoriety. However, Russo participated effectively with Berman's group and won some real recognition.[27]

Russo, given his formal positions, personal alliances, and a growing power base within the House, is well placed to improve his policy credibility. Congressman John LaFalce, on the other hand, faces a different problem, largely as a result of his past record as an entrepreneur. LaFalce's expertise in banking and loan guarantee policy (for example, Chrysler Corporation) is not questioned, nor are his day-to-day political skills, which landed him a chair of the Economic Stabilization subcommittee of the Banking, Finance, and Urban Affairs Committee.[28] Nonetheless, LaFalce must confront the fact that his entrepreneurial efforts failed, almost completely, to set either the congressional or the Democratic party agenda on a national industrial policy.

Although LaFalce's subcommittee provided him with the base to devise such an agenda, almost from the beginning of the debate, there was little chance of forging a broad consensus. Without either a perceived crisis (for example, pollution in the late 1960s) or a persuasive underlying concept (equitable tax "simplification" in the 1980s), LaFalce could not weave together all the disparate threads of industrial policy.[29] The most profound policy and political divisions developed over the centerpiece of LaFalce's initiative, a national development bank. Entrepreneurs must convince their colleagues that an idea has merit. Otherwise, as political scientist Ross Baker observes, "the perception that an issue or a program has substantive flaws—this was surely the case with industrial policy—may well cause members to move on to other issues."[30]

In the end, LaFalce's aggressive style, coupled with an unworkable policy vision, has left him with a mixed reputation in the House. Had he been more successful with industrial policy, LaFalce might well have led a revolt against autocratic Banking Committee chair Fernand St Germain (D-R.I.), who has faced ethics charges. At the same time, the still-operating seniority system has rewarded LaFalce with the chairmanship of the Small Business Committee and the congressman can take heart that the involvement of Tim Wirth and Dick Gephardt in industrial policy has not hindered their careers. Still, one of the marks of a successful entrepreneur is to know when to cut one's losses, and neither of these activists kept their grip on the industrial policy agenda as it slid from national consideration.

In addition, as John Kingdon persuasively argues—and the Bradleys and Waxmans of the world convincingly demonstrate—sheer persistence often determines the success of a policy entrepreneur.[31] The economic conditions that prompted the industrial policy proposals have not disappeared. In the late 1980s many similar issues have resurfaced in the rhetoric of trade and competitiveness, and Gephardt, among others, has sought to attach his political fortunes to these concerns. His was a high-risk strategy, tied to a presidential campaign that briefly took off in Iowa but quickly spattered. The great difficulties in integrating the myriad strands of trade or industrial policy also illustrate why many newcomers, at least those with the Democratic label, are so difficult to categorize along traditional right-left, liberal-conservative policy dimensions.

Individuals and Issues: New Politicians and New Labels

The attention attracted by individual entrepreneurs such as Bradley, Wirth, Tsongas, Gephardt, and Hart has engendered attempts to lump together their approaches to government under a single label. With the promotion and active support of *Washington Monthly* editor Charles Peters, the term "neoliberals" evolved in the early 1980s, culminating in Randall Rothenberg's generally positive assessment in his 1984 book, *The Neoliberals: Creating the New American Politics.*

In dozens of interviews, I have never heard a single individual—elected official, staff aide, or journalist—use the term "neoliberal" as part of any normal conversation. Indeed, Rothenberg concedes that the so-called neoliberals reject the label. To the extent that any grouping does exist Gephardt concludes, "It's a group without a charter, without even a self-identification."[32]

Rothenberg embarks upon a twofold strategy to delineate the nebulous boundaries of neoliberalism. First, and most telling, he identifies a handful of (mostly) young politicians, journalists, and academics who "constitute the congregation."[33] The class of '74 provides some of his major suspects, such as Gary Hart, Paul Tsongas, and Tim Wirth, who are listed as the congressional core, along with Albert Gore, Jr. (D-Tenn.) (1976), Richard Gephardt (1976), and Bill Bradley (1978). To the extent that "neoliberalism" retains any meaning in the late 1980s, it must rely on an association with active policy entrepreneurs, many of whom are real or prospective 1988 presidential candidates. For example, as the 1988 presidential campaign progressed, *The New Republic*'s TRB columnist observed that Michael Dukakis's approach to government was "to let capitalism do its powerful thing, but [not to] shy away from using the state to nurture it and spread its blessings more fairly. This used to be called 'neoliberalism' a couple years ago, before that became a term of contempt having more to do with hairstyles than political philosophy."[34]

The second, even less concrete manifestation of neoliberalism derives from some overarching approaches to issues. Without question the new pols of the 1970s brought some fresh perspectives to the national policy debate. Coming into office in an era of limits rather than of growth, these politicians rejected many of the tenets of New Deal and Great Society liberalism. Within their pragmatic approach, Rothenberg identifies three broad organizing trends in the neoliberals' thinking: investment, not redistribution; appropriate technologies, not rigid centralization; and cooperation, not interest group competition.[35]

In general, however, individual politicians have experienced more success than has any set of neoliberal nostrums. The policy impacts of a Bradley on tax reform and a Wirth on cable television are scarcely the mark of a successful ideology, no matter how loosely defined. Rather, they represent the results of tenacious, knowledgeable policy entrepreneurs moving a major policy onto the congressional agenda and, with lots of help, through the legislative process.

A brief reexamination of industrial policy, a major item on

the neoliberal agenda of the early 1980s, is instructive. Among their class of '74 peers, in the House John LaFalce and Tim Wirth invested the most political capital in this broad issue. Working through the normal channel of a major House subcommittee, LaFalce attempted to establish a national development bank. This went nowhere, and the congressman benefited little, if at all, from the application of his substantive expertise.

Tim Wirth generated nothing more concrete than LaFalce. Nevertheless, his career was given a boost by his task force work in overseeing the Democrats' efforts to develop long-term economic policy. In 1981–82, Wirth succeeded in weaving both political and policy threads through the process and into the ultimate report, the "yellow book."

In the end, Wirth could take credit for helping move a broadly based set of items, which roughly reflected an industrial policy initiative, onto the governmental agenda. Agenda setting is almost always easier than coalition building, and LaFalce was left with the less enviable task of forging legislation. Wirth retained an identification with industrial policy, but through good fortune or prescience, he avoided the pitfalls of trying to pass legislation in this extraordinarily difficult issue area.

For Wirth, LaFalce, and the so-called neoliberals, as for any group of youngish politicians, Jonathan Yardley writes, there is a "question that won't go away: Is their real interest progress for the country or power for themselves?"[36] The answer is both. Ideas are identified with individuals who want to govern. One peculiar characteristic of this era, when congressional authority is dispersed and executive leadership is questioned, is that individual policy entrepreneurs have shouldered the burden of putting forward possible solutions to difficult problems. It is scarcely surprising that these politicians—the Gephardts, Kemps, Harts, Simons, Bradleys—are projected as presidential material.

Party as Forum

One of the best lines from the 1988 presidential campaign came in Senator Paul Simon's announcement speech, when he stated flatly, "I am not a neo-anything. I am a Democrat."[37] Although Simon's comments on party were meant to strike a traditional chord, they capture one essence of contemporary issue-based politics, that most activists conduct their policy debates within a partisan context, even though subsequent legislative initiatives may require bipartisan support. Developing the party into a series of forums is especially prevalent inside the House, as opposed to the more individualistic Senate, where each member strives to set his own agenda.

Increasingly, legislative parties structure policy debates, and entrepreneurs operate within the party-based arenas. The Democratic whip operation, which now includes more than seventy members, acts like a weekly caucus, at which more than one-fourth of all House Democrats can have their say. Such a forum does not ordinarily resolve policy debates; rather, middle management leaders are given continuing opportunities to make their case. Likewise, the Democratic Caucus's Committee on Party Effectiveness offers members an opportunity, in one aide's words, "to range beyond their committees and to have a sense of the dynamism . . . in the House."[38]

Given their distance from the levers of power, House Republicans have somewhat fewer formal channels for expression, but the thrust of the GOP Policy Committee and Conference activities is similar. Congressmen Jack Kemp (former Policy Committee chair) and Richard Cheney (R-Wyo.) (Conference chair), despite stylistic differences, are comfortable in encouraging policy debates within their ranks.

Ironically, it was the entrepreneurial House of the late 1970s that strengthened the party's role in providing the forum for developing alternatives. During the tenure of Speaker Tip

O'Neill, the class of '74 and their junior colleagues became full partners in the policy debate. The House did not develop into a complete meritocracy in that seniority and an active apprenticeship remained significant. But the Robert Kruegers, the Henry Waxmans, the Henry Hydes demonstrated that policy expertise, coupled with political skills, could take legislators a long way, even within the House. For others, like a Paul Simon, a Charles Grassley, or a Tim Wirth, the House served as a stepping-stone to the Senate, the policy entrepreneur's promised land.

The Rise of the Idea Merchants

The class of '74 and other new pols have reached political maturity within a fragmented Congress that encourages participation as much as that of the 1950s required patience. Legislators continue to value expertise, but the context for obtaining and using information has changed a great deal.

In the past, legislators became policy experts through extended committee service. With increased staff, expanded research capacities, and a breakdown of the apprenticeship norm, newcomers and backbenchers now are expected to participate fully in the legislative process. Although the Congress has greatly expanded the number of formal opportunities for participation, the currency of this activity is competence on the issues. As Congressman George Miller notes, "Substance gets you a shot. You get an opportunity to play. You have to earn that." Such a circumstance prompts increasing numbers of legislators to engage in retail politics, in which support is solicited through a series of almost endless one-on-one conversations.

This issue-based style can work within the Congress, especially for those who mix patience and persistence with their expertise, but progress is often excruciatingly slow. In addition to the problems it poses for majority building, the retail politics style has severe limitations for those with ambitions toward the presidency. Congressman Richard Gephardt, widely regarded as an extremely capable retail politician, did not succeed in converting his legislative assets into presidential campaign strengths. Even in Iowa, which lends itself to one-on-one politicking, Gephardt succeeded only with a populist-oriented media barrage. The pragmatism that has marked Gephardt's actions in the House created problems when his target expanded from specific pieces of legislation to some broader vision. As one presidential strategist comments, "Gephardt's record has been all over the place. All of his proposals . . . leave questions of who he is."[39]

In contrast, Gary Hart, who eschewed the Congress's retail politics, successfully articulated a new generation theme in his strong 1984 presidential bid. Hart's policy competence came through in the broad brushstrokes of "new ideas, new approaches, new issues," which began to cut many Democratic ties to the New Deal.[40] Though atypical of his congressional colleagues, Hart at least sketched the outlines of how expertise can be communicated in "wholesale" terms. Hart's expertise on military policy is widely recognized, but he has not actively built coalitions to push his ideas. This does not mean that Hart has not had influence. As Congressman Les Aspin argues, "There is no Gary Hart military reorganization act that passed Congress, but there are an awful lot of Gary Hart ideas in what we're doing."[41] Few other members of Hart's political generation have succeeded in articulating any broad vision of American politics. Focusing on specific issues and concrete problems may well limit their capacities to set the national agenda and capture the reins of executive power.

4

Entrepreneurs and the Public Eye

TALKING ABOUT the post-1974 Congress, *New York Times* reporter Martin Tolchin observes that the pragmatic new generation of legislators "use reporters like they use anything else." He continues:

> It's like Russell Long said when he was asked about morality and politics. Long said, roughly, "If it works, use it. You can use morality like you can use anything else." . . . Getting publicity is part of the necessary equipment of being a politician today.

If anything, shunning publicity, formerly the norm for power-seekers on Capitol Hill, has become newsworthy in itself, as a *Congressional Quarterly* profile on Congressman John Murtha (D-Pa.) suggests.[1] Elected in a 1974 special election, Murtha has developed into a powerful inside broker by eschewing any outside recognition.

Much more typical is Congressman George Miller's assessment that publicity provides an integral link between competence on issues and ultimate policy effectiveness. "Absolutely, you need [attention]," he asserts. "You have to have it around here. Visibility leads to credibility." At the same time, he acknowledges, as do most of his peers, the risks of attracting publicity. "Now you can go too far. Once people see that you're a hot dog, you've got problems." What has changed dramatically on Capitol Hill is how far is too far. Gregg Easterbrook writes, "The penalties for being a glory-seeker have been all but eliminated."[2]

Contemporary legislators deal with reporters in more regular and sophisticated ways than their predecessors. Even Lyndon Johnson (D-Tex.), as Senate majority leader, did not use the press—especially the electronic media—as a major tool in advancing his policy goals or his personal ambitions. In the 1950s, a senator such as William Proxmire (D-Wisc.), who appealed directly to the media, was labeled a maverick or a "showhorse" and summarily dismissed as a legislative force.[3] When Richard Bolling ran a publicity-oriented, "outside" 1962 campaign for majority leader, he demonstrated the essential weakness of his position within the House.[4]

Recent changes have probably affected the House of Representatives more profoundly than the Senate, many of whose members have cultivated press attention, although more often as presidential hopefuls than as legislative entrepreneurs.[5] House Majority Leader Tom Foley observes, "Sam Rayburn could have walked down the streets of Spokane, Washington, without anyone noticing him. Tip O'Neill couldn't do that, and it's very unlikely that any future Speaker will be anonymous to the country."[6] Not only is the leadership affected, notes Foley's colleague, Congressman Tony Coelho. Televised since 1979, the House has become "a goldfish bowl," in which the media play important, continuing roles in their relationships with almost all members. In addition, much of what the 535 members of Congress know of each other and their policy initiatives comes through the media, not person-to-person contact.

Congress and the Media: Beyond Stereotypes

Two complementary, but incomplete, images of Congress-media relations have arisen since the mid-1970s. The first and most public view roughly corresponds to the witless "Washingtoon" comic character, Bob Forehead. A political consultant provides an almost perfect description of this type:

> [You] get the guys with the blow-dried hair who read the script well. . . . You've got a guy who is not concerned with issues; who is not concerned about the mechanics of government; who doesn't attend committee meetings; who avoids taking positions at any opportunity and yet is a master at getting his face in the newspapers and television.[7]

Such statements lead media analyst Michael Robinson to assert, "The greatest effect of the new media mix . . . has been to attract a new kind of congressman."[8]

Without a doubt, any congressional reporter, member, or staffer can identify more than a few legislators who could pass for Bob Forehead. There is no denying that television has shaped the ways in which candidates and sitting officeholders have acted. But the outright contention that the media, and especially television, have dramatically changed the nature of who runs for Congress and how members act once elected requires close scrutiny. A strong argument can be made that more intense coverage has improved, not diminished, the quality of legislators. Not only is there no place to hide, but the media open up any numbers of opportunities for those with patience, wit, and talent. "I've never considered how they look," notes Karen Sughrue, the executive producer of "Face the Nation." "It's more important that they have something to say and how forthcoming they are."[9] Peggy Robinson,

"McNeil-Lehrer News Hour" producer, adds, "Is Claude Pepper telegenic?"[10]

A Jack Kemp or a Dick Gephardt is indeed telegenic, but no one would suggest that Phil Gramm or John Dingell fills any ideal of a "blow-dried" media star. All these legislators have become national political figures by reaching their audiences with issue-based appeals rather than "show boat" activities.

Among academics, there is a second perspective in viewing the treatment of the Congress by the press, one that emphasizes the institutional position of legislators. Because leaders receive a major share of the coverage, the media's treatment of the Congress becomes a key element in the centralization of power, rather than in its diffusion. The data compiled by Steven Hess and others paint a clear picture of top-heavy coverage in which formal leaders (for example, Bob Dole, Tip O'Neill) and serious presidential candidates receive by far the most attention among legislators.[11] At the same time, however, a few key policy entrepreneurs do appear near the top of the scholars' lists. In the early 1980s, Phil Gramm ranked inordinately high, due to his activities in writing an alternative budget. For 1985–86, the names of relatively junior senators Gramm and Bradley would rank toward the top, given their central, and well-publicized, roles on spending and tax policies, respectively.

These findings contradict the telegenic interpretation of contemporary politicians in various ways. Hess demonstrates that formal position is far more important than image in determining levels of coverage. Relatively few highly image-conscious senators (and even fewer congressmen) receive significant national attention. Moreover, the distinction between showhorses and workhorses is misleading to the point of being almost totally wrong. Hess concludes, "Today those who do the work get most of the publicity."[12]

In one essential conclusion, however, Hess and the purveyors of the telegenic perspective do agree—using publicity to promote specific policies does not work. As Hess puts it,

> Trying to use the media to get legislation through the Congress is a Rube Goldberg design based on (A) legislator influencing (B) reporter to get information into (C) news outlet so as to convince (D) voters who will then put pressure on (E) other legislators.[13]

Still, legions of senators and congressmen acting as policy entrepreneurs energetically attempt to use the press as one tool to further their goals, both personal and issue based. Neither considering patterns of coverage, which emphasize the formal leadership, nor stereotyping congressional behavior, which focuses on the mindless pursuit of attention, adequately accounts for the ways in which the new politicians understand, use, and relate to the media.

Most policy-oriented legislators see the media as essential. Tom Downey emphatically argues:

> Seeking publicity is one way—an important way—of conveying your message. Ultimately that results in good legislation. There are a lot of people who do good work around here, but that doesn't necessarily mean that you'll get recognized for it. *Not getting publicity limits your effectiveness. . . . I can't think of someone around here who's effective just by being on the inside* [emphasis added].

COVERING THE CONGRESS

There are a few accepted rules of the game in how Congress is covered by the media today. First, with a few important exceptions, senators receive more attention than do members of the House.[14] Second, most coverage of individual members is local, and most of this is favorable.[15] Correspondingly, assessments of the Congress as a whole are usually negative.[16] Third, legislators and journalists maintain both adversarial and symbiotic relationships, with the latter coming to dominate most communications.[17] In the Congress of the 1930s or the 1950s, top-ranking members did not need to maintain good relations with journalists in order to exercise power. Today, the ability to establish such ties has become a virtual necessity for most legislators as they struggle to influence policy.

Although the traditional notion that reporters and members of Congress are adversaries remains true to some extent, this is far overshadowed by their mutual needs. In a fragmented Congress, where information is often at a premium, media representatives and legislators regularly help each other perform their jobs. From the journalists' perspective, members of Congress, most of whom crave publicity, either for themselves or their favored issues, represent an endless set of sources. However, not all members receive the same amount of coverage, nor are they all equally useful to the press. Far from it. Leaders are the preferred sources, followed by those who are seen as "newsworthy," such as New York's quotable and well-informed Senate Democrat, Daniel Patrick Moynihan.[18]

Moreover, the national press and metropolitan media outlets prefer to cover senators. A senator is simply a bigger catch. "Face the Nation"'s Sughrue notes with elegant simplicity, "We tend to go for senators because there are fewer of them." In addition, senators are "more well-known nationally and tend frankly to speak out more on national policy than members of the House."[19] As former Congressman Floyd Fithian puts it:

> If I'm a reporter, if I can get a senator [to comment], I will. . . . For example, if I'm a reporter and I can get a senator from Illinois, then I've got the whole state. What does someone from the suburbs care about what [inner city House member] Charles Hayes [D-Ill.] has to say?

In short, there are members of Congress and then there are members of Congress. Even within the House, is it any wonder that House Speaker Jim Wright and junior Republican Congressman Joe Barton, who represent nearby Texas districts, receive vastly different amounts of attention?

Congressional Sources. Policy entrepreneurs can advance themselves and their favored issues by shaping their stories for the most attentive national reporters. An entrepreneur wants to gain acceptance as a "good source," which Martin Tolchin defines as

> someone who you can call at 6:00 P.M. after a tough five-hour committee meeting, who'll tell you what happened behind closed doors, even though he's sworn to his colleagues that he wouldn't. He's a guy who'll tell you what happened and get it right.

Such a trusting relationship can serve both member and reporter; yet familiarity can be dangerous. National Public Radio's Cokie Roberts notes that a good source is

> someone who's accessible. You keep going back to them. In fact, as a reporter you have to try to avoid that. . . . You don't want to use the same people over and over. . . . [Still,] the people who get coverage around here are the ones that are accessible. I know, for example, if I call [Congressman] Henry Hyde in the middle of Illinois on a weekend, he'll get back to me.

Accessibility and persistence have their benefits, although they are often long-term, not immediate. By meeting with reporters after Finance Committee meetings, Bill Bradley, scarcely a media natural, kept his version of tax reform alive throughout the Senate's lengthy markup process. Such extended, conscientious care and feeding of the national press is unusual. Most legislators spend much more of their time and resources on the local press, who report back, after all, to their constituents.

The Local/National Press Distinction. Just as journalists do not lump together all members of Congress, legislators do not view the press as some undifferentiated mass. For most members—most of the time—the local media are considerably more important than their national counterparts. Press secretaries, as key parts of the congressional enterprise, give most of their attention to local reporters and their district outlets.[20] Press aides establish regular links to all the media operations within their districts or states—ranging from major television stations and daily newspapers to small radio stations and rural weekly papers.

The local press provides virtually automatic attention to even the most junior legislators, especially outside major metropolitan areas. Such coverage is central to building a strong re-election base—news stories legitimize congressional activity, almost regardless of content. One press secretary observes:

> It personalizes it that way. The other way [direct communication] depersonalizes it; all you've got is four [newsletter] pages of "aren't I wonderful." If you go to the news, you get the balance of it—you can say you're wonderful and get someone else saying it, and then maybe someone else saying you're a dirtbag. It's more important to know that [members of Congress] are working—important to see them on the news.[21]

As this press secretary knows, legislators rarely get labeled "dirtbags" by the local press. Almost by definition local coverage is positive, often as submitted by the legislator's staff. Indeed, a substantial proportion of congressional news releases are printed verbatim or with only the most modest editing.

What distinguishes many, though not all, newer congressmen and senators from most of their senior colleagues is their assiduous cultivation of the national press. For some legislators this may simply mean getting their names displayed prominently. During 1975–76, one ambitious member of the class of

'74 was exceedingly pleased to have his name appear in either *Time* or *Newsweek* for nine weeks running. A decade later, another junior congressman expressed very similar sentiments after a measure of national attention. He noted:

> In the last couple of weeks I've had my picture in the *New York Times* twice—prominently. The New York delegation went wild. A couple even gave me a copy of the paper. . . . [At home, there's] no significance at all just to be in the *Times*. . . . it's of no consequence to your district, but it may have an [ultimate] impact on your district.

Such a reaction, however, represents only a lowest common denominator of impact. More commonly, legislators see the national press as a means of communicating with their colleagues and influential policy makers like the White House staff and top-level bureaucrats. Regardless of the ultimate goal of this attention, such as a quest for higher office, politicians obtain publicity by dealing in substantive issues, such as environmental policy or tax law. In this sense, newsworthy information on important or interesting issues becomes the coin of the realm. Political scientist Tim Cook finds that one major outcropping of political ambition is the desire of House members to gain status as a "national spokesperson" on a significant issue.[22]

Talking Heads. In 1960, roughly 1,550 journalists possessed congressional press credentials; by 1976, that number had risen to about 2,550, and by 1987, to over 4,000. Although these figures grossly inflate the actual number of congressional correspondents, because most of them have much wider beats, the growth demonstrates that since the 1970s legislators have entered an institution receiving increasing attention.

At the same time, local television stations have rapidly expanded their live coverage of Capitol Hill politics. With relatively inexpensive satellite hookups, local reporters from Wichita and Sacramento can conduct timely, on-the-spot interviews with their districts' representatives. For many House members, such coverage becomes regular and rewarding. Congressman Dan Glickman (D-Kans.) notes:

> Television stations come to me when there is an issue. . . . They know I'm available, and that I'm the one voters and viewers will identify with. . . . I can be on Tom Brokaw, but it is not as important to my re-election as being on the NBC affiliate in Wichita. . . . On national TV, you don't get more than a short bite. On local TV, it's often two or three minutes.[23]

At the national level, the changes in congressional coverage have had much more substantive implications. Although their ranks have grown somewhat over the past twenty years, there are no more than a hundred full-time national congressional correspondents. At the same time, many newspapers have bolstered their Washington staffs and have sought to play up the regional aspects of national stories. As a result, there are more reporters concentrating on the same number of legislators.

Since the early 1970s, both the electronic and print media have greatly increased the opportunities for individual members to appear before a national audience.[24] In 1975 there were precious few outlets for most members of Congress to present their favorite legislation in print or on television. Twenty-two minutes of network news each evening, plus the morning network shows and the Sunday interview programs, represented all the possibilities for regular television coverage. With the occasional exception of the morning shows, few senators and even fewer congressmen were likely to be asked to comment on a specific policy or development. For the nightly network news and the Sunday interview shows, this remains the case,[25] but coverage of Congress beyond these basic programs has proliferated tremendously in the last ten years. Public radio, for example, provides three and a half hours of national news programming each weekday. PBS's "McNeil-Lehrer News Hour," with five hours of programming each week, employs a format requiring up to a dozen spokespersons every evening. Cable News Network (CNN) has a similar hunger for knowledgeable and authoritative-sounding individuals, and where better to find cheap, accessible, and willing talking heads than within the Congress? The list of opportunities for media exposure does not stop with public radio, PBS, and CNN. ABC's "Nightline" must have its nightly quota of spokespersons, and C-SPAN likewise needs well-informed commentators on the day's events to complement its coverage of congressional floor activity.

The print media have also provided more possibilities for members of Congress to present their policy perspectives. The *Washington Post* and many other papers have adopted the two-page op-ed format made popular by the *New York Times.* An op-ed piece in the *Post, Times,* or *Wall Street Journal* can advance both a legislator's issue position and his or her standing as a significant player in the policy debate. Finally, there are the dual "insider" weeklies that devote a great deal of coverage to the Congress: *Congressional Quarterly Weekly Report (CQ)* and *National Journal.* Even more than the national daily newspapers, these authoritative and densely written magazines provide lines of communication for policy entrepreneurs both inside and outside the government.

The proliferation of media opportunities has coincided with the press's recognition of the fragmented nature of congressional decision making. Although the process of change had begun before the class of '74 arrived on Capitol Hill, no single event more exemplified the changes than the unceremonious dumping of three senior committee chairmen during the 1975 organization of the House. Coupled with other reforms, this action of the Democratic Caucus told congressional correspondents and other interested parties that to understand the chances of a key piece of environmental legislation, talking to the chair of Energy and Commerce was no longer enough, even when the relatively powerful John Dingell came to occupy that seat. Subcommittee chairman Henry Waxman (after 1979) and even junior subcommittee members, such as Dennis Eckart (D-Ohio), might hold the key to explaining how policies would be resolved. Indeed, on some occasions, the central actors might not even hold seats on the relevant committees, as was the case for Jack Kemp and "supply side" tax cuts in the early days of the Reagan administration.

Publicity and the Class of 1974

Freshman members of Congress have traditionally arrived in Washington to a bit of ceremony and attention and subsequently shuffled off to learn the tangled ropes of the legislative process. In the 1950s, a first-term member might not reappear in the press until he had spent a decade-long apprenticeship practicing that arcane art of being seen but not heard. In the early 1970s the apprenticeship norm was observed more in name than practice, but first-term members of Congress could not anticipate wielding real power or receiving substantial attention from the press.

The class of '74, however, did both, almost from the moment its members were elected, well in advance of being sworn in. NPR's Cokie Roberts notes that "this group [beginning with the class of '74] understands television. They came in understanding television, and when the technology advanced, with the local TV stations providing coverage, it took the members about fifteen seconds to see what was going on." In the wake of the 1974 election, the new members quickly became accustomed to media attention. As one top leadership aide observes, this was a watershed for the Congress. "The big difference between the pre-'74 people and the ones since then [is that] they're good at getting attention." For a handful of these politicians, obtaining good coverage was as natural as breathing, but for most dealing effectively with the press required early lessons and expert instructors. Both, fortunately, were available.

In her work on political campaigning, Marjorie Hershey uses social learning theory to explain how candidates and their managers learn from both their own experiences and those of other successful campaigns. She notes that "in observational learning (. . . or modelling), people watch, read, or hear about the behavior of others—their actions, their words, their feelings and strategies—and form an image in their minds of how that behavior is performed."[26]

The 1974 congressional neophytes acted in much this way; they were not, for the most part, practiced politicians. In the aftermath of their often surprising electoral victories, they found their models where they could, within their own ranks and among incumbent legislators. Three such models stand out, although there were many others. The first comprises the collective experiences of the class in the first few months after the 1974 election. The second model is Connecticut's Toby Moffett, whose name crops up time and time again in conversations with his classmates. Finally, and perhaps most important, is Congressman Les Aspin, who, more than any single legislator, has instructed contemporary members of both chambers on how to play the game of inside policy influence through outside, media-based channels.

THE INITIAL EXPERIENCE

Even before the class of '74 members took their oaths of office, they were learning about the alluring power of the press. Former Congressman Ned Pattison reminisced that by early December 1974,

> the press was paying more and more attention to the phenomenon of the freshman. Martin Agronsky . . . invited Martha Keys of Kansas, Andy Maguire of New Jersey, and me to appear on [the nationally syndicated program "Eve-

> ning Edition"]. . . . It was very heady stuff to be on national TV for a halfhour program. I received favorable comments for many months from people back home who had seen it. I began to better understand the comment that Henry Kissinger made about politics being the "ultimate aphrodisiac."[27]

Pattison's experience was reenacted by any number of other class members; even the most awkward politicians received at least a bit of coverage. More significant in the long run, however, has been the media depictions of the 1974 election victors as an identifiable unit. The intensity and amount of early press coverage has meant that the "Watergate" class label (or the less flattering title of "Watergate babies") has remained with the class long after it ceased to operate as any kind of cohesive unit.[28]

A general impression developed within the press that these post-Watergate legislators did represent something different. The *National Journal* observed in its first-year assessment of the class that the techniques used "by the new Members—such as writing newspaper columns and doing television shows—are also done by their seniors, but with less frequency," and Congressman Pattison concluded that no "other class has understood the techniques of communication as well as this one."[29]

For journalists, Colorado's Tim Wirth came to represent the archetype of the emerging public style of the mid-1970s. Former Congressman Jerome Ambro (D-N.Y.), a class of '74 colleague, recounts, "When we came in, the press was calling Wirth the 'pick of the litter.' After that, when he'd come in a room, we'd all bark or go 'oink-oink.' But look—he's a natural." Wirth reflects the ease with which new pols weave issues into their media performances, especially on television. Indeed, the willingness to exploit television, while feeling comfortable about it, is a central characteristic of the new generations of national politicians. "I don't see [TV] as a conspiracy of a generation to figure out what to do to succeed," notes Congressman

Dennis Eckart, an attractive, aggressive junior legislator. "I see it as endemic in our very makeup."[30] For no recent member of Congress does this statement apply more accurately, or more ironically, than to former Congressman Toby Moffett.

TOBY MOFFETT: FROM CONGRESSMAN TO ANCHORMAN

By late 1986, Toby Moffett's issue-oriented, publicity-driven political career had ground to a halt. A local press report explained:

> In Washington [Moffett] displayed a high-voltage personality and was known for having press conferences first and consulting with colleagues second. Despite his tender years [thirty in 1974], the national press treated him as a savant and ticketed him for great things, but . . . many [now] question whether he has any political future left at all.[31]

A narrow loser in his 1982 attempt to unseat liberal Republican Senator Lowell Weicker, four years later Moffett made a quixotic effort to defeat fellow Democrat William O'Neill, the incumbent governor of Connecticut. Failing to force a primary election, Moffett became, in October 1986, an anchorman for the six and eleven o'clock news on Hartford's WVIT. In many ways, nothing could have been more appropriate.

No class of '74 member was more comfortable with the press than Toby Moffett, whose experiences as head of a statewide public interest group led him to understand the value of obtaining good coverage, especially when one possessed few other resources. Although Moffett's argumentative, publicity-oriented style drew criticism, his classmates generally viewed him favorably. A former aide fondly recounted Moffett's parking a "lemon" at the foot of the Capitol and holding a press conference there to dramatize the difficulties consumers faced in forcing automobile manufacturers to honor their warranties. "Of course," he went on, "when you're a subcommittee chairman, you don't need to do that any more"—which is exactly the point for Moffett and many of his colleagues. Much of their publicity-seeking resulted from their lowly position as junior members and a fervent desire to have an immediate impact on policy.

After the class of '74 members had moved into subcommittee chairmanships, their need to attract publicity through stunts or provocative statements diminished sharply, but their visibility did not. Moffett, as a subcommittee chair on the investigation-oriented Government Operations Committee, could easily hold hearings that would attract press attention, especially on energy policy—a fact Moffett and his colleagues both understood and exploited. The *New York Times*'s coverage of Moffett more than doubled in the years following his rise to chairman status, even though he was speaking out on roughly the same issues as before.[32]

Several years after leaving the Congress, Moffett retains an indirect effect on congressional agenda setting. Classmate Congressman Norm Mineta notes:

> Moffett could really get publicity. He really understood it. First of all he had the best press secretary of all of us, Willie Blacklow. And second, he just knew how to do it. . . . When we're talking among ourselves now [1987], we're always saying among ourselves, "Hold it, how do we get this thing across. No matter how good our idea is, how do we get these 2 minutes and 15 seconds in prime time?"

Moffett's penchant for obtaining publicity, along with the similar talents of other younger members, served an additional important purpose for many of his colleagues, which became apparent only after he had left the House. He and a few other "bomb-throwers" outflanked most of their fellow classmates in calling for reform and government-imposed solutions to problems of energy prices and consumer protection. Almost wistfully, Congressman Jim Florio, no shrinking violet himself, reflected in 1984:

> I miss Moffett and [former Congressman Andy] Maguire . . . and now [Senator Al] Gore, too. I need them to be the crazies. Then someone like me comes in and looks more reasonable. . . . You want them to be the Bolsheviks. The trouble is, now I'm out on the flank.

In 1985–86, Florio's fears came true, as he played the "Moffett" role on superfund legislation, while Congressman Eckart inherited the "Florio" position of presenting a more moderate policy alternative as a basis for a winning coalition.

Toby Moffett's issue-based, publicity-oriented style, placed within an open institution, has contributed a great deal to how contemporary legislators conduct themselves. Both junior Republicans, like Newt Gingrich, and their Democratic counterparts, such as Oklahoma's Congressman David McCurdy, have thrust themselves into the front ranks of issue debates, simultaneously seeking policy impact and personal attention. Like Moffett, Gingrich and McCurdy have paid a price for the publicity-oriented style. Elizabeth Drew captures this part of the new style, noting in 1986 that

> McCurdy, who is thirty-six and was first elected to the House in 1980, is one of a number of junior members who [have] become prominent by carving out an issue and working hard at it. By definition, some members see these people as a bit pushy, as seeking the limelight. The line between earnestness and pushiness is a hard one to draw, and while many members like McCurdy, some have grown tired of his being in the limelight.[33]

Moffett had demonstrated to members like McCurdy that bruising a few egos can be acceptable if the work being done had some real substance, although the dividing line between the successes of Moffett and—to a greater extent—Senator Albert Gore are offset by the truncated careers of such a highly visible activist as former Congressman Andy Maguire. Even for Moffett, the question of means and ends in obtaining publicity may have ultimately become confused. As one of Governer O'Neill's aides waggishly noted in 1986, upon learning of Moffett's impending television news job, "Well, O'Neill gets what he wants, to be governor, and Toby gets what he wants, all the TV time he can use."

Finally, if Toby Moffett and his colleagues are any indication, the most effective publicity seekers within the House eventually seek a more prominent soapbox—usually the Senate but, on occasion, the presidency. Texas's Robert Krueger, Colorado's Tim Wirth, Connecticut's Moffett and Chris Dodd, and in a lesser key, Iowa's Tom Harkin and Illinois's Paul Simon, all sought publicity with alacrity, weaving it into their career development. Although the House can and does sustain this style, it is the Senate's individualism that most rewards such behavior. As many House members continue to demonstrate, however, a Senate seat is not a prerequisite for effective action as a policy entrepreneur. No one illustrates this fact so well as that past master of congressional media relations, Congressman Les Aspin, who helped create the issue-based, public style adopted by many post-Watergate activists.

LES ASPIN: THE OUTSIDER AS INSIDER

In scores of interviews, no class of '74 member has ever spontaneously suggested that Les Aspin has had a profound effect on the way legislators deal with the press. Yet, acknowledged or not, Aspin has affected the styles of literally hundreds of individual members. There have been many skilled cultivators of press attention, but Aspin demonstrates most effectively that using the press is a strategic possibility for even the most junior of policy entrepreneurs.

Ever since his 1970 arrival on Capitol Hill, Aspin has understood that, in his words, "no congressman is a source story in Washington."[34] Even the most powerful member of Congress cannot make news simply as the source of that information. Only the president can truly be regarded in such terms, at least for the national press. Members of Congress must provide the press with new or different information. Much of this revolves around anticipation of where a story is headed and what the press's interest may be. For Aspin,

> a story is like a sailing ship—it can only stay on one tack so long. You've got to know when it's going to come about and make the other tack, and be there with your report or your speech. . . . There are not more than a half a dozen reporters who understand what you're saying. Hell, I don't know how many readers of the *New York Times* understand the stuff, but the *Times* and the *Washington Post* write for the aficionados—of the defense department, for example. This operation is all aimed at them. . . . *You're trying to influence the debate on the subject* [emphasis added].[35]

For the class of '74, Aspin's influence was profound, if somewhat indirect. From their earliest days in Congress, the Watergate babies viewed the combination of hard work and substantive expertise as the keys to achieving policy success. Aspin embodied those traits. A Ph.D. in economics with a background in Robert McNamara's Defense Department, Aspin worked diligently to master defense policy and to obtain national press coverage. He saw such attention as essential to make him a major player on an Armed Services Committee that discouraged deviations from the senior members' conservative positions. Many younger policy activists both supported and learned from Aspin's willingness to risk internal (the Congress and the committee) sanctions and disapproval by employing an outside strategy. That Aspin regularly succeeded in affecting the American defense policy agenda sent a clear message to impatient younger members such as Downey, Moffett, and Maguire that this behavior could be effective and, broadly speaking, acceptable.

In the 1980s, Aspin has continued to serve as an important model for his less senior colleagues, although not so much from a press-related perspective. Over the years his approach to the military became less sharp and more conciliatory as he slowly moved into positions of some formal power on the Armed Services Committee—to the point that he could emerge, through a series of coincidences, as a legitimate and ultimately successful candidate for committee chair in 1985.

Even under a strong challenge to his chairmanship in 1987, Aspin could do what he had to—in this instance, fight his battles privately. As veteran Speaker O'Neill aide Chris Matthews notes with unsuppressed glee:

> The man who had risen to power on the press release shifted to the personal approach, telephoning one member of Congress at a time. The state-of-the-art pol was forced to salvage his ambitions the old way. The man who loves the Brinkley show was forced to stand at the little congressional subway, holding out palm cards.[36]

Matthews characterizes Aspin's actions as the mark of a desperate man. Perhaps, but over the long term he is an individual who has successfully tested the limits of tolerance within the contemporary Congress as well as any legislator, and he was simply doing what was necessary—to retain his chairmanship, affect defense policy, and appear on the Brinkley show again and again.

PUTTING THE LESSONS TO WORK: THE POLITICS OF FOREIGN POLICY

Finding Senator Chris Dodd and Congressman Stephen Solarz, two of the class's most skilled publicity mongers, operating in the sphere of foreign policy comes as no surprise. The

Congress's post-Vietnam role in foreign affairs has never been completely clarified. As a result, publicity-oriented policy entrepreneurs often attempt to influence the debate, even if they harbor few hopes of producing immediate, concrete accomplishments. Broadening the scope of the conflict, on South Africa or contra aid, may be the only real weapon that opponents of administration policy can bring to bear.

Senator Chris Dodd: Exploiting the Senate's Advantages. With apparent irony, Dodd, as a senator, has employed a modified version of the traditional House strategy of committee-based specialization to reach a position as key congressional spokesman on Central American issues. Dodd's visibility as a senator has allowed him to attract press coverage on his own agenda of Central American concerns. For example, the congressional Democratic leadership selected Dodd to respond to a 1983 Reagan speech on Latin America, and he then became a fixture on the weekend news programs as an articulate opponent of Republican policies. With a Peace Corps stint in the Dominican Republic and fluency in Spanish, Dodd has the background and expertise to question administration policies. In addition, he commands the "tremendous forum" of the Senate.[37]

Dodd's status on Latin America has grown since the Democrats won a Senate majority in 1986, projecting him into the Foreign Relations subcommittee chair on Latin America. In advance of his tenure, he visited five Central American countries and Mexico, speaking with the chief of state in each instance. During the trip, Nicaraguan President Daniel Ortega personally handed over captured pilot Eugene Hasenfus to Dodd. With this kind of access, combined with his language skills and long-term experience, Dodd does not need to seek publicity. Rather, from his Senate Foreign Relations Committee position, he can attempt to exert serious inside influence on Latin American policy, knowing that he can publicize these issues almost whenever he desires.

Congressman Steve Solarz: Pushing the Limits. Since his 1974 election, Solarz has fought the long odds against a House member exerting much influence over foreign policy. He has acted much more like a Senate Foreign Relations Committee member of the 1960s, such as George McGovern (D-S.Dak.) or Frank Church (D-Idaho), than a typical House policy specialist. As a subcommittee chair on the Foreign Affairs Committee, Solarz has become an important legislative player in many emerging foreign policy debates. However, if a congressman is to attract the attention usually reserved for key senators, that member must be inordinately skilled at serving the needs of the press—and Solarz is nothing if not accommodating.

Solarz has mastered many of Aspin's lessons on attracting media attention and has developed a few innovations of his own. Above all, he knows what he is talking about, as does his staff. His administrative assistant explains how the Solarz enterprise meshes with his entrepreneurial style:

> We have seven staffers who do foreign policy, four on the [House Foreign Affairs] subcommittee, one State Department detailee, one Budget Committee person who has a Ph.D. on Latin America, one legislative assistant who has a long-term interest in refugee matters. By definition he covers the committee area better than anyone else. Plus, over the years he's gone to dozens and dozens—hundreds—of briefings with everyone. He really knows the issues.

Beyond this, Solarz has traveled more extensively and has probably gained more from his trips than any other legislator in the post-1974 period. As Solarz describes his strategy, "Information and knowledge are the key to influence. My knowledge has been enhanced by the trips I've taken abroad."[38] On this score, his behavior occasions no serious debate.

A combination of committee position and knowledge does not, however, guarantee press coverage or even interest. Solarz's fellow subcommittee chair, the well-liked and thoughtful Congressman Lee Hamilton (D-Ind.), gets much less attention because he seeks much less. Solarz is accessible, knowledgeable, and quotable—an almost irresistible mix; he is also relentless in his quest for press coverage. It may appear that someone like Solarz bursts upon the scene when a major news story like the fall of Philippine president Marcos comes along. Nothing could be further from the truth.

Rather, Solarz continually anticipated the Marcos story by a few days. On occasion, however, this could not be done, as when the congressman had to race to the Philippines after the Marcos regime toppled thus gaining a *Newsweek* photograph as he embraced Corazon Aquino. Such behavior earns Solarz the label of an unbridled media hound. Nevertheless, this type of hustling is the exception, both because the press would not regularly cover it and because Solarz represents an extremely well-informed and accessible source. As the Marcos-Aquino-Philippines story unraveled, Solarz stayed ahead of the curve, especially in his investigation of Marcos's wealth. "He played the story well," observed Harrison Rainie of the *New York Daily News.* "He was very careful to ration the stuff. And yet there was real news attached to each event he orchestrated."[39]

Solarz has paid an undetermined price for his media-conscious behavior (see chapter 3). By temperament a loner, he has built few strong personal ties to his fellow members of Congress. One congressman noted that Solarz's "approach is not always collegial." But the ability to play the inside game is important to any House member, and Solarz's isolation renders him less influential than his stature and subcommittee chair might suggest.

Most members are unwilling to make public judgments about the actions of their colleagues, but Solarz does not receive this consideration. In interviews with a wide range of members and staff, a relatively consistent picture of Solarz emerges—one that acknowledges his expertise, but resents his single-minded efforts to promote himself and his foreign policy agenda. Congressman Marty Russo states:

> Everyone fits in a niche around here, but Solarz is so caught up in foreign policy, that's all he deals with. Plus, he's got the tendency to be smart ass, which can interfere with the programs that he's pushing. Downey [a Russo friend] can be a smart ass too, but he can joke about it. You can get away with more if the other members know you more.

Democratic Study Group executive director Dick Conlon strikes a similar note, although he emphasizes Solarz's ambition. "There are a lot of ambitious people around here, but it's just so obvious with Steve." Aspin, he notes, is successful because he is willing, on occasion, to hide his ambition, "plus, Aspin's personable. He's likable. He can josh around. He's good at it."

In addition, Solarz does not suffer fools easily, which translates to a reputation for arrogance, a liability within the House. One lobbyist observes that "Steve thinks he's smarter than everyone else."[40] A House Foreign Affairs committee staffer commented, early in Solarz's career, "There's a saying on the staff that no bill can pass [the committee] without a 'Solarz amendment.' No matter what the issue, whatever comes past, he tacks on an amendment."

Still, wielding influence within the House may be less significant for Solarz than for most of his colleagues. As Congressman Robert Torricelli (D-N.J.) observes:

> What makes him different than most members of the [Foreign Affairs] Committee is that he has a real interest in influencing policy beyond the committee. He has developed the kind of relations with foreign leaders and Administration officials that give him much broader influ-

> ence. . . . He has used his time in Congress to get a good education. This is not it for Steve Solarz.[41]

Such ambition, of course, fits thoroughly with the entrepreneurial style and the actions of the class of '74. Solarz's sights are more likely set on the secretary of state's office than a Senate seat, much as Les Aspin's ambitions and policy concerns might lead him to become secretary of defense, rather than to any higher elective office.

Despite Solarz's relentless attempts to obtain press coverage, the congressman remains virtually an essential source on many foreign policy stories. He and the journalists covering him do not need to like each other, but they do need each other. Through this symbiotic relationship, Solarz has made himself one of a number of (mostly) younger congressmen and senators who are highly regarded for their effectiveness in dealing with the press. In a 1986 article on Congress and the media, political reporter Paul West listed twenty-eight legislators considered to be especially effective: only four of those listed were elected before 1974, and seven (Senator Dodd and Congressmen Solarz, Les AuCoin [D-Oreg.], Florio, Miller, Waxman, and Wirth) are members of the class of '74.[42]

Policy Entrepreneurs and the Media Connection

Congressmen and senators can lose sight of why they are seeking press attention. Chris Matthews, as a former press secretary, sees a generational trend among younger legislators. "You ask these guys why they want to be on TV, and it's like asking a moth why he likes a light bulb. It's why they're there."[43] Perhaps, but in the end, Les Aspin argues, the most important result of his sophisticated press techniques has allowed him to "influence the debate." He notes that a legislator must always bear in mind that "even if you're a subcommittee chairman or a full committee chairman, at the end of the process, the question is, what difference have you made?"[44] For policy entrepreneurs this is not, as Aspin acknowledges, an easy question to answer.

Class of '74 member Floyd Fithian, for eight years an Indiana representative, and for more than four a staff member in the House and Senate, observes that

> you get publicity around here for three reasons: First, to get re-elected. Second, on behalf of a cause; there are 435 people there, [and] it's tough to get them interested. . . . [if you get the media] other members pay attention, especially if you're down on the lower half of the order. Third, there's political advancement.

Policy entrepreneurs need to use the press, and the best ones are good at it and enjoy the process. Being a public figure is part of the game. As a campaign consultant advised Congressman Bob Edgar as he prepared to mount his Senate candidacy, "You should become a nonobnoxious media hound."

INFLUENCING THE DEBATE

Academic evidence to the contrary, most contemporary national legislators think that issues can be raised, that the agenda can be set, that alternatives can be framed through the skillful use of the media.[45] This is not to say that they see themselves as manipulating either the press or the debate; rather, they view their role as participants, trying to move an issue in one direction or another. This is accepted not only as possible but virtually essential. Consider the statements of two former House members, neither of whom remotely qualify as a publicity hound. Berkley Bedell noted:

> On many issues you need real national attention for the issue, if you're going to be successful. It's got a lot to do with staff. Success in raising issues often relates directly to staff.

Martha Keys (D-Kans.) commented:

> If you're an activist, a person who went into politics to solve problems, like I am, there aren't many chances [to have an impact] at present. . . . Raising issues is about the only way to demonstrate the failings of the [Reagan] administration. [Its] voice gets attention, so I don't know of any other way.

Bedell and Keys see publicity as important, if somewhat dependent on circumstance or staff efforts. For them, as for other low-key legislators, seeking press coverage is not a natural act. It's a lot like raising money—something that needs to be done, but that few members perform easily or well. For increasing numbers of national political figures, however, engaging in publicity-oriented maneuvers is simply part of the day's work. Media strategies have become vital means for politicians to meet their legislative goals. Not only are one's colleagues alerted, but so are key outsiders who can help to frame the debate. One press secretary insightfully noted, "Define the political landscape to include your goals, and then it's easier to respond to that landscape."[46]

One problem in assessing the ultimate success of media strategies is that they are frequently lumped together, with little attempt to differentiate among them. For example, Jack Kemp's broad 1978–79 attempts to set the agenda on supply-side economics differ categorically from the efforts of a subcommittee chair to influence a few votes on a specific piece of legislation. Another problem is time span and issue specificity, which come into play as soon as one begins to discuss media

TABLE 4.1

Time and Specificity of Issues and Media Strategy

		Time	
		Short	Long
Specificity	High	Key vote (contra aid)	Complex agenda (immigration)
	Low	Partisan appeal (judicial appointment)	Broad agenda (stronger defense)

strategies (see table 4.1). When Congressman Jim Florio sought publicity, one aide observed, there was either a long-term agenda-setting goal or an immediate desire to "shake free a few votes," on a particular bill, such as toxic waste.

Ordinarily, short-term considerations are specific ones; long-term attempts to influence the agenda are more general, even though frequently phrased in specifics. Thus, Senator Bill Bradley has always promoted tax reform in relatively specific terms, but the underlying ideas of broadening the tax base and reducing the rates have been far more important than any particular detail. Other issues, such as immigration reform or acid rain, are so complex that basic principles or simplifications are inadequate to further the idea. In these circumstances, even a proficient media-oriented entrepreneur, such as Wyoming's Republican Senator Alan Simpson on immigration law, has encountered grave difficulties in promoting a major policy change. The complex immigration reform act was finally enacted only after it became a low visibility political problem upon which inside pressures were brought to bear. (See the discussion of Charles Schumer's involvement in immigration policy in chapter 5.)

For most representatives and senators, the basic lesson is that policies can be moved—onto the agenda and through the legislative process—by the skillful use of a media strategy. Regardless of the difficulties inherent in such an approach, the fact remains that the Jack Kemps, Phil Gramms, Dick Gephardts, and Bill Bradleys of the contemporary Congress have succeeded in bringing major policies into the arena of national discussion and decision. The continuing willingness of Republican Finance Committee Chairman Bob Packwood (R-Oreg.) to share tax reform credit with Bradley, a relatively junior Democrat, demonstrates the extent to which normal party and seniority lines can be ignored. Such a lesson—like the one provided by Senators Gramm, Rudman, and Hollings on deficit reduction—is unlikely to be lost upon legions of policy activists.

At the same time, a much larger group of politicians—larger than those who have pushed through comprehensive policy changes—have used similar publicity-based tactics to obtain a hearing for any number of less earth-shaking policy proposals. One staff member, who has worked as an aide for four class of '74 members, concludes that

> the question around here is: How does one of 435 [representatives] assert credibility? Especially when there are 6000 bills introduced each Congress and only a small percentage pass—and most of those are "must pass" pieces of legislation. . . . These "must pass" bills are not emblematic of individual legislation. It's well nigh impossible to make your mark with legislative ability. Access to the press leads to credibility with various groups—interest groups, fellow legislators. There's a snowball effect. It increases his opportunities and his effectiveness.

These sentiments echo those of Willie Blacklow, former press aide to Moffett and George Miller, who notes that on occasion he has sought media coverage with no pressing or clear policy aim.

> Sometimes there's no legislative goal, at least not immediate. That was often the case on the Education and Labor

> Committee, and the "kiddie committee" [The Select Committee on Children and the Family], that's got no legislative authority at all.

Rather, extensive coverage and an effective press operation have helped to make George Miller a more important national politician. Good information, attractively packaged, would bring the reporters back when the congressman did have a policy that he wished to move.

Conversely, other politicians seek to move policies without having their names attached. Cokie Roberts notes that

> often a [Majority Leader] Tom Foley or a Matt McHugh will not be cited but will move an issue forward with a significant comment or valuable information. Foley is constitutionally unwilling to be quoted, but he'll give you very, very good interviews and you'll be able to use it.

On the record or off, the new generation has come to accept the media as a major vehicle for pressing their policy agenda—within the electorate, the Congress, and the broader Washington community. "Sometimes," notes Foley, "you have to change the attitude of the country." At the same time, Congressman Downey concludes, "If you want to reach your colleagues . . . the best way [may be] to let them see you on TV or to read your name in the paper."[47] Not all such attempts succeed, of course, but Congress today is filled with skilled entrepreneurs who commit considerable time, effort, and resources to push their favored issues onto the policy agenda.

POLICY, PUBLICITY, AND PERSONAL GOALS

Policy entrepreneurs do not lead one dimensional political lives. In fact, those who promote issues most aggressively are often politicians with a complex mix of motivations. For example, in 1977 second-term Congressman Chris Dodd won appointment to the Rules Committee, probably the subunit with the greatest attraction to careerist House insiders. Three years later he campaigned for and won a Senate seat, subsequently becoming one of that chamber's most visible members.

Politicians live in a world of continual uncertainty. They may win occasional legislative victories, and they must, of course, win reelection at regular intervals. But on a day-to-day basis, there is little to reassure them that they are making headway. Obtaining publicity—especially national coverage—thus can serve as a proximate goal, one that can be reached before the next election or without passing any legislation. Martin Tolchin states, "There has got to be a lot of insecurity in the [politician's] job . . . a member of Congress . . . can say 'I'm in the *New York Times,* therefore I am.' "

In talking about the "generic member of Congress" and the press, one administrative assistant explained,

> First, there's an ego component—instant gratification. Other than the election every two years [in the House], they don't know "how they're doing." Mayor Koch has used that for years as a question. Members want to know. . . . You see your name in print, and journalists take you seriously. . . . The presumption is that your name in the press connotes activity and effectiveness.

Generalizing about politicians' motivations is risky, but to the extent that the policy entrepreneur style does incorporate press-related strategies, getting coverage probably has become a useful gauge of progress.[48] Media attention does connote a type of success, in that legislators feel they are being taken seriously and, perhaps, getting their message across. The best entrepreneurs, however, usually remember that publicity is almost always nothing more than a means to an end.

Moreover, press coverage can have electoral consequences. Local press coverage, the conventional wisdom goes, helps incumbents win reelection; national coverage is of uncertain value—it can even hurt, rather than help, an activist legislator. Congressional leaders who obtain a good deal of publicity have faced, on occasion, strong and well-financed challengers able to benefit from an ability to focus attention on the differences between local sentiments and the incumbent's national issue positions. Challengers have been especially successful at unseating a series of well-publicized Senate Foreign Relations Committee chairmen, from J. William Fulbright (D-Ark.) to Frank Church and Charles Percy.

More generally, political scientist Tim Cook has found that, for House members, obtaining national press attention has no systematic reelection value.[49] Nor is this kind of coverage sought for any such purpose. Members and press secretaries alike understand that few of their constituents read the *New York Times* or *Washington Post.* National coverage is valuable for pursuing national policy goals or seeking the presidency; beyond that, it has little use for election purposes. This is also true for House members eyeing Senate seats. Such representatives need broader local coverage. Pennsylvania's Bob Edgar, in running for the Senate, for example, required statewide publicity beyond his home in the Philadelphia suburbs. Similarly, when Paul Simon represented a downstate district in the House, he kept in close touch with Chicago newspapers, in part because he foresaw the possibility of running for higher office.

For the most part, policy entrepreneurs are ambitious. They must, of course, win reelection; and, as a rule, their egos require generous attention. Put all this together, and you get someone who enjoys the game and hopes to profit, somehow, at some time, from gaining an enhanced national reputation. As Les Aspin responded when asked if he had ever leaked a story without having his name attached to it "No. There's no benefit in that. (chortles) Who needs that? (laughs)"[50]

5

Levels of the Game

IN 1987 Bill Bradley reflected on how the Senate works. He observed:

> I was in the Senate in about my third or fourth month and it was late at night. I was in the Democratic cloakroom, which is right off the Senate floor. I was new and had never been in a legislative body. . . . I saw one senator who was angry, . . . one who was pacing, . . . one who was reading, . . . one on the phone, and one . . . telling a joke.
>
> So, I looked around and said to myself, "You know, this isn't a lot different from the Knick locker room." And in that sense, it isn't, because both jobs are about getting people from diverse backgrounds with different individual agendas to work together toward a common objective. So, club? No. Team? In the best sense, yes.[1]

Basketball is not the sport traditionally associated with Washington and national politicians. As fans, members of Congress pay homage to baseball and follow football, embracing the hometown Redskins. As participants, politicians have ordinarily favored golf and hunting, pastimes that encourage extended conversations among small groups of congenial souls.

Indeed, the preferences for hunting among House powers such as Speaker Jim Wright and committee chairs John Dingell and Jack Brooks (D-Tex.) indicates a changing of the guard on Capitol Hill. "Tip O'Neill was the golf era," concludes Congressman Ron Wyden (D-Oreg.), and "1987 launches the hunting era."[2]

For the younger members of the congressional middle management, however, basketball is the chosen pastime. Not only does the sport bring them together in the House gym, but it also serves as a common metaphor for explaining how the policy game is played on Capitol Hill. Time and time again, junior legislators employ basketball imagery to interpret the fast pace and rapid changes of congressional politics. Like basketball, the political game itself must hold some real attraction, as well as offering the chance to win. In addition, basketball, more than any other sport, encourages individualism while simultaneously rewarding teamwork. If members of Congress cannot appreciate such tension, no one can.

Four basketball metaphors can be used to explore the policy-making skills of the new pols. Although some younger members seek to (1) "free-lance" with the wit and inventiveness of a Julius Erving, most simply want to (2) "get into the game." In the end, it is often the (3) "patterned offense" of a Bobby Knight, or John Dingell, his congressional alter ego, that carries the day when major victories are to be won. Still, even in a disciplined system, individual players must continue to improve if their team is to succeed, and some class of '74 members have discovered that their levels of legislative performance have risen as their vertical jumps, never high, have become even more leaden. As increasingly important policy entrepreneurs, they can play the political game, figuratively at least, (4) "above the rim."

Free-Lancing: The Senate Style

Well before the House dispersed power through its series of reforms in the 1970s, the Senate allowed its members to press for their agendas, regardless of position, party, or seniority. In 1974 Senator Philip Hart (D-Mich.) could conclude, with his characteristic optimism, "We are all constructively free-wheeling individuals."[3] Alternatively, one House member offered the pithy comment, "The Senate is a zoo."[4]

Through a combination of choice and circumstance, most senators have developed into policy free-lancers who seek to influence a wide range of issues throughout the policy-making process.[5] This has affected how all legislators operate. First, always attractive to ambitious House members, the Senate offers special lures to those like Colorado's Tim Wirth and Illinois's Paul Simon, whose policy interests are more diverse than even the decentralized House can reasonably accommodate. As Congressman (later Senator) Richard Shelby (D-Ala.) noted, "In the Senate the arena is smaller, the players are fewer. The power is awesome."[6] Second, the public, multiple-issue style of many senators increasingly serves as a powerful model for House members to emulate, even if they publicly deprecate such behavior. Writing in 1977, Jack Walker noted, "Only a minority of Senators . . . can be described as activists or promoters of legislative innovation."[7] Not only does this no longer hold for the Senate, but a great many House members currently view themselves in policy entrepreneur terms.

Most senators with prior House experience see the two chambers as moving closer together, largely due to the televising of House proceedings, the advent of the congressional budget process, the growing stature of formal and informal House leaders, and the breakdown of Senate discipline, which leads ultimately to the free-lancing style.[8] Major differences remain, of course, but many House members, from top leaders to inexperienced freshmen, find themselves emulating a style best suited to entrepreneurs from the other chamber.

This can create a no-win situation for House members; senators almost automatically obtain more attention and ordinarily can command more staff resources. Even the most aggressive representatives understand their disadvantages. On one occasion, Congressman Jim Florio, a key Energy and Commerce subcommittee chair, accompanied Senator John Heinz (R-Pa.) on a helicopter tour of a polluted section in Pennsylvania's Susquehanna River. "After we looked over the situation," a former Florio aide recounts,

> We came back down and the press came up to us, and here they had a real United States Senator. It didn't matter that Florio was the best-informed member of the House on the subject. The EPA had given Heinz a quick and dirty briefing on the way up, and he did a pretty good job—fifteen or so twenty-second sound bites. Just right for TV. I looked over at Florio and he just shrugged. He knew what was going on.

As an experienced Senate free-lancer playing at home, Heinz had all the advantages when it came to attracting media coverage.

Much free-lancing revolves around setting the policy agenda because this part of the game is open to all, with almost no restrictions and few penalties for playing. A Senator Howard Metzenbaum does free-lance in the decision-making phase, but he must be willing to endure his colleagues' animosities and the collective ill-will of the Senate. Despite these costs, he perseveres, employing Senate rules that permit maneuvers the House denies its members.[9]

Senator Chris Dodd, as the Democratic point man on Latin America throughout the 1980s, offers one illustration of how far Senate free-lancing can extend. Not only did he provide the Democrats' response to a crucial Reagan message on Nicaragua in 1983, but he and Senator Paul Tsongas, a class of '74 colleague, demanded a secret Senate session on Nicaraguan policy, which flew directly in the face of the preferences of both Majority Leader Howard Baker (R-Tenn.) and Minority Leader Robert Byrd (D-W.Va.). Dodd felt very much at home in attempting to set the Senate's Latin America agenda as an independent entrepreneur, viewing the Senate as "such a tremendous forum, a place where you really can accomplish things."[10] Dodd mixes the notions of forum and accomplishment, a characteristic of the free-lancing style. Not that setting the agenda is an insignificant feat. But timely, concrete results do not always flow from an entrepreneur's free-lancing activities, regardless of the publicity received.

Free-lancing encourages innovation in mixing policies with politics. By 1986, Tom Harkin, a senator only since 1985, had developed the major alternative to the Reagan administration's farm policies. From his overlapping memberships on the Agriculture and Appropriations committees—a combination that he could never have held in the House, due to its more restrictive rules—Harkin has been in an ideal position to promote tough, mandatory production controls, even though his legislation does not yet command majority support in either chamber. As a free-lancer, however, Harkin is scarcely content to push from these strategic heights. In 1986 he campaigned actively for fellow agrarian Senate candidates Kent Conrad and Congressman Tom Daschle, in North and South Dakota, respectively. Their subsequent victories strengthened his hand, both in the Senate and nationally. With 1988 approaching, Harkin's bill was adopted and cosponsored in the House by presidential aspirant Richard Gephardt, who spent more time in Iowa than any other candidate. Harkin's overall strategy in educating the presidential candidates and the nation as a whole was anything but subtle:

> There are seven or eight presidential candidates in each party, and it all starts in Iowa. I'm trying to set the stage

> for that. I'm trying to tell them if they want to be president, they'd better pay attention to what's happening in the heartland.[11]

In the end, the candidates did come, and the Harkin-Gephardt bill was thoroughly aired—without, however, any immediate substantive result.

Despite their emphasis on and identification with a single major issue, both Senators Harkin and Dodd have spread their talents much farther. Harkin, a former military pilot, actively backs legislation supporting Civil Air Patrol surveillance of the busiest routes of the drug trade. Although he has no committee base for such concerns, his press secretary explains that Harkin, who has flown surveillance flights in Florida, ties this publicity-oriented activity to his legislation and to his record of "work days" that focus on particular jobs and problems. His press aide notes, "There are a hell of a lot of easier ways to get national attention than to go through all of this [flying in Florida]." Still, Harkin could choose exactly what part of the drug issue he wished to carve out as he developed policy proposals in line with his own interests, experience, and expertise.

For Dodd, being part of the post-1986 Democratic Senate majority means that, in addition to heading the Latin America subcommittee on Foreign Relations, he became chair of the Labor and Human Resources subcommittee on Children, Families, Drugs, and Alcoholism. As its name suggests, this subcommittee can attract great attention on a wide variety of social issues, and as its chair, Dodd can command substantial staff to organize hearings, publicize his issues, and push his policy alternatives.[12]

Less than a month after the start of the 100th Congress, Dodd introduced a parental leave bill, which would require employers to give time off to new parents. Harkin was following his own agenda on drugs; Dodd responded to the Senate's agenda on the parental leave issue. As one Senate aide notes, "There are issues that senators 'ride' and issues that they 'create.' "[13] Dodd rode the maternal leave issue in the wake of a key January 1987, Supreme Court decision. In 1986, with a Republican Senate, Dodd tried and failed to schedule hearings on parental leave. In 1987, as a subcommittee chair in a Democratic chamber, he immediately held a Washington hearing, to an "overflow crowd," got his picture in the *New York Times* twice in two weeks, and announced hearings around the country.[14]

"The way the Senate is set up," observes Senator William Armstrong (R-Colo.),

> it rewards a member who gets involved in everything. . . . You get a certain leverage on a lot of different deals. So even though it's impossible really to participate in three committees, four committees, ten subcommittees . . . if your interest is in affecting the outcome of legislation, there's an incentive to be on every committee you can get on.[15]

In short, the Senate encourages free-lancing throughout the legislative process. A hundred-member body holds out the promise all senators' interests can be accommodated, even when legislation is on the Senate floor. The much larger House offers no such hope, but this has not stopped the Congressmen from adopting the free-lancing style and making it common, if not prevalent.

Getting into the Game: Coming Off the (Back) Bench

Senators have provided role models for House policy entrepreneurs, and many House members have simply used their considerable resources to pursue their policy interests. Nevertheless, as former congressman Robert Krueger demonstrated (see chapter 2), some personal expertise is essential for House entrepreneurs. This sets them apart from many senators, who can often rely on their individual leverage within the chamber to affect policies. Moreover, entrepreneurs generally see publicity as essential to moving policies and setting the agenda, and the average senator's advantages remain overwhelming. Where does this leave House policy activists? Rarely can they dominate a policy game. Rather, entrepreneurs in the House must rely on persistence, focus, and knowledge. Perhaps the greatest contribution of the class of '74 has been to demonstrate how its members have an impact on policy making at the various stages of their congressional careers.

CONGRESSMAN BOB EDGAR: THE POWER OF PERSISTENCE

Political scientist John Kingdon observes:

> Successful entrepreneurs are persistent. Many potentially influential people have expertise and political skill, but sheer tenacity pays off. . . . Persistence alone does not carry the day, but in combination with other qualities, it is disarmingly important . . . [and] implies a willingness to invest large and sometimes remarkable quantities of one's resources.[16]

While Congressmen Toby Moffett, Andy Maguire, and Bob Carr confronted the House leadership and often alienated the House establishment in 1975–76 with their criticisms and penchant for publicity, Bob Edgar pushed ahead with his own, less-publicized attack on the status quo of pork barrel politics. As a first-term member of the Public Works Committee, he proposed deleting various water projects, many near and dear to the hearts and pocketbooks of his committee colleagues. Not surprisingly, Edgar lost. On some tallies, his amendments received only his single vote. Congressman Norman Mineta comments, "I always called Bob Edgar a '37-mission kamikaze pilot.' " Phoenix-like, Edgar set off on a decade-long effort to effect radical change in the content and context of water policy decision making. A long-time opponent from the Water Resources Council observes, "I don't agree with a lot of things that Edgar's trying to accomplish. But I'll have to say he's persistent. He comes back and back and back. He never knows when he's beaten."[17]

Edgar's substantive knowledge and his reputation for honesty served as the foundations for his entrepreneurial efforts, but information and integrity in themselves cannot sway a Congress filled with self-interested politicians. Edgar needed allies, and simple opposition to pork barrel projects, or even to bad projects, was not enough. Consequently, he began to make water projects policy a strong regional issue, much as western legislators have historically done with their own water issues. Edgar spoke increasingly about water projects as part of a declining Northeastern and Midwestern infrastructure and brought up the issue of regional equity in funding water projects. His rhetoric did not generate good copy or easy television exposure. Speaking to civil engineers, he stated:

> We're going to see a coalition built between those who want meritorious water projects and those who are willing to accept some new directions in water policy . . . that meets both a new infrastructure needs test and a rehabilitation of the older areas that need to be addressed.[18]

Like most skilled entrepreneurs, Edgar possesses a sense of his audience, and he brought politics to the engineers, much as he introduced politicians to "meritorious" criteria for water project decisions.

Edgar's proposals to rationalize the allocation of water project funds met stiff opposition throughout the 1970s and early 1980s. In 1980 Edgar introduced 184 amendments in an attempt to stop a water projects appropriations bill, and he made a serious 1981 effort to sidetrack a $4.4 billion appropriations measure on the House floor. His amendment to delete twenty projects (including three in Pennsylvania) lost on a 133 to 271 vote. "I consider today my Don Quixote day," Edgar noted.[19] However, public defeats sometimes lead to private triumphs. Six months later he and conservative Republican Gerald Solomon (R-N.Y.) helped pass legislation requiring some cost-sharing by beneficiaries for safety repairs to federal dams.[20] Edgar's tough-minded attitude on the merits of water project expenditures meshed with the conservative Solomon's reluctance to spend federal funds.

In his final three years in the House, Edgar did win some further, broader policy victories. Most notably, in June 1985, he offered an amendment that succeeded in temporarily overturning the funding for thirty-one projects that had not yet received authorization. The 203 to 202 count did not reflect any final recognition of Edgar's water policy perspective by the House. Instead, Edgar noted that

> the vote for his amendment represented a combination of forces: . . . fiscal austerity, . . . desire to reform the system of financing for large public works projects, jealousy by authorizing committees . . . , administration pressure and opposition from members whose projects were not included."[21]

Political circumstances permitted this victory, more than any major shift in the way the House viewed water policy. Thus Bob Edgar, with his 100 percent rating by the liberal Americans for Democratic Action, was ready and willing to join forces with the losers in the process (members from authorizing committees and districts with unfunded projects), Reagan administration supporters, and fiscal conservatives. Such opportunism is central to the entrepreneurial style.

During his 1974–86 House tenure Edgar became an effective coalition-builder on water issues without losing his focus on reform. Indeed, his classmates almost unanimously regard him as the epitome of the reformist spirit of the class of '74.[22] Still, his twelve-year colleague on the Public Works Committee, Congressman Norm Mineta, concludes that Edgar learned a great deal:

> When Bob Edgar was first making his water projects in committee, he was about as popular as a skunk in church. The chairman would have an $80 million project to do something, and Bob would start asking questions about why this was needed, what the environmental impact was. And this really affected the things that he undertook. Yet, in the last two years he was in the House he was as strong as ever on environment. But if he wanted a mass transit subsidy [another Edgar cause], he would end up getting it into a bill. He was still as principled and forceful as ever. But he didn't enrage the other members. He'd learned how to play the game without compromising his principles.

CONGRESSMAN GEORGE MILLER: A MULTIPLE OFFENSE

In playing a word association game with most policy entrepreneurs' names, a consensus will develop around the issue an individual is most identified with. Senator Tom Harkin is linked to agriculture, former Congressman Michael Barnes (D-Md.) and Senator Chris Dodd to Latin America, Congressman Ed Jenkins (D-Ga.) to trade, Congressman Les Aspin to defense, and so on. But when Congressman George Miller's name comes up, there is little agreement. Miller is active on water policy, a host of family issues, support for the minimum wage, Latin America, and the pay-as-you-go budget concept.

Miller's interests sometimes seem arcane. The *New York Times,* for example, highlighted Miller's work with the headline, "Congressman Criticizes Funds for Bowling Alley."[23] Given his myriad interests and a first-class press secretary, it came as no surprise to find that Miller had attacked a bowling alley, nor that the *Times* had covered his broadside. The bowling alley was constructed in conjunction with a federal water project, originally authorized by the House Interior subcommittee that Miller chairs. As part of the controversial Central Utah Project, Miller had used the bowling alley to focus attention on waste in federal water projects and the often unresponsive Bureau of Reclamation. Miller dryly commented, "You ask them for a dam, and they give you a bowling alley."[24]

Although Miller has involved himself heavily in a wider range of policies than he likes to admit, he sees three general issues as constituting his core agenda.

> Since the beginning of my House career, I've focused on resources [including water], children, and Nicaragua. . . . Each of these issues has been with me since I got here. I've stayed with them. I can support my involvement. I've got separate support staff for all of them, except for Nicaragua, and even on Latin America I probably have the most knowledgeable person on the Hill [on my personal staff].

Miller has responded effectively to the diverse mixture before the contemporary Congress. As one freshman noted in the late 1970s: "It's a giant smorgasbord . . . in terms of having this fantastic variety of things you can get involved in. . . ."[25] Congressman Marty Russo, a close friend, notes that "George is not really full of a lot of issues. He's focused on one issue here, one there. . . . He's got a carefully thought out plate—it's full, but well thought out." Miller chimes in, "That's right. Even though I have strong feelings on it, I don't do arms control. There's just no time. We all have different spheres of influence."

Miller now emphasizes the links between resources and focus, but in his first six years of service, without a subcommittee chair or any other position of influence, he forged an image of competence and energy, while making his Northern California seat relatively safe. He has become much more of a legislative force during the 1980s, as either subcommittee or select committee chair, on three committees, in addition to serving on the Budget panel. The active apprenticeship served by almost all class of '74 members has proven valuable to Miller in his command of increasing amounts of resources. One top leadership aide observes, "Miller has always had something. For a while he was the guru on Latin America. He's always been taken seriously on policy issues."

Miller will continue to be taken seriously—he stands next in line to chair the Interior Committee, a position which will come through the ordinary workings of the seniority system. Perhaps more interesting is how the entrepreneurial Miller created his own select committee. Miller has forcefully articulated children's and family issues since his initial days in the House. In the early 1980s, he lobbied for the formation of a select committee on children's and family policy; upon its creation in 1983, he was named chairman. Given the political significance of family issues, Miller's success illustrates his generally good relations with the House leadership, who trusted him on these key policies. Moreover, Miller has paid his dues inside the House. One leadership aide observed that he "had gotten out front on the pay raise. . . . He helped carry the Speaker's water on that [in 1982]. And it helped him with his select committee." Policy expertise always comes into play within the contexts of personal relationships and political considerations. Congressman Tom Downey, widely regarded as an arms control expert but also as somewhat obnoxious, lost a Democratic caucus vote on his proposal to establish a House select committee on this subject.

As he has moved into positions of greater power, Miller's political skills have increased in value. During his Budget Committee service, Miller developed the "pay-as-you-go" idea, which would have tied new spending to increased taxes or reductions in current spending levels. This gave many liberals a most useful umbrella for their protection on difficult budget issues; they could use the proposal to argue for defense cuts to offset new domestic spending. New York's Matt McHugh, who comes from a heavily Republican upstate district, notes: "Pay-as-you-go is a nice mechanism. I think some members try to explain things, while others rely more on the phrase. I tend to try to explain it."

Miller's pragmatic liberalism is especially well suited for Interior Committee work, where environmental interests come into sharp, continuing conflict with those of water users. As subcommittee chair, Miller has pushed policies toward a resolution, rather than simply placing them on the agenda. In 1986, for example, he modified his previous complete opposition to the massive Garrison Diversion project in North Dakota in order to fashion construction much reduced in scale and environmental impact. Farmers, fiscal conservatives, environmentalists, and even the Canadian government all got something from the Miller proposal. Although environmentalists did not unanimously agree with Miller, most groups did come down on his side. Like many of his class of '74 colleagues, Miller as subcommittee chair has moved from setting agendas to building coalitions that produce a legislative product.

THE LIMITED IMPACT OF SOLO EFFORTS

Within the postreform House, though not the Senate, loners do not do well. In the midst of an overall decline in comity, the ability to get along with one's peers may have become, ironically, more important than it was in an era of committee barons and long apprenticeships.[26] As one veteran congressional aide points out,

> [Former Congressman Andy] Maguire is a brooder, a loner, that's just the way he is. Toby Moffett, on the other hand, was more likable. Civil to everyone, staff of all sorts. When they played basketball, if [conservative Congressman] Dan Crane [R-Ill.] was open under the basket, he'd pass it to him.

For the class of '74, only Congressmen Steve Solarz and Jim Florio have both remained in the House and generally had a real impact on policy while gaining reputations as loners. In one member's words, Solarz would "rather talk to the *New York Times* than hang around with his colleagues."

Florio, who chairs a major Energy and Commerce subcommittee, is a more difficult case because he does not share Solarz's reputation as an unbridled show horse. One leadership aide observed that Florio's two unsuccessful attempts to win the New Jersey governorship have left him with the indelible image of an individual who keeps looking beyond the House. Another veteran staff aide, very familiar with the entire class, sees Florio as "another guy, like Maguire, who is a loner. He has the respect of his colleagues, but they aren't close to him."

While Solarz and Florio remain in the House and continue to have an impact, loners such as Maguire and Elliot Levitas (D-Ga.) have lost both their seats and their potential for influence. In the House, these members were loners by temperament, although Maguire was a major figure in the class's efforts over the first few years, putting forward strong policy views on a wide range of issues. A strong constituency operation helped account for Maguire's electoral survival (see chapter 8), but the 1980 Reagan landslide and an articulate, well-funded opponent overcame his efforts. Even among his like-minded colleagues, Maguire never completely fit in, unlike Toby Moffett or Tim Wirth, both of whom felt more at home within the institution.

Levitas, somewhat older than many other class of '74 members, did serve as part of the Democratic whip organization and had some major policy successes (for example, as a sponsor of airline deregulation). In the 1980s, Levitas focused increasing amounts of attention on the legislative veto and the overall question of regulatory reform. As a former Rhodes scholar and member of a prominent Atlanta law firm, Levitas enjoyed dealing with the complexities and broad implications of these policies.[27] Levitas's passion for the legislative veto was not shared by large numbers of other House members, and he played down the coalition-building necessities in devising solutions to the Supreme Court's finding that most such veto provisions were unconstitutional. Discussing the legislative veto, Levitas noted that "some issues build their own coalitions." One cannot imagine a policy entrepreneur like Henry Waxman or Dick Gephardt making such a statement. A similar kind of arrogance allowed Levitas to ignore a successful challenge at home in 1984, and he departed the Congress with legislative veto action still pending.

Both Maguire and Levitas acted independently, and their peers perceived them as loners. Their individual performances were different, to be sure. No one could confuse the aggressive, active Maguire with the more traditional, subdued Levitas. In the end, however, neither fit all that well in a House that places an increasing value on effective communication. Competence on the issues is only a beginning. Maguire and Levitas failed to establish the firm one-on-one bonds required by contemporary "retail politics" inside the Congress.

Opening up to one's colleagues can count a great deal in creating strong personal ties. Marty Russo notes, "We're very public people who act very privately." George Miller argues for the importance of breaking down ordinary barriers in an institution where everyone is wary. "Take the simple catalyst of basketball," he says,

> It really does make a difference. When you're in the gym, you just open up more. If you were coming out of a committee meeting [with another member], you wouldn't say certain things. But if you're in the gym, you're tired, you'll say things.

Beyond generating mere camaraderie, "participation [in policy debates or basketball games] is important," Miller continues.

> Take the simple question, "Why did you vote that way?" on some issue. If you don't know someone, you might

think, "That asshole," but if you know him, you'll understand, or you'll ask, "Do you know something?" To the point that you know members, you'll come to trust them in degrees.

Every style of behavior has its costs. Some legislators surely distrust the gregarious Miller. But being a loner may mean that you never have the opportunity to generate the trust that the House has always required.

A Patterned Offense and a Team Effort

After his 1987 selection by Speaker Jim Wright to the highest appointive party position in the House, Congressman David Bonoir (D-Mich.) commented that it "may be a message to Members about recognizing those who hustle."[28] The choice of Bonoir also exemplifies the rewards that come to those who can combine partisanship with the pace and flexibility of the free-lance style. Bonoir notes, "The Boston Celtics are great because they also take pride in passing and defense. I will maintain a decent visibility, but I operate best when I'm quiet."[29] Bonoir's success in acting effectively across the wide range of Rules Committee policy debates and heading an anti-contra aid task force illustrates one way that broad interests in policy and a willingness to take risks (on contra aid) can be harnessed, if not controlled, by the party leadership.

Only through recruiting such able individuals as Bonoir into their ranks can House leaders hope to move policies through that body, which demands high levels of participation from the entire leadership. Although the class of '74 has given the Congress much more than its share of policy entrepreneurs, it is the next cohort—those who entered the House in 1977—

that has provided a disproportionate number of leaders, most notably Bonoir, Panetta, and Gephardt. It may be purely accidental that a group of coalition builders followed so closely a set of agenda setters, but without question there were few "bomb-throwers" in the cohort that entered the House after the reformist class of '74.

The archetype of this policy entrepreneur-cum-party-leader style is Missouri's Democratic Congressman Richard Gephardt, first elected to the House in 1976. Although best known for his 1988 presidential candidacy, Gephardt has played a major role in developing an activist leadership style that suits the openness and fragmentation of the postreform House. As a member of the Ways and Means Committee, the Budget Committee, and the House whip structure in the early 1980s, Gephardt could put his coalition-building talents to work on a variety of personal and partisan initiatives.

The *National Journal*'s Richard Cohen spent a day with Gephardt in 1983, before he had become Democratic Caucus chair or an active presidential candidate, and Cohen's account of a single day provides substantial insights into how a policy entrepreneur operates. Mostly, he (or she) talks, then listens some, and talks some more—ad infinitum.[30]

With seats on the Ways and Means and Budget committees and a position as a deputy whip, Gephardt did spend some time in committee meetings and on the House floor, but his main efforts came in other arenas, where he participated in policy development and coalition-building activities. In these party task forces, committee caucuses, lobbyists' working groups, and issue-oriented lunch (and breakfast) meetings the policy game is played. Like basketball, it's an indoor sport and the pace is fast. Just counting the formal meetings with other House members or policy activists (but not constituents) and key leadership contacts, Gephardt's day proceeded as follows:[31]

1. 8:00 A.M. Breakfast meeting of health group that he helped to create.

2. 8:50. Meeting with five members of the House Democratic Caucus's committee on party effectiveness, to update a revised version of the party's "yellow book" on new policy directions.
3. 10:10. Talks with Ways and Means Chair Dan Rostenkowski about polling Democrats on the deficit.
4. 10:15. Committee staffer notes meeting for next day with Senator Bill Bradley on tax reform.
5. 10:30. Makes seven calls to wavering Democratic members concerning a public service jobs bill.
6. 10:50. Attends closed meeting of Ways and Means Democrats and acts as key congressional spokesman for auto workers' position.
7. 11:15. Democratic task force meeting on jobs bill, which he chairs in Whip Tom Foley's absence; then returns to Ways and Means meeting.
8. Noon. Closed luncheon meeting of party effectiveness committee on revising industrial policy initiative ("yellow book").
9. 1:30 P.M. Meets briefly with Speaker to gain approval of his poll of Democrats on deficit.
10. 2:30. Arrives late for Ways and Means meeting, where he is on the losing side of a key vote (on domestic content), taken before he had his say.
11. 5:00. Meets in Capitol with Budget Committee Chair Congressman James Jones (D-Okla.), key Budget member Leon Panetta, and "a flock of aides from the leadership and Budget and Ways and Means Committees."
12. 8:00. Dinner at former Congressman Jim Corman's (D-Calif.) house to raise funds from business community for Congressman Vic Fazio (D-Calif.); also attending, Congressmen Jones and Wirth.

Gephardt met briefly with a couple of groups of constituents and dropped in on a reception for a former aide, but most of his time was spent discussing policy substance, strategy, and tactics with fellow activists, generally from Congress. Throughout the day, the threads of party and policy were continually interwoven. On this day, at least, Cohen's reporting shows Gephardt talking seriously with no Republicans.

Although Gephardt does more policy brokering than most members, his schedule resembles those of many middle management legislators, and it stands in real contrast to the way committees and constituents dominated congressional business in the past. For example, political scientist Charles Jones tracked senior congressman Morris Udall and third-term member William Cohen (R-Maine) through two legislative days in 1977.[32] Udall, as chair of the Interior Committee, was extremely busy, but in two days he had no meetings scheduled with any party leaders. His only partisan meeting was a subcommittee caucus. Cohen, an energetic and ambitious member, essentially tended to his committee business and met only once in a partisan setting—with the moderate Republican House Wednesday group.

Even if Udall and Cohen met informally with their partisan colleagues, the differences are striking between their 1977 schedules and Gephardt's 1983 routine. By the early 1980s, especially in the House, the Democratic leaders, with their inclusive strategy, had begun to recast the nature of policy making. By bringing scores of low and midseniority Democrats into the whip structure, into task forces, into a reinvigorated campaign committee, as well as into positions of committee authority, the Democrats in the O'Neill era created a leadership system for an activist, participatory age.[33]

This consultative leadership format offers no legislative panaceas. Rather, it provides Democrats with a wide variety of forums in which to hash out policies and come to agreement. Such a system makes good sense in a chamber where the younger members value hard work and expertise much more than other, traditional legislative norms. In addition, the congressional party forums often overlap with those offered by informal groups (caucuses) and the party outside the House (for example, the Democratic Leadership Council). Given the continuing, if diminished, strength of hierarchy and seniority in congressional committees, the House has moved a long way toward creating its own kind of political meritocracy, where "cream and bastards rise." The problem is to distinguish the former from the latter.

Above the Rim: New Players and a Different Game

It's March 1987 and my last round of interviews with members of the class of '74 is about finished. I'm talking with Congressmen George Miller and Marty Russo, who are becoming animated as they discuss the 1986 tax bill and the overall opportunities for effective participation in today's House. Both in their early forties, these still-young men have seen the future of their chamber, and they like what they see. Miller expounds:

> After we were here for a period of time, we discovered that there's a whole different level of game to be played. In basketball terminology, "There's a game that's played above the hoop." You find that you can dunk the ball. ["Slam it!" Russo interjects.] Although sometimes you miss.

Metaphors cannot replace analysis, but on occasion they do capture a central truth. Perhaps the success of tax reform has imbued Russo and Miller with too much optimism, given their strong ties to Ways and Means chair Dan Rostenkowski. Still, detached observers have come to a roughly similar conclusion about the decision-making capacities of Congress. The *Wall Street Journal*'s Jeffrey Birnbaum and Allen Murray conclude,

"Legislators say they learned from tax overhaul that a comprehensive idea designed to help the general interest can, under the right circumstance, overwhelm obstacles posed by special interests."[34] To the extent this is so, policy entrepreneurs will find reasons to participate with energy and elan.

Much of the Senate game continues to be played by freelancers, who seek to set their own agendas and cut their own deals. Although some senators are more equal than others, individualism continues as the order of the day. Most senators (actual and would-be) see themselves as able to play "above the rim" from the moment of their entrance into the chamber. Congressman Bob Edgar noted that giving up a powerful House subcommittee chair would not be difficult. "As a first-term senator, I'd have as much clout on [the subcommittee's veterans'] issues as I would as a seventh-term representative."

In the House, however, distinct "levels of the game" do exist. As a veteran liberal policy broker, Matt McHugh argues that to affect major legislation—a crucial aspect of high-level play—

> You need to engage the leadership early. . . . So there are two ways to go. The first method is to impact on key players and have them incorporate you and your point of view. Second, you protect your right to offer alternatives. This is less satisfactory. A lot of members will "go with the flow" with the leadership.

Engaging the leadership is especially important because large numbers of key policy decisions are made on the House floor, not in committee or subcommittee.[35] Increasing numbers of floor votes and levels of amending activities have led to rising uncertainties over the outcome of legislation passed out of committee. In turn, a growing number of floor decisions requires, ironically, more collegiality in decision making. The Congressional Research Service's Stan Bach argues that the decline in control by top committee leaders and the "political individualism and entrepreneurship" among members "have contributed to bringing the House of Representatives back toward what it was originally intended to be—a forum for collective decision-making."[36] At the same time, party leaders have increased their abilities to control the shape of these collective decisions, often by writing complex rules that structure debates and votes.[37]

Political scientist Steve Smith points out that more floor activity has meant that policy entrepreneurs have had to find ways to influence the results. "Much of the growth of single-issue caucuses, party caucus and committee activity, and ad hoc groups of other kinds [has] occurred because of opportunities to pursue policy interests on the [House] floor. . . . [T]he enhanced role of the floor encourages continual formation and reformation of participation and decision-making."[38]

In sum, once having demonstrated their policy competence and thus having qualified as players in the continuing series of policy games, new pols must show acute political skills to advance into the next echelon of decision making. For many House members, this may mean rising to an "inner circle" of party leaders,[39] but the focus here remains on members' actions, rather than on their formal positions. One key asset for any entrepreneur—whether free-lancer or team player—is to understand what constitutes an opportunity for effective action. Bill Bradley continued to see an opening for tax reform when all around him were dubious at best. Even less likely as a successful policy broker was third-term Congressman Charles Schumer, who sought to breathe life into a moribund 1986 immigration reform measure.

Accurately labeled a "public insider" by the *National Journal,*[40] Schumer is a direct descendant of both the publicity-consciousness of a Steve Solarz and the intense insider style of a Marty Russo. Barring the onset of schizophrenia, this combination will continue to propel Schumer into the ranks of emerging policy entrepreneurs. With his frequent appearances on PBS's "McNeil-Lehrer" show and access to the *New York Times* op-ed page, Schumer has proven himself a first-rate practitioner of agenda-setting politics. Such a style hardly qualifies, however, as a base for building a coalition on immigration policy, which required patient negotiation and a willingness to avoid the spotlight.

Although Schumer came to understand the intricacies of immigration policy through extended conversations with fellow Capitol Hill townhouse residents Miller and Panetta,[41] his greatest contribution to an ultimate settlement came from having no direct interest in the issue. In addition, Schumer understood that perceptions and timing were crucial to building coalitions. Schumer argued first that the 1986 legislation should be viewed as a "left-center" bill, compared to the 1984 effort, which was more "right-center."[42] Second, he posited that the 1986 bill was preferable to anything that most Hispanic interests would likely win in the foreseeable future. Schumer proved persuasive, winning both an unexpected legislative victory and accolades from all involved.

Winning, Losing, and Playing the Game

Former Rules Committee chair and long-time congressional observer Richard Bolling concludes,

> In the end, the thing the House needs most is legislators. What's important is getting things through—then you've done everything. . . . Running the House is the only thing that makes a difference. The subcommittees, in the end, become special interests. A legislator needs to function as a generalist.

Bolling's conclusions ring true, regardless of legislative era. Yet the ideas of "running the House" and even functioning as a "generalist" have meaning only in specific contexts. New politicians have helped to create new, participatory ways of running the House and have redefined the notion of who can act as a generalist. Beyond the commanding heights of the top party leadership or the Rules Committee, Bolling could have found few true legislative generalists before the mid-1970s. Since then, generalists and those members with multiple expertise, like George Miller, have come to dominate the entire middle management of the Congress.

Whatever the satisfactions of particular legislative successes, playing the game at a high level offers real rewards to this new generation of politicians. To be sure, winning is important. Schumer comments that "it was so fulfilling to get [immigration] done. It felt so good." Issues are important, Miller notes, but there's also the possibility of closure, of success. "After several years," he said in 1987, "it's so much fun to get things done."[43] Senators from the class of '74 express similar sentiments, even though their game remains more an exercise in free-lancing than in team playing. Still, losses, disappointments, and delays are more commonplace than sweeping victories. Participation must have some attraction of its own. One congressional entrepreneur concluded: "We're a privileged group of people, who get a chance to have an impact on policy. . . . If you're there, you can go for it. It's amazing to think of the chances we have to affect things."

The ultimate question remains, how many legislators truly have a chance to influence outcomes within a House that increasingly resolves issues by attaching amendments or spending proposals to a few major omnibus pieces of legislation (for example, budget reconciliation, continuing resolutions). With money committee members holding the keys to these bills, along with the House leadership, some legislators see visions of an earlier era of decision making. Congressman Phil Sharp argues that "the natural tendency of this institution is toward oligarchy. What we have now is a technique for returning to a closed system where a few people make all the decisions."[44]

Despite this trend, the oligarchy of the 1980s is a permeable one, subject to frequent penetration by skilled, activist members.

In the end, the new pols get a chance to affect policies, as long as they suit up—in gray pinstripes, not Celtic green—and come to play a difficult game at a high level.

6

The Congressional Enterprise: Offices and Caucuses

DURING THE 1970s, as members of Congress sought to recapture policy leadership from the executive, they also consistently voted themselves more resources, ranging from staff to computers and trips back to their constituencies.[1] Legislators also banded together in innovative ways to affect policy decisions. On their own they formed informal groups—often labeled caucuses—to represent specific interests that ranged from Mountain states (High Altitude Coalition) to automobile constituencies (Auto Task Force) to demographic groupings (Congressional Black and Hispanic caucuses, and the Congressional Caucus on Women's Issues).[2]

Expanded personal offices and caucuses constituted important new elements in the complex game of congressional politics. Coupled with the decentralizing reforms that have strengthened subcommittees (see chapter 7) and the substantial increases in campaign spending and political action committee contributions (see chapter 8), legislators have faced a series of often-bewildering choices in building and organizing their enterprises. Nonetheless, the personal office remains the heart of almost every congressional operation.

Personal Offices: Worth a Million—and More

As of the 100th Congress (1987–88), Congressmen Steve Bartlett (R-Tex.) and Jim Slattery (D-Kans.), both initially elected in 1982, chair no subcommittees. Nor do they occupy any high party position or major informal caucus leadership slot. They control little more than those basic resources that any rank-and-file member of the House can command. Yet, in their third terms, these congressmen have moved quickly into numerous major policy debates, all the while maintaining (for Bartlett) or greatly improving (for Slattery) the strength of their home political bases. Although these are attractive and energetic young legislators, they are scarcely exceptional. Rather, they demonstrate that the foundation of democratization in the Congress, more than committee reforms or the broadly inclusive style of party leadership, lies with the substantial staff resources and other perquisites of the personal office.

A small businessman in private life, Steve Bartlett lost no time in organizing his House office to pursue his goal of almost immediate policy impact. Elected from a safe Republican district near Dallas, Bartlett enjoyed the luxury of planning an overall strategy for using his office resources well before the general election. His electoral security allowed him to hire a set of strong legislative aides, while employing, at least initially, only a minimal district staff. Despite his status as a minority-party freshman, Bartlett concluded that an individual member "can make a difference," especially with a capable staff. Bartlett observed that, within his first eighteen months of service, he had helped to pass

> in committee and on the floor, over thirty amendments, and had impact on a lot of other legislation. To do this takes good staff work. On an amendment, the staff mobilizes. We deliver "Dear Colleagues" by hand, and a staff member answers the phone immediately on calls that ask about the amendments' implications.[3]

Bartlett has continued to make a legislative impact through the tactics of sponsoring key amendments and building unlikely coalitions that sometimes tie the Democratic leaders of the Banking, Finance, and Urban Affairs Committee in knots. His successes in affecting both agendas and outcomes have been recognized to the extent that in 1987 *National Journal* named him one of the Congress's "rising stars."[4]

In contrast to Bartlett's safe-seat organization, Congressman Slattery's personal office staff offers a textbook illustration of how resources can be reallocated as political circumstances change. Serving in a marginal seat that changed hands three times in the 1970s, Slattery, with his business background, has consistently recognized the need for a strong home base. His administrative assistant, for example, has remained in Kansas, rather than moving to Capitol Hill. At the same time, Slattery has won prized memberships on the Energy and Commerce and Budget committees. With the additional staffer granted to each Budget Committee member, by his third term Slattery can call upon five fairly well-seasoned legislative aides, as opposed to his initial legislative complement of three raw recruits.

This level of assistance has permitted Slattery to move into new policy areas, most notably Central America. In early 1987 he traveled to Honduras, Costa Rica, and Nicaragua, accompanied by two staffers, three journalists (from Kansas), and several private citizens from his district. Upon his return, he sought to participate actively in the Central America peace process, even though he had no formal congressional position from which to operate. All his policy and publicity initiatives, including proposed outlines for negotiated settlements, have rested upon the work of his personal office staff, which include no foreign policy experts at all. Nevertheless, Slattery has received generally positive reactions to his entrepreneurial actions, both on Capitol Hill and back in his district (where he had won election in 1986 with 72 percent of the vote). Although it remains an open question as to whether he will become a major player in Central America politics, Slattery has made an entrance into that policy arena with relative ease and few obvious costs.

Beyond hard work and strong political skills, Bartlett, Slattery, and literally dozens of low-seniority congressional policy entrepreneurs can rely upon legislative aides and other personal office resources worth more than a million dollars a year—and that only applies to House members. With their larger constituencies and broader legislative responsibilities, senators receive substantially more resources.

THE BASIC ENTERPRISE

As of 1987, in the 100th Congress, every member of the House is entitled to a truly formidable array of resources. Including the member's own wages, annual office salaries approach $500,000; added to this is a set of fringe benefits that increases the value of the package to about $600,000. Beyond this, official expenses for everything ranging from plane tickets to coffee filters average about $200,000 annually. Moreover, the value of franked mail comes to approximately $220,000 per House office (1986 figures).[5]

The growth of congressional resources should make clear that democratization on Capitol Hill does not rest solely upon rules and procedures. Rather, all members can use their resources in bringing expertise to bear on policy matters as well as in insulating themselves against the potential retribution of

TABLE 6.1

Personal Staff of Representatives and Senators, 1947–1986

Year	House Total	Average Per Member	Senate Total	Average Per Senator
1947	1440	3.5	590	6.1
1957	2441	5.6	1115	11.6
1967	4055	9.3	1749	17.5
1977	6942	15.9	3554	35.5
1986	7920	18.2	3774	37.7

SOURCE: Adapted from Norman J. Ornstein, Thomas E. Mann, Michael J. Malbin, *Vital Statistics in Congress, 1987–1988* (Washington, D.C.: Congressional Quarterly, Inc., 1987), p. 142.

committee or party leaders. Not only have staff numbers risen sharply (see table 6.1), but the contemporary Congress has also granted itself considerable "overhead" resources to help it keep pace with an expanded executive branch, unending technological advances, and an increasingly complex budget process.

Again, the class of '74 benefited tremendously from changes that occurred before its members ever took their oath of office. When these policy activists sought expert advice, the Congressional Research Service (CRS), the Congressional Budget Office (CBO), and the Office of Technology Assessment (OTA) were available to provide reasonably high-quality information in a timely and relatively routine manner. Although CRS and CBO studies do not convert the average member into a full-blown policy expert, these congressional agencies can insure that all members and staffers have the opportunity to understand the issues at hand. Indeed, many offices encountered an overload of policy information, not a shortage.[6]

Crucial to understanding the congressional enterprise is the amount of control that legislators have in hiring, firing, and setting office policies. Although the House Administration Committee does stringently enforce some technical limitations in certain areas (for example, lease and purchase of computers), members have great flexibility in deciding how—or if—they will employ their considerable resources. For the most part, Congress has exempted itself from restrictive laws, such as antidiscrimination statutes, that apply to the private sector. Aides serve at the pleasure of the elected official, and the enterprise notion, which ties together the fortunes of members and their staff, makes especially good sense in assessing the day-to-day world of office operations.

The growth of staff numbers, however important, reflects only one side of the change in the nature of the congressional enterprise. Equally significant have been the perquisites of office (such as trips home and WATS lines) and the increasing professionalism and technological sophistication of legislators' offices. The post-Watergate entrants to Congress have reinvented the very nature of the congressional office. Although some pre-1974 members, such as Senator Mark Hatfield (R-Oreg.) and Congressman Charlie Rose (D-N.C.), have broken much new ground in applying technology to their enterprises, it is the younger members and their aides who have consistently pressured the Congress to move into the computer age.[7] Changes come with each succeeding wave of new members, who are amazed that state-of-the art technology in business, science, or academia have barely touched the Congress. In the early 1980s, for example, the only personal computers (PCs) on Capitol Hill were those purchased by members or staff on their own. By 1987, the House had developed some software (an adaptation of Lotus 1-2-3) that made PCs an attractive option in office management.[8] More generally, as of 1986, all but two Senate offices and a handful (thirty-five) of House units had computer systems of one kind or another, which cost more than $30 million annually to operate.[9]

Combined with the television coverage of both chambers, computers have made continuously updated information on the policy-making process much more available to all interested parties—members and staff, to be sure, but also lobbyists and constituents. Furthermore, in the hands of a sophisticated politician, computers can do much more than grind out personalized mailing labels. Back in his North Carolina district, for example, Congressman Rose uses his portable computer to "let local officials peek into the federal pork barrel, [where] the goodies are listed in a federal grants data base."[10] Although this may be sensible district politics, such focused access can create great pressures to deliver those goodies. In fact, lots of congressional resources provide members with the capacity to alert their constituencies of impending problems (for example, program cutbacks) or emerging opportunities (federal grants).

All in all, the control and manipulation of information has profoundly affected the Congress, where legislative aides, despite an annual turnover rate of more than 40 percent, can monitor the progress of bills and amendments and inform themselves on arcane subjects.[11] The control of intelligence and data has traditionally bolstered the power of party leaders and committee chairs, who stand as the major losers from a timely, decentralized access to both procedural and substantive information. In addition, politicians can respond in seemingly personal, yet routine, ways to constituent requests for information and assistance. Word-processing technologies offer endless permutations and combinations in fashioning a countless number of explanations on votes, positions, and other actions that constitute the essence of a legislator's home style.[12]

MANAGING THE ENTERPRISE

The expansion of the overall congressional enterprise during the 1970s was expressed in various ways—more specialized jobs (like computer operator), rising expenditures, an avalanche of mail, and, most visibly, the growing number and diversity of district (or state) activities. Even the most tradition-bound senators and representatives came to realize million-dollar operations could no longer be run in totally idiosyncratic ways. Enhanced resources and automation have led the post-Watergate generations of legislators to build enterprises that are hierarchical, specialized, and decentralized. Correspondingly, the oxymoronic term "congressional management" has crept into the lexicon of Capitol Hill.

Hierarchy: The Administrative Assistant as Manager. When Congressman Jim Moody (D-Wis.) arrived on Capitol Hill, fresh from an arduous 1982 campaign, he carefully recruited an experienced administrative assistant, to whom he immediately delegated most authority for (and virtually all of the work in) hiring the remainder of his Washington staff. Moody concentrated on obtaining the best committee assignments possible. Even before serving a day in the Congress, Moody understood that delegation and hierarchy within his enterprise were essential if he was to achieve his goal of taking on immediate legislative responsibilities.[13]

Although offices differ, given the wide variety of district demands and member styles, most congressional enterprises have become much more hierarchical in the past two decades. Ironically, it is in the House that the trend toward increased hierarchy and delegation is most striking. In the early to mid-1970s, about two of every five House offices employed an explicitly hierarchical style in which the administrative assistant (AA) monitored all communications between staff and House member.[14] A subsequent sampling of House offices found that almost 60 percent had adopted such a pattern by the early 1980s.[15] But Senate offices, which command many more resources and considerably larger staffs, continue to resemble free-for-alls, where legislative aides often struggle to catch their senator's ear. Of course, there is great delegation within a senator's office, but as any number of case studies illustrate, it is as likely to occur by default as by choice.

Why do congressmen choose the more orderly, hierarchical style? Largely because one or two staff members, usually an administrative assistant and/or a legislative director, can grasp the diverse strands of a House member's enterprise. In the Senate, even a strong and talented AA is unlikely to be able to manage the enterprise while simultaneously staying abreast of its major legislative initiatives. This is almost certainly so when the enterprise revolves around a majority party senator who sits on ten or twelve subcommittees, chairs a couple of them, and represents a populous state.

The highly developed individualism of Senate politics emphasizes personalities and dealings among senators that frequently resemble the relations among sovereign states. Much of the day-to-day negotiations among Senate enterprises occurs at the staff level, subject only to ratification by the principals.[16] Michael Malbin concluded in 1980 that "House members [also] seem to be delegating more than they used to, hiring more entrepreneurial activists and letting staff-to-staff conversations begin to replace direct communication between members."[17] Perhaps, but a good part of delegation in the House frees the legislator to carry on exactly the kind of one-on-one politicking that only principals can conduct.

In addition, personal ties among House members have become increasingly significant as key authority figures—party leaders and committee chairs—have lost some formal power to move policies through the legislative process. Within the 435-member House, politics has often moved to the "retail" level, where the leadership, the committee chairs, and other individual entrepreneurs build coalitions one vote at a time. In such a context, members who aspire to influence the process must be free to do their own negotiating. Effective entrepreneurs will thus delegate as much routine office-based responsibility as possible. A Steve Bartlett or a Jim Moody can emerge quickly as an effective force in part because each freed himself from the daily requirements of management.

Specialization: The Demise of the Clerk. Seeking to recapture an earlier era, Congressman Jim Slattery has taken to composing several personal, handwritten notes each evening in response to difficult or special constituency problems. However politically valuable this tactic may be, the fact remains that the great bulk of his replies are printed out in a flexible word-processing format, which allows his legislative aides and a computer operator to mesh a set of available paragraphs into a coherent set of remarks.

Within the memory of some Capitol Hill veterans, most replies to constituent mail were written by hand, and the only assistance that most legislators had was a clerk or a secretary.[18] A clerk was ordinarily a jack-of-all-trades who might answer legislative mail one moment, greet a visiting constituent the next, and draft an amendment the next. By the 1950s and early 1960s, personal offices still had their share of clerks and secretaries, sometimes presided over by an administrative assistant. In 1957, for example, the average House enterprise employed only 5.6 staffers, while senators got by with fewer than 12 per office (see table 6.1). In other words, House offices, with approximately 18 aides per office, have far outstripped the Senate operations of the Eisenhower administration. The bureaucratization of the Congress has more than paralleled similar trends in the executive.

The best information on staff specialization comes from the Congressional Management Foundation's (CMF) annual salary survey of congressional offices. In 1987 CMF listed twenty separate positions commonly found in House offices.[19] Virtually all operations had an AA, a couple of legislative assistants (LAs), and some caseworkers (usually in the district). In addition, press aides, personal secretaries, receptionists, and district representatives are found in almost all offices. And most members employ either a computer operator or a "systems manager."

If automation has forced the hand of many legislators, even more widespread are the practices of using staff to accomplish policy and constituency service goals. The enterprise has evolved in three distinct ways since the 1960s. First, the press secretary role has become institutionalized. Virtually all House offices have such a position, although some members continue to resist labeling any staffer as a press secretary or aide.[20] Senatorial offices frequently employ one or two aides who assist the press secretary. Second, district operations require both more personnel and some hierarchy of their own. Again, the post-Watergate congressional generation has led the way here, with most casework going to the district, where service can be more personal. During the 1970s, district caseworkers created new jobs within (and new responsibilities for) the congressional enterprise as they brought the office to the constituents.

Finally, and perhaps most important, staff growth has meant that a backbench member of Congress could choose to hire enough legislative assistants for specialized assignments so that he or she could participate actively and effectively in all stages of the process. Jim Moody, for example, hired six LAs in his first term. None would get rich on the salaries he offered, but young, smart, and ambitious talent is abundant in Washington. As Moody's AA recounted, "I read 1200 resumes and interviewed 100 to 150 folks, some three to four times. . . . I tried to hire intelligent people and teach them what to do. And I tried to hire people who would put up with this crap." With his six LAs, Moody employed a larger legislative staff than did some full committees in the 1950s. And they could offer him specialized assistance as he sought to wield influence as an activist entrepreneur. Moody's AA observed with satisfaction that his six LAs had become increasingly competent and professional over their initial eighteen months of service. "In the first year, we'd want to do something, and I might make six suggestions and an LA might add one. Now it's the reverse."

Legislative assistants provide the most tangible link between the overall enterprise and the individual member as entrepreneur. In many ways this is what makes the lure of a Senate office so great for an ambitious House entrepreneur. Senator Paul Simon's AA, former Congressman Floyd Fithian, observes, "Over here [in the Senate], if we want to get involved with something, I can just assign a couple of interns and an LA to it, and pretty soon, if it's not too big a subject, they'll know more about it than anyone else." With 434 competitors and more rigid committee jurisdictions, such freedom does not exist within the House. But if a policy has even a tangential committee or constituency handle on it, House entrepreneurs can, with the help of their staff, propel themselves into the middle of policy debates.

Decentralization: The Legislator as Ward Boss. "Each one of us—the newer people who were so critical of the power structures—has created our own little power structures," observes class of '74 member Chris Dodd.

> Call it what you want, but basically it is the old spoils system, only this time it's not jobs or contracts we're handing out, but constituent service. I think it's worthwhile . . . But I also know that the political spinoffs are most positive.[21]

As Senate and House staffs have grown and communications capacities have improved, more and more aides have worked within their members' home constituencies. In 1972, House offices averaged 2.7 staffers in the district, and in-state Senate operations averaged a mere 3 staffers. A decade later, House members allocated 6.2 aides to the district, while senators employed an average of 10.5 staffers in their home states.[22] As younger legislators replaced their senior predecessors, this trend accelerated, in that the new members were often: (1) electorally insecure; (2) comfortable with decentralized constituent services; and (3) situated in cramped Capitol Hill quarters that encouraged placing staffers in district or state offices.

Again, the mid-1970s served as a turning point. Not only did newly elected members perform more of their casework in the district, but constituency demands rose as well, both in response to governmental largesse and regulation and to the increasing local visibility of congressional offices. Indeed, one continuing goal of many legislative enterprises is to solicit as much business from constituents as possible. At the most mundane, this may simply reflect a desire to build a large list of eligible voters, classified by demographic characteristics and issue concerns. Thus many freshman legislators may set a specific goal, such as getting 100,000 or so names in their computers by the end of their first term.

More broadly, the enterprise can develop into an integral part of a local community and perhaps even serve to define the boundaries of an unwieldy district. In the wake of his February 1974 special election victory for a central Pennsylvania House seat, Democrat John Murtha immediately added four district offices to his predecessor's single location. With lots of activities, a continuing presence, and an activist local press strategy, the Murtha enterprise, argues an aide, has helped "to alleviate a serious void in the governmental process."[23] By the mid-1970s, the decentralized enterprise was often taking on many tasks beyond the normal advertising and constituency service activities. On occasion the district-state offices actually sponsor or deliver services, as when former Congressman Barry Goldwater, Jr. (R-Calif.), instituted a transportation system to get his constituents to the beach (about twenty miles from his district) and back.[24]

Such a specific service remains the exception, but virtually all congressional enterprises play major roles in obtaining federal funds and in providing the nitty-gritty casework that consumes the major share of district staff time and efforts. In some instances, the office can actually resolve a constituent's problem, but much more frequently the enterprise dispenses information and advice about how—and if—a solution can be reached.[25]

In that most legislators invest a lot of resources in their district operations and act as policy entrepreneurs, can any connections between these two trends be found, save for the notion that most members see constituency service as almost pure political gain? Two possible links stand out.

First, for some midseniority members, casework leads directly to subsequent policy initiatives.[26] Newly elected legislators have little feeling if a given constituency problem has general applicability; senior members are often burdened with committee responsibilities. But midlevel policy entrepreneurs, such as Slattery or Bartlett, have the experience, the resources, and the time to pursue a locally based initiative. Political scientist John Johannes notes:

> The offices of "up-and-coming" members, many of whom are beginning to move into positions of institutional responsibility and power, may be precisely the ones who most successfully utilize—or seek to utilize—casework for legislative and oversight purposes.[27]

Effective policy entrepreneurs can connect the policy and political strands of public problems and have the resources to take some action. No group better fits this description than middle management legislators. Moving an issue along may be somewhat easier for those chairing subcommittees, but the experienced backbencher—a Bartlett, a Slattery—has the staff, information, and other resources for setting the congressional agenda and framing attractive policy alternatives.

Second, in an era of weak parties and indifferent bureaucracies, congressional enterprises are frequently the most responsive units of the national government in addressing citizen demands and problems. Indeed, with their open-door policies and willingness to offer assistance, district offices represent the modern-day equivalent of old-line political machines. The district staff can offer access to the wide range of governmental programs and agencies; the cost to the constituent is nil; and enterprises provide information and counsel that are part of the ordinary congressional overhead. In addition, the members of the class of '74 and their colleagues have offered their own regular, personal involvement.

Both political scientists and practicing politicos have come to see the decentralized enterprise as promoting, if not absolutely guaranteeing, the reelection of incumbents.[28] Personalized attention, information, and occasional favors can be traded for votes—the classic machine politics exchange. This trade is especially attractive for policy activists, who can, with their resources and apparently limitless personal energies, provide electoral insulation from an ideologically incompatible constituency.[29]

The class of '74 seemed to make this work; in 1976, only two of seventy-five freshman Democrats lost their bids for reelection, and one of these was caught in a minor sexual solicitation scandal. Young, visible activists like New Jersey's Andy Maguire, New York's Tom Downey, and Michigan's Bob Carr, all representing strongly Republican districts, held onto their seats throughout the 1970s, largely on the strength of the district operations. Similarly, such low-key 1974 Democratic newcomers as Matt McHugh and Bob Edgar compiled consistently liberal voting records in heavily Republican areas, while delivering first-rate constituency service.

Virtually all legislative enterprises begin with the personal office, but few end there. As Salisbury and Shepsle observe, "It is dangerous . . . to stress [too much] the pattern of personal staff arrangements, precisely because a large proportion of the members have additional staff components within their total enterprise."[30] Exactly so. The enterprise concept incorporates both other resources and the complex relationships between and among members and their staffs. On the one hand, the million dollar or more enterprise requires management; on the other, the essence of effectiveness within the Congress is rarely a management question. Rather, the enterprise must support its principal, as he or she seeks reelection, advancement, entrepreneurial success, power, or compensation. Despite the temptation to consider the personal office as mainly a reelection tool, that is only a single, albeit important, dimension of a broader enterprise.

Caucuses as Enterprises

During the 1970s, freshmen legislators were no longer expected to be seen and not heard. In addition, majority party legislators could legitimately anticipate that they would chair a subcommittee within a few years of their arrival on Capitol Hill. What else could they possibly want? Or use? Caucuses, that's what. In many ways, the proliferation of caucuses reflects the energy, innovation, formlessness, and confusion within the Congress of the 1970s, and these bodies remain important forces, with ninety-four separate caucuses existing in 1985.[31]

Ironically, the explosion in the number of congressional caucuses (also known as "informal" or nonofficial groups) within the Congress was directly related to the growth of resources and the proliferation of subcommittees. Resources to help support caucuses were controlled by legislators who could simply take on a leadership role in a caucus and designate one of their staffers as the contact person for that group.

Many caucuses, however, have used members' personal office resources in more imaginative ways, by pooling financial resources, both through dues and the use of individual members' clerk-hire funds. Thus, the Congressional Sunbelt Council, qualifying as a Legislative Service Organization (LSO) under House rules, receives office space and uses members' pooled office resources to support its staff and efforts. The Council has a staff of two and separate (if spartan) space in that "Siberia" of office buildings—House Annex II, a shuttle bus ride away from most Capitol Hill operations. Although some of these informal groups, including the granddaddy of them all, the House Democratic Study Group, have grown into large, powerful units, most LSOs have two or three staffers, who generally work for a few key caucus leaders.

Finally, a few sizable caucuses rely on outside fund-raising for a large part of their budgets. The Congressional Black Caucus, the Congressional Hispanic Caucus, and the Northeast-Midwest Congressional Coalition can offer considerable assistance to their leaders. The Black, Hispanic, and Northeast-Midwest groups are tied to parallel tax-exempt institutes, which attract both donations and foundation grants. Therefore, heading a caucus of this sort provides a backbencher with both additional resources and prestige—dual weapons for an effective policy entrepreneur.

Caucuses offer would-be policy entrepreneurs ideal vehicles for their work—especially when their initiatives take them beyond the normal committee subject matter. One veteran caucus staffer explained, "My definition of a caucus activist is someone who is too big for his district and too small for the national stage." Thus, in 1987, when "competitiveness" became the policy catchword, a Competitiveness Caucus sprang up, with more than 150 members and cochaired by Montana's Democratic Senator Max Baucus (class of '74) and Congressman Buddy McKay. For such leaders, there were some important opportunities to participate in the debate and expand their issue agendas.

Caucuses allow rank-and-file members to demonstrate their concerns on a host of issues. Back in their districts they can cite their membership in the Competitiveness Caucus or the Auto Task Force or the Caucus on Women's Issues as demonstrating their concerns on the groups' issues. "As a member of the [Congressional] Arts Caucus," Congressman Bill Richardson (D-N.Mex.) notes, "I can tell my constituents who are interested in the arts that I'm with them. . . . You can use it to expand your base. If someone writes me on arts issues, I can write back and say I'm in the Congressional Arts Caucus."[32]

Caucuses encourage adaptation within the Congress because seniority, committee structures, and party leaders do not control their activities. Instead, caucuses provide direct, timely, and low-cost connections between the outside environment and the Congress. As the institution becomes more fragmented, with bits of subcommittee turf divided among increasingly large numbers of legislators, most emerging policy problems do not fit neatly into a single subcommittee's jurisdiction. Political scientist Eric Uslaner points out, for example, "In the 95th Congress (1977–78), 83 committees and subcommittees in the House . . . held hearings on some aspect of energy policy."[33]

Rather than trying to create a new subcommittee or select committee, it is much simpler to put together a caucus, which requires little more than a letterhead and a presiding officer.[34] In the late 1970s, the industry-oriented Auto Task Force and Congressional Steel Caucus provided avenues for legislators who chose not to wait for electoral results or committee action to place trade and import issues on the policy agenda. In addition, these caucuses focused much of their attention on executive-branch actions, which are crucial in trade matters. However problematic it is for an individual entrepreneur to move an issue through the Congress, affecting the administration is even more difficult. Caucuses can and do help. Both the auto and steel groups succeeded in changing executive policies—trigger prices on steel and so-called voluntary imported automobile quotas, respectively.

Caucuses can serve individual entrepreneurs with more than conventional agenda setting. Susan Hammond notes that many caucuses and their activist leaders seek either to keep issues on the congressional agenda or to block their advancement.[35] A single legislator from New York may have little say in opposing the closing of the Brooklyn Navy Yard, but the Northeast-Midwest (NEMW) Coalition can make a difference by redefining the question in terms of the regional distribution of defense dollars. In addition, caucus participants ordinarily cut across committee memberships and often across party lines. If an entrepreneur can mobilize caucus activists on a variety of relevant committees and subcommittees, some informal, ad hoc coordination is likely. Within either the fragmented House or the individualistic Senate, any organized collaboration is a valuable policy tool.

CAUCUSES AND THE CLASS OF 1974

As with much of the restructuring of the Congress during the 1970s, the class of '74 members embraced the new caucus opportunities and developed innovative ways to take advantage of these circumstances. Most notably, the class put together its own caucus before its members formally took the oath of office (see chapter 2). The New Members Caucus (NMC) gave visibility and organization to class activities, providing a forum for airing both substantive matters and reelection concerns. With its functioning whip organization, NMC leaders provided the Democratic leadership with estimates of the breadth and depth of class support on specific votes.

Finally, the NMC set a precedent by remaining active, as the 94th Caucus, for several years after the first term. This earned for the class the ire of Tip O'Neill, who notes that

> what really annoyed me about this group is that as late as 1979 they still had their own caucus. . . . I had naturally assumed that after their first term was over, the new members would join the mainstream. But almost overnight Congress was crowded with all kinds of caucuses. . . . I used to meet with them all.[36]

Caucuses thus provide one more set of potential channels for communication between party leaders and backbenchers. Caucus leaders can use their positions both to set the agenda and to build coalitions—and to promote their own careers.

Bob Edgar: The Caucus Activist. Few contemporary legislators have understood the virtues of caucuses more than former Congressman Bob Edgar, whose leadership activities in two major groups served to define much of his congressional career. Edgar tied his caucus activities directly to his class of '74 experiences. "We invented the caucus—the Northeast-Midwest Coalition. We expanded the MCPL (Members of Congress for Peace

Through Law), and we started the Energy and Environment Conference." Edgar was a bit weak on the facts; for example, the Democratic Study Group and the Republican Wednesday Group predated the Energy and Environment Conference (1973). Yet he is essentially correct in asserting that the post-1974 newcomers engineered the contemporary caucus format that emphasizes rapid organizational responses to emerging policy problems.

Whatever their impact on the processes and policies of Congress, there is little doubt that individual members, usually from the rank and file, can prosper with the addition of caucus resources and prestige. As Edgar notes, "When I was Chairman of the [then 212-member] Northeast-Midwest Coalition, I had a staff of twenty. I could get lots of extra things done. And I had some leverage—something to bargain with." Edgar recognized the opportunity that a major caucus chair offered to junior members, and he sought the NEMW position despite his status as an outsider—a marginal-seat legislator with a reputation as a moralistic, anti-porkbarrel, reformer. Edgar recounts, "I went around and got commitments from everybody. At the last moment [classmate Congressman James] Oberstar [D-Wisc.] jumped in, and I won by one vote. Some of my support was not all that strong, due to my water projects stand. The next time I was elected unanimously." After his elevation to NEMW chair, described in the *Washington Post* as "a national podium which is the envy of his more anonymous colleagues,"[37] Edgar moved to integrate completely his NEMW position within his overall enterprise—including his committees and the Congressional Clearinghouse on the Future, his other major caucus.

The caucuses afforded Edgar the opportunity to make a substantial long-term policy investment. He observed that the Clearinghouse and the NEMW Coalition

> allowed me to be more effective earlier [in my career]. I didn't have to be chairman of the Public Works Committee [or even a subcommittee] to have an impact on water is-

sues. I had eyes and ears and people available to go after issues.[38]

By defining policy problems in terms of either region (for the Coalition) or the future (for the Clearinghouse) Edgar could, simultaneously, mitigate the effects of his liberalism within his district and hope to set the agenda on broad national issues—all without having any traditional party or committee seat of power.

In addition, Edgar relied on caucus activity in his 1986 campaign for statewide office. "In a sense," Edgar argued, "I've [already] been the third senator from Pennsylvania because of these coalitions. I've been able to address the issues of steel and coal and the infrastructure and the other areas that senators, who represent whole states, deal with."[39] Edgar's environmental image and entrepreneurial style paid some very tangible dividends for his electoral enterprise. His issue positions, visibility, and record obtained for him entrée into a statewide network of policy activists, whose assistance was crucial for his primary campaign. In fact, the Pennsylvania League of Conservation Voters became, legally, the Conservationists for Edgar during his Senate campaign, reclaiming its nonpartisan status when the election was over.[40]

Although this expansion of the Edgar enterprise was unusual, caucuses often provide resources and opportunities that allow relatively junior members to affect important policy debates and outcomes. Many of the most successful individual efforts, like Edgar's, build upon strong issue positions, derived either from personal interest or district-state needs. Caucus leaders, regardless of their ideology, party, region, or special interests, often gain valuable expertise and legislative experience early in their congressional tenure.

Congressman Bob Carr: An Artistic Change. In 1980, after an often stormy six years in the House of Representatives, Bob Carr lost a close election in his marginal district. Carr had led a minor insurrection against Speaker Albert during his first year in the House, and, as a member of the Armed Services Committee, he had spoken out frequently against excessive military spending and waste. Carr was a perfect example of a congressional "bomb-thrower" whose ability to use his personal office resources did not prevent his ultimate defeat.

After narrowly recapturing his seat in 1982, Bob Carr returned to the House an apparently changed man. He received an appointment to the Appropriations Committee, and unlike Tom Downey, who moved from Armed Services to Ways and Means, Carr has not continued to speak out publicly on military policy. Rather, he has used his position and resources to forge a different, low-key style that eschews the confrontations of his earlier years. Few members can make this kind of switch, but the flexibility of personal resources does allow for such a change. In addition, Carr altered his own issue agenda and commitments. Typical here is his 1987 election as chair of the Congressional Arts Caucus, which has been, since its inception in 1981, the province of the class of '74 (Congressman Fred Richmond [D-N.Y.] organized the group, and Downey succeeded him).

It was Carr's choice to become identified with this caucus, to seek its chair, and ultimately, to help control its considerable resources ($300 dues per member, plus the receipts from a major fund-raiser). Carr thus benefits in three ways from his role in the Arts Caucus. First, he creates firm ties to a popular subject that cuts across normal political boundaries, much as Bob Edgar did with environmentalism. Second, he controls additional resources and staff. Third, as the leader of an important caucus, Carr can take credit for services and favors to his colleagues, such as assisting on a difficult grant proposal or in obtaining an invitation to a luncheon with prominent members of the arts community.

In a district that will always require a lot of attention, Bob Carr has fashioned, through his Appropriations position, personal staff, and caucus commitments, a legislative enterprise that serves him well. With his major committee assignment and varied interests, Carr remains a player in many key decisions, if not an energetic policy entrepreneur.

Enterprising Politics: Protection and Projection

Enterprises serve two general purposes for members of Congress today. They can both protect legislators from defeat at the polls and project entrepreneurs into policy debates and political arenas extending far beyond their usual committee and constituency concerns. Despite the attention paid to the protection elements of enterprises, such as incumbency, campaign contributions, and the political uses of staff (see chapter 8), the ability to project influence may be more important.

Inside the Congress this means that backbenchers can command enough personal resources to understand issues outside their committee and constituency domains; such knowledge allows them to play a role in floor action and informal negotiations. In addition, chairing a major caucus propels many junior members into key roles within leadership coalitions. Indeed, the class of '74's caucus rules called for a six-month term of office for its president. To an extent this reflected the class's democratic instincts, but it also recognized the value of a position that allowed access to the councils of the party leadership.

The ability to project one's influence extends far beyond the insider politics of Capitol Hill. As Republicans like Newt Gingrich, Vin Weber (R-Minn.) and others have demonstrated, a visible, publicity-conscious caucus, such as the Conservative Opportunity Society, can be forged quickly with relatively few expenses. Their central asset is the ability to appear on television, even when the House chamber is empty and only 200,000 or so C-SPAN addicts are tuned in. As with other resources shared by all in the House, obtaining television time was quickly established as a right possessed by all members (although some had to wait longer than others to exercise it).

The most profound democratization of the Congress has come not in procedural reforms, however important, but in the resources and positions available to all members—House or Senate, majority or minority. At the same time, opportunities are cumulative, and the greatest benefits belong to those who hold majorities in the respective chambers. In the House, for example, Republicans have chaired no committees or subcommittees since 1955. In other words, throughout the entire growth-of-government period, since the 1960s, they have never been able to exert control over the chamber's agenda. Beyond this, in a publicity-driven system, formal leadership positions remain highly valuable in attracting the kind of attention—from the press, special interests, and administration officials—that makes it possible to set the policy agenda and to build the essential coalitions.

7

Enterprise, Position, and Influence

THE HOUSE OF REPRESENTATIVES is not the House of Lords; rather, it is full of elected officials on a two-year leash. This can impose severe restrictions on policy entrepreneurs, as Congressman Henry Waxman discovered in 1984:

> One by one, a dozen or so U.S. representatives approached their colleague from California, Henry Waxman . . . and told him why they had voted down his bill to allow doctors to use heroin for terminal cancer pain. . . . Their opposition was based on fear. "They explained to me," Waxman says, "that with the November election coming up, a vote for the bill would allow their opponents to brand them 'heroin pushers.' "[1]

Waxman lost this tally by a large margin (55 to 355), as he knew he would. Nevertheless, that he could and would press for such a vote is enlightening. First, it demonstrates that a skilled subcommittee chair can bring a difficult, even impossible, piece of legislation to a floor vote. Second, it shows that a highly regarded legislator can lose a vote by a wide margin and suffer no loss of respect. And third, Waxman's action illustrates that the power of key subcommittee and full committee chairs in the House (and even more so in the Senate) ultimately resides in the ability to influence their peers. If Richard Neustadt's dictum that presidential power is "the power to persuade" rings true in the White House, it also strikes a responsive chord within the Congress of the postreform era.[2] Waxman's efforts at persuasion had just begun. He could bring back a heroin bill (formally, the Compassionate Pain Relief Act), or he might rewrite the proposal and insert it, with the chamber's tacit approval, into a $600 billion supplemental appropriations bill, never to be seen again, save by the medical profession and its ultimate recipients.

In a Position to Play

Congressional enterprises bring to mind a set of staff members, other resources, and a network of connections. This makes sense, yet it omits a crucial element for most policy entrepreneurs—a position from which to expand their influence. However substantial personal office resources may be and regardless of the significance of informal caucuses, positions within the formal structures of Congress provide regular channels for policy entrepreneurs. As House Majority Leader Thomas Foley puts it, "A committee or a leadership position must inform one's expertise. Otherwise you're not taken seriously." Subcommittee chairs, "power" committee assignments, and party leadership slots represent the most common positions, and the proliferation of these opportunities reflects a major change within the contemporary Congress, especially the House. Even a minority party's freshman senators can expect a

TABLE 7.1

Chairs and Power Committee Slots in the House of Representatives, 1955–1988

Congress	Number Chairing Standing Committees/Subcommittees	Number of "Power Committee" Positions
84th (1955–56)	63 (27.2%)[a]	92[b]
90th (1967–68)	111 (44.9%)	95
92nd (1971–72)	120 (47.2%)	95
94th (1975–76)	142 (49.1%)	108 / 133(w/Budget)[c]
96th (1979–80)	144 (52.2%)	131
98th (1983–84)	124 (46.4%)	136
100th (1987–88)	128 (49.6%)	141

SOURCE: Compiled by author from *CQ Almanacs* (various years).
NOTES: a. Percentage of majority party holding at least one chair
b. Total number on Appropriations, Rules, Ways and Means
c. Total of above three committees, plus Budget from 94th Congress on (both figures provided for 94th Congress, when Budget's status was uncertain)

decent committee assignment and the designation as ranking member on one or two subcommittees.

Central to House reforms in the mid-1970s was a substantial increase in the number of available subcommittee chairs and "power committee" positions (see table 7.1).[3] Under most circumstances, members could chair only one legislative subcommittee; in addition, Ways and Means grew much larger (and created subcommittees), and Budget took its place by the late 1970s as a major committee.

In fact, the conventional wisdom of proliferating subcommittee chairs is not applicable into the 1980s.[4] Rather, more growth has come in the expansion of power committees: Appropriations, Ways and Means, Rules, and, since the mid-1970s, Budget. This has different implications than does a rise in the number of subcommittees or subcommittee chairs, which, when coupled with the greater authority granted subcommittees in the 1970s, contributes to what Smith and Deering see as

> a system of independent but not wholly autonomous subcommittees in the House. The leaders of these panels serve in positions of power and influence but they are answerable to numerous colleagues. These new leaders in Congress are less senior, more active, and generally more representative of their party colleagues than were their predecessors. But they hold positions of initiative rather than positions of ultimate authority.[5]

One top leadership aide observes, "Things don't work from the top down around here. It's from down up." In this decentralized setting, the party leaders have moved to institute procedures, channels, and positions that allow—even require—a great deal of participation by those middle management and low seniority members who wish to have a significant impact on policy. Although it is not true, at least in the House, that everyone on the Democratic side is a chairman, between whips, task force heads, Rules and Budget committee members, and the top elected leaders, almost everyone who wants to serve in a leadership role has some opportunity to do so.[6]

SUBCOMMITTEES: THE CLASS OF 1974's BASE OF OPERATIONS

Former Congressman Bob Edgar observes, "The base of this group—the class of 1974—is the subcommittees. If you look to see who is managing bills, it's one class member after another."

The Watergate babies assumed these positions of power soon after arriving on Capitol Hill. In the 94th Congress, immediately upon entering the House, Congressman Steve Neal (D-N.C.) became a subcommittee chairman, a most unusual achievement, but understandable on a Banking Committee that included thirteen new Democrats within its twenty-nine-member majority. Six years later, of the forty-four class of '74 Democrats left in the House, all but three either sat on a power committee (twelve) or chaired a subcommittee (twenty-nine). To place this rapid advancement in perspective, ten years earlier the large class of '64 was also entering its fourth term. Of its twenty-seven surviving House members, only nine held subcommittee chairs, and a mere two sat on power committees.

The 1974 group has incorporated subcommittee chairs into their enterprises at a unparalleled rate for the modern Congress. Although many of their number, such as Washington's Don Bonker (on trade) and New Jersey's William Hughes (on crime), head important panels, nowhere has the overall significance of subcommittee chairs and the progress of the class of '74 come together more clearly than on the Energy and Commerce Committee. Between 1981 and 1986, full committee chair John Dingell was the only non-1974 entrant to lead any subcommittee, save for the 1985–86 tenure of Congressman Ed Markey (D-Mass.), who, coming to the Congress in 1976, is a spiritual cousin of the 1974 group.

At the same time, the Energy and Commerce Committee illustrates the great differences among subcommittee chair positions, especially when combined with electoral and personality factors. A veteran committee staffer pointed out in 1984 that

> [Tim] Wirth and [Henry] Waxman are much more comfortable wheeling and dealing [than some others]. [Phil] Sharp is much more oriented toward consensus, at least among Democrats. He's unable to get *outside* groups to support his positions. Wirth and Waxman are hard and heavy hitters with liberal groups.

Building political support means using one's enterprise as effectively as possible, and no one unites entrepreneurial talents with enterprise resources more productively than California's Henry Waxman.

Congressman Henry Waxman: Policy Entrepreneur as Subcommittee Chair. Although no single legislator can stand for all members of the large and disparate class of '74, Congressman Henry

Waxman can certainly serve as a model subcommittee chair. A policy entrepreneur par excellence, much of Waxman's strength in Congress derives from his position as head of the Energy and Commerce Committee's important subcommittee on Health and the Environment. Although he has other positions and commands other resources (through his California-based political organization), Waxman's subcommittee chair lies at the center of his entire enterprise. In this, he resembles many of his class of '74 peers. Still, Waxman in particular, and the other Energy and Commerce subcommittee chairs in general, have enjoyed great opportunities to mine a rich and controversial lode of issues.[7]

Waxman demonstrates the potential that a well-staffed subcommittee offers an activist chair. Not only can he promote a pet project, as with his heroin proposal, but he can push legislation to fruition through obtaining publicity (orphan drugs), tack on a program to a budget reconciliation bill (maternity benefits), and seek long-term political solutions to intractable policy problems (clear air, acid rain). If Waxman does not always emerge victorious—and he surely doesn't—he always comes to play, and a key subcommittee gives him lots of leeway to find a way to win.

The amount of publicity he and his subcommittee receive notwithstanding, Waxman has no reputation as a media hound. Fellow subcommittee chair Phil Sharp comments, "He's got his eye on the ultimate product. Publicity is a tool to use." Commenting on the use of publicity to push policy, Waxman observes:

> You use publicity to get public support behind [an idea]. The public's got to know something's a problem before you do anything. . . . The best example is probably orphan drugs—when there are rare diseases and the drug companies simply wouldn't produce the drugs if they had them, or do the research. Another failure of the market, yet people suffer both from the nemesis and the frustration of

> knowing that solutions might be available. So, we had some hearings, brought in Jack Klugman to testify and we got some public attention, made the problem visible and then wrote some legislation that gives some incentives to pharmaceutical companies to manufacture the drugs so they could break even. It's been a great success . . . [with] over a hundred new drugs produced in response after this legislation was passed.

"More generally," Waxman continues, "members think that visibility in legislation helps them. Someone always had to do it, outside groups maybe in the past." Members are more publicity conscious at present, he observes, and "they end up being showboats and it can have some costs."

Two points bear some emphasis here. First, Waxman did put on a bit of a show, with Klugman's appearance, in order to attract attention to an important, if obscure, problem. Second, the visibility of a member and the issue at hand blend together, almost seamlessly. Waxman and other talented entrepreneurs keep this firmly in mind. For skillful subcommittee chairs, claiming credit is rarely a problem, especially when a legislative product, like the orphan drug bill, emerges.

Many issues do not receive the closure that the drug legislation did. Waxman's handling of extended policy debates—on clean air, and especially acid rain—demonstrate his dual drives, to promote legislative solutions and to win.

After five years of shaping a series of policy alternatives, by 1987 Waxman had developed an acid rain package that appealed to a broad array of Democrats and moderate Republicans. In 1986 an acid rain bill, cosponsored by more than 170 House members, passed his Health and Environment subcommittee for the first time. Waxman commented that defining the problem was not the issue; rather, it was coming up with an acceptable political solution. "Over the last couple of years (1985–86) we've been developing legislation that's got a lot of support . . . local rate payers [of utilities] are protected, so are other rate payers nationally."

Decisions on what kind of coal to burn, what kind of technology to adopt, fall upon utilities and local officials, who are encouraged to adopt the cheapest clean system available. Waxman continues, sounding like a textbook entrepreneur,

> [Acid rain] is a political problem, [that requires] a political solution. It's not like orphan drugs, where there was a policy solution. I think some acid rain legislation can pass. If you don't try, you've already lost . . . it's a dynamic process. If the public supports acid rain legislation, and a bill is sent to the President, . . . he might sign it. He signed the superfund bill . . . you keep developing support.

Finally, as a subcommittee chair who attends to issues of interest to everyone in the Congress, Waxman is in an excellent position to move policy into the massive budget reconciliation measures and appropriations bills that have become late-session fixtures in recent Congresses. After passing through the House, a Waxman-sponsored measure to provide maternity benefits for the poor died in the Senate in 1980. Five years later, he built a coalition that spanned parties and ideologies to hold in place a similar policy initiative within the comprehensive budget reconciliation bill.[8]

With a large majority staff (eighteen members), a wide jurisdiction, and a heavy workload, Waxman can operate much like a senator who identifies a problem and allows his staff to pursue solutions.[9] In their reports on hearings that dealt with the cost of prescription drugs, both the *Wall Street Journal* and the *New York Times* quote extensively from his subcommittee's staff report. Indeed, their stories lead with staff findings and use the congressman's statements only in later paragraphs. As much as any House member, Waxman has combined his own skill, the importance of his jurisdiction, and a large staff to create a subcommittee-based enterprise that extends his influence beyond that of many full committee chairs.

Congressman Phil Sharp: An Academic Chair. Twice an unsuccessful House candidate before winning a seat in 1974, Phil Sharp has remained a prime Republican target ever since. His marginal district reinforces Sharp's cautious personality and academic style (appropriate for a former political science professor). A long-time aide says, "We've got a saying that every issue has two sides, and Phil sees all three of them. He never wants to look foolish." In 1981, Sharp became chairman of a key Energy and Commerce subcommittee, with "fossil fuels" jurisdiction. He has thus received a great deal of attention from the energy industry, especially after 1982, when, a staff member notes, Sharp "replaced [the departed] Toby Moffett as the great threat in the campaign literature of the oil companies, the Texas groups."

Sharp's caution and precarious electoral situation surface continually in the way he uses his subcommittee position. As he has gained seniority and experience, Sharp seems comfortable with his role as a low-key broker and majority builder; on a committee with a John Dingell, a Henry Waxman, and various other aggressive policy activists, Sharp's style is distinct. Still, like all his Energy and Commerce colleagues, policy results are central to his work. He observes:

> What I've come to see is that there are lots of different functions to be played around here. Some of us are more interested in finding solutions—to work out solutions to problems with others. We have to produce policy—or else, in terms of our own standards for success. Others have different roles to play. . . . They have to make their statement, regardless of the end product.

Sharp resembles the average subcommittee chair much more than Waxman in his tendency to specialize a great deal—a trade-off of position for range of policy interests. Sharp notes that serving as chair "forced me to focus more tightly on one set of issues. It may have made me a little too narrow. We've spent two years on natural gas." In the end, however, such committee-based specialization remains at the heart of House policy making. Sharp won plaudits for piloting a natural gas deregulation bill through the committee and the House in 1984, a feat that many observers thought impossible, especially given the opposition of Energy and Commerce Chairman John Dingell. Nevertheless, a good reputation does not replace policy accomplishments; Sharp's subcommittee staff director notes that the chairman's political education continued in the 1984 process. Subsequently, in 1985,

> Sharp knew he needed three Republican votes (on the full committee), so he got the twenty-two supporters [of his bill] to take a "blood oath" to oppose every amendment to the package. . . . You know, this might have been the coming of age of Phil Sharp. He values openness and open intellectual discussions so much. But sometimes that's not the best way to get things done.

The bill made it out of Energy and Commerce but failed to progress beyond that; the urgency of the issue had waned.

Jim Florio: Pugilist as Subcommittee Chair. The dateline on the *New York Times* column was Atlantic City, and a reader found it in the sports section, not on the op-ed pages. New Jersey Congressman (and candidate for governor) Jim Florio had taken his subcommittee on Commerce, Travel, and Tourism to the Jersey shore to hold hearings on, as he called it, the "prizefighting industry."[10] Little came of these efforts, save a nice column, but the entire episode—exploring the boxing business with a bunch of characters worthy of a latter-day Damon Runyon—illustrates the possibilities afforded an energetic entrepreneur like Florio.

If Sharp's approach to his subcommittee is to build consensus, Florio's is to move forward, pushing toward a policy goal or a new issue for his subcommittee to delve into. Discussing his subcommittee in 1984, Florio said:

> We're expanding our jurisdiction. We've got authority over the FTC [Federal Trade Commission], and that gets you to antitrust and regulation. We've begun to deal with some trade issues. There was a headline the other day, "Florio on Trade." *The legislative credentials and the jurisdiction give you a forum on almost everything.* From the forum you affect public opinion and from that you get clout [emphasis added].

Such a pugilistic approach to his subcommittee position has helped Florio win some major legislative victories (the original superfund legislation, the Rail Act of 1980, and a toxic substances control statute, for example). In addition, in 1986 his tenacity on superfund reauthorization enabled him to rebound from defeats within both his own subcommittee and the full Energy and Commerce Committee. Florio won a substantial strengthening of the superfund bill after it was referred to Public Works in the wake of Energy and Commerce actions.

Florio's challenges to Dingell and a majority of committee Democrats has had repercussions for the congressman's subcommittee enterprise. At the start of the 100th Congress in January 1987, Dingell and the committee's party caucus forced Florio to choose between chairing one of two subcommittees with redrawn policy jurisdictions. Florio selected the panel on Commerce, Consumer Protection, and Competitiveness over one that included hazardous waste and rail issues, in which he had been intimately involved. Although Chairman Dingell denied any retribution, one committee aide commented, "The fact of the matter is that [Florio] lost a big piece of his jurisdiction."[11] A consumer lobbyist concluded: "If there was overwhelming support for Jim Florio on that committee, Dingell wouldn't be able to do that stuff. . . . To slice someone's committee in half, you really have to have lost support."[12]

Despite his expertise and his past policy accomplishments, Florio could not protect himself against a tough chairman and an antagonistic committee caucus. Subcommittee chairmanships remain important positions, but they are scarcely immutable grants of authority. In a sense, Florio's enterprise has suffered for the style more than the substance of his entrepreneurial actions.

THE LIMITS OF POSITION

Subcommittee chairs are extremely valuable parts of any member's enterprise. A chair can command at least a bit of attention, and sometimes a good deal. A chairmanship grants staff resources, which are often substantial. Chairs are well situated to set the agenda, to make deals, and to oversee the bureaucracy. But this does not mean that subcommittee chairs dominate the House or even their full committees. Rather, like other positions and resources, a subcommittee chairmanship allows members to participate actively, and with a stronger hand, in the continuing political game. As Deering and Smith conclude, "There are more opportunities for rank-and-file members, especially subcommittee chairs, to place demands on [party leaders]."[13] At the same time, "on major issues, subcommittee leaders are in no position to guarantee party leaders that certain legislation will be reported to the floor in a particular form at a particular time."[14]

In short, House and Senate subcommittees allow their chairs to expand their entrepreneurial activities. As long as they can build majorities, policy impact will follow. Nevertheless, coalition building in a multitiered system is no mean feat. This is especially true within Energy and Commerce, where strong subcommittee chairs continually must contend with a full committee leader, John Dingell, who seeks expanded roles for himself and who has his own policy agenda for the entire committee. Ironically, the Energy and Commerce Committee rules, which devolve much authority to subcommittees, were written by Dingell and others during the era of a weak and ineffective chairman. "John inherited the boundaries that he helped to create," a staff member observed. "Once you've let the quicksilver out of the thermometer, you'll never get it all back in."[15]

THE BUDGET COMMITTEE: ELUSIVE INFLUENCE

If subcommittee chairs provide policy entrepreneurs with substantial resources and specialized vantage points for their activities, Budget Committee seats confer an opposite blend. Serving on Budget provides few resources but does offer an excellent position for an entrepreneur to address a host of issues and, on occasion, to fashion coalitions. Indeed, as Speaker Jim Wright notes, a Budget Committee seat "is a prize, it is a plum, it is a leadership position."[16] Still, a seat on the committee is no unmixed blessing. Senator Tim Wirth contends, "The pleasure I felt when I got on the [House] Budget Committee was exceeded only by the pleasure I had getting off it."[17] As Wirth's exasperation implies, the interminable budget process may take its toll on even the most dedicated, ambitious, and forceful entrepreneurs. Ironically, upon his election to the Senate in 1986, Wirth was appointed to that chamber's Budget panel.

One glance down the roster of present and former House committee members (who must rotate off the panel after six years' service) demonstrates how desirable this committee is to all House members, but especially to activist junior representatives. Early in their careers, talented representatives such as Democrats Wirth, Mineta, Gephardt, David Obey (D-Wisc.) Panetta, Gray (chair in 1985–88), and Pat Williams (D-Mont.), and Republicans Bill Frenzel (R-Minn.), Ed Bethune (R-Ark.), Gramm, and Loeffler, among many others, won seats on Budget. No congressional cohort has been better represented than the class of '74, which has provided fifteen members, including twelve majority Democrats.[18]

The Budget Committee's attraction derives from its unique status within the House. Not even the Rules Committee deals with all the issues addressed by Budget. In addition, members who might have waited for years to make a major impact on the Appropriations Committee can have an immediate effect on Budget; the 1980s budget process has allowed Budget, with approval from the leadership and the chamber, to dictate spending cuts to both authorizing and appropriations committees.[19]

Budget membership also encourages legislators to move outside their committee-based specialization. For a Tom Downey, this has meant that his switch from Armed Services to Ways and Means did not keep him from having a position to speak on defense spending issues. Given his expertise and his commitment, Downey would have remained outspoken, regardless of his position, but the Budget slot, with an attendant task force chair, gives him a piece of turf on which to place his podium. Thus, not only does the Budget Committee provide a member with almost limitless policy scope, it also confers legitimacy. Because the committee's jurisdiction covers the whole of the budget, any member can speak out on any part. As Congressman David Obey grumbled from his Appropriations Committee position, "The budget process offers endless opportunities for cheap shots from free-lance artists."[20]

Just as congressional agenda setters are attracted to the Budget panel, so too are some coalition builders. In the early years of the budget process, it became apparent that in the House budgets pass only with the painstaking creation of highly partisan coalitions. Even party-based brokerage, worked out in private, requires great sensitivity to coalitional requirements of those whose priorities differ greatly.[21] Individual committee members, such as Buddy McKay, and caucus heads, like the Democratic Study Group's Matt McHugh, have invested much time and effort in offering detailed proposals for deficit reductions.

The entrepreneurial possibilities of Budget Committee membership are best illustrated by the performance of the "gang of four" in 1980, who held up the process in order to have their policy concerns addressed. Congressmen Gephardt, Panetta, Mineta, and Wirth, all archetypal new-style politicians from the classes of '74 or '76, stubbornly refused to endorse a budget compromise that made them uncomfortable. Senator Pete Domenici (R-N.Mex.), ranking member of the Senate Budget Committee, provided them with celebrity, at least inside the capital's beltway, by declaring, "If this gang of five [sic] thinks that by shooting down our negotiations . . . , that they will get further concessions, they are dead wrong."[22] Weathering public criticism and private entreaties, these moderates did force a rearrangement of priorities and gained immediate notoriety as they commanded the key congressional veto point within a House-Senate conference committee. It is instructive that four junior representatives could bring the entire process to a halt. The domination of the House Budget Committee by activist junior members allowed the gang to employ their weapons of policy expertise and political savvy. Martin Tolchin wrote at the time (June 1980) that the gang's members are "serious-minded and well-respected by their colleagues, and their opposition to the House-Senate compromise budget . . . presaged the measure's defeat on the House floor."[23]

As the gang of four experience illustrates, the Budget Committee offers great possibilities for gaining visibility. The budget is news, year in, year out, and the press continually needs new angles and new spokespersons to approach what frequently becomes the same old story. Couple these requirements with the entrepreneurial types who often end up on the committee, and most any member who wants some coverage can get it. In his years of sitting on the panel, Congressman George Miller could relate almost all of his myriad policy interests to the budget debate.

Somewhat at odds with the publicity possibilities inherent in Budget Committee membership is the panel's status as part of the leadership. Most House budgets, in and out of the committee, have been partisan documents, and party leaders, especially Democrats, have a substantial stake in committee outcomes.[24] The Budget Committee often serves as an incubator for future party leaders, as the top leadership seeks legislators who can participate effectively in numerous ways. Indeed, Budget panel members take on an assortment of responsibilities that mirrors those confronting the House in general and the leadership in particular. They must understand innumerable policy complexities, accommodate the contradictory requirements of the overall budget with the specifics advocated by full and subcommittee chairs, and decide whether to make political statements in the midst of economic policy making. Such a mix of roles corresponds closely to the views of one top House leader, who sees a need for the next generation of leaders to be thoughtful and effective and to serve as "articulate spokesmen, who can use the media." Less charitably, Congressman David Bonoir concludes that Budget politics need not be taken "very seriously, . . . in that the numbers get changed later anyway. The Budget Committee is a talker's shop."[25]

The transitory nature of House Budget Committee membership also fits into the entrepreneurial style. Although a Budget appointment means that a legislator will take a leave of absence from another committee, about one-half of the Budget members who rotate off the panel have transferred to either Appropriations or Ways and Means.[26] Such movement illustrates how the committee serves as a testing ground for nascent leaders. At the same time, Budget service does not diminish a legislator's accumulation of seniority on other committees. This is especially significant for junior members, who can deal themselves into budgetary politics while waiting for a subcommittee chair.

The add-on nature of a Budget assignment allows legislators a great deal of flexibility in defining how they will approach the job. Most of these issue activists throw themselves into the budget process with great energy, but this is not universal. Congressman Steve Solarz, as a subcommittee chair on Foreign Affairs, used his Budget position to reassure his urban constituents. One staff aide noted that Solarz

> sees himself as the representative of two interest groups. . . . He's committed to distributing foreign aid. . . . Second, he's an urban congressman. . . . The people of Borough Park . . . are not living and dying over whether Rhodesia becomes Zimbabwe. Budget is a fabulous complement to his foreign policy interests.

Beyond its range of issues, the Budget Committee also offers its members something a bit more tangible—an additional staffer, paid from committee funds but located in the member's office. These staff tend "to have more political experience than economic training," and they are frequently used as general legislative assistants rather than as budget specialists.[27]

Despite an extra staff member, despite a policy domain that covers almost the entire range of government policies, and despite its leadership status (at least within the House), Budget Committee members often express great frustrations at their inability to affect policies. Much of their time is spent manipulating figures with little connection to reality. This produces what Senator Don Reigle (D-Mich.) calls "a gentleman's agreement to live with phony numbers."[28] The Gramm-Rudman-Hollings deficit reduction measure has exacerbated these tendencies, and Budget Committee members understand that their actions will have little effect on the broad, macroeconomic policies. Nevertheless, entrepreneurs remain drawn to the Budget Committee due to its status within the House, its subject matter, and the education, both formal and informal, that takes place there.[29] More than anything else, a committee seat here has become a stepping-stone to positions of greater power, both on prestige committees and within the party leadership.

PARTIES AND ENTERPRISES: INFORMATION AND NETWORKS

Although resources and committee positions are important to any congressional enterprise, these are useful only to the extent that channels exist for coalition building and pushing policy alternatives. A greatly expanded party leadership structure increasingly provides the avenues for the retail politics of the contemporary House. As one Democratic leadership aide commented,

> We added about ten to fifteen appointed whips [in the 99th Congress]. There was a lot of demand. People just came up to the leadership and asked. None of the [appointed] whips lost, and only one quit. Some of them don't work too hard, or at all. But it's hard—impossible—to fire them. So you just add some.

Although Republicans have a number of partisan groupings where policies are discussed, the House Democrats, the majority party since 1955, retain their status as the most important party group on Capitol Hill. For the House to work, the majority party must be able to lead; in the postreform House, this has been no easy chore.

In the end, as politicians and political scientists alike have concluded, leadership in the Congress demands a strategy of inclusion.[30] By the 100th Congress of 1987–88, no Democrat interested in leading is left out (see table 7.2). Beyond the top leadership organizations such as Steering and Policy Committee, and the entire caucus, the politics of inclusion come into play most notably in the ever-expanding whip operation and the party task forces. As of the 100th Congress, more than a fourth of all House Democrats belong to the whip organization. A leadership aide notes, "The whip organization, with seventy or eighty members, is now a mini-[party] caucus every week. Often issues are discussed and decisions reversed during the whip caucus."

What party leaders and middle management members (the whips) get from their weekly meetings is an exchange of information. The lower echelons receive some insight into the direction the party is taking, and what is happening in other policy

TABLE 7.2

House Democratic Legislative Leadership Positions, 92nd and 100th Congresses

92nd Congress (1971–72)[a]	100th Congress (1987–88)[b]
Speaker	Speaker
Floor leader	Floor leader
Whip	Whip
Caucus chair	Caucus chair
Deputy whips (2)	Chief deputy whip
Zone whips (19)	Deputy whips (10)
	Whip task force chairs (4)
	At-large whips (44)
	Zone whips (22)
	Steering and policy (31)
Total = 25	Total = 114*

SOURCES: a. *CQ Almanac 1971* (Washington, D.C.: Congressional Quarterly Inc., 1971), p. 10. b. Alan Ehrenhalt, ed. *Politics in America: The 100th Congress* (Washington, D.C.: CQ Press, 1987), pp. 1716–17.
*Occupied by 98 individuals.

domains. The leaders obtain views from their troops, whose opinions get an immediate, public airing. One class of '74 member noted that, early in Speaker Jim Wright's tenure,

> Bob Carr [another 1974 entrant] stood up and told [Speaker] Jim Wright that however he saw the tax [increase] issue that his [Carr's] constituents saw it as more Democratic "tax and spend" policy. Wright got angry, but in Carr's district, which is very marginal, he'd be dead. The whip meetings can get you away from the inside the beltway mentality.

In short, the whip system allows for the regular exchange of ideas—up and down. Both top and middle management can benefit from this, but rarely in terms of obvious, immediate rewards. For all involved, it is more like a continuing conversation. Few concrete benefits accrue to whips, even those fairly high up the ladder. Congressman Mineta, a deputy whip, sees his slot as providing some status and some access, but little else. He goes on:

> Among my colleagues, I'm given some recognition for having some information, being connected. Like Ivy League eating clubs, . . . well, I'm part of the Speaker's eating club. . . . People say to me, "You're part of the leadership, what's going on?" And then I say, "Gee I don't know," and I go and find out. I think you're part of the inside track in asking questions.

Mineta noted that as a whip he could get better information from top leadership aides, who often knew when and if important votes would come up. A great many of the day-to-day benefits of being a member of the leadership's lower, even middle, echelons come in slight, though sometimes significant, communication advantages. As one leader notes, the whip system

> is a great vehicle for [communication]. But the whip operation today is different than in previous years. Now what we do to lobby a bill through is to set up a task force. The task forces are now the old whip organization.[31]

The growth and consolidation of the Democratic Caucus's task forces, which are organized around single issues or pieces of legislation, has paralleled the whip system's expansion.[32] Like serving on the Budget Committee, leading a task force gives a junior member a real opportunity to demonstrate a range of talents. Simultaneously, task force service brings junior members into the process and increases their overall party loyalty.[33] Devised under Tip O'Neill's leadership in the late 1970s, task forces provided the class of '74 members with excellent coalition-building experiences early in their careers. Of the twenty such ad hoc groups appointed in 1977–80, eleven were headed by 1974 entrants, and only two chairs came from the pre-1974 era.[34]

By the mid-1980s, task forces had become almost totally open to any member with the time or inclination to join. One House majority aide states that

> if you want to be on [a task force], you're on. All you have to do is ask. [Congressman] Vic Fazio called yesterday and wanted to be included in the Nicaraguan group. By tomorrow, when they meet, he'll be there. That's all there is to it.

Although these task forces offer real opportunities for learning and influence, they also give members one more way to explain to their constituents what they do. Like the informal caucuses, task forces can provide symbolic associations (industrial policy, arms control) for a member as well as the possibility of influencing policy.

With such a proliferation of nominal leadership positions, the notion of "core leadership" takes on increased meaning.[35] Only a few members obtain real resources and greatly enhanced access to information within the Democrats' broadly inclusive structure. For most members, a leadership post offers an additional avenue of influence and communication, to be used in conjunction with the other parts of their enterprises. Increasingly, however, the party forums and channels of communication serve to structure the coalitions policy entrepreneurs seek to build.

Enterprises and Influence

Individualism run rampant in the Senate and fragmentation within the House have created milieux for members of Congress in which most formal positions add relatively little to one's influence. One Democrat notes that "there are only 10 or 15 people who have real power as a result of their positions" in the House.[36] A similar figure for the Senate would be no higher. Some positions, like committee chairmanships, do confer substantial resources and the power to move things onto the agenda. Nevertheless, chairs cannot keep issues from legislative consideration, and they too must build coalitions on a member-by-member, "retail" basis, like any congressional entrepreneur.

In such a policy-making context, positions—within committees, parties, or informal caucuses—provide openings for legislators to participate in a system of almost constant entrepreneurial activity. For Phil Gramm, an obscure second-term House member in 1981, a Budget Committee seat allowed him access to the most important game in town, and he proved himself a most substantial player. Henry Waxman, as a third-term Energy and Commerce Committee member, demonstrated his understanding of the new House rules and the value of the Health and Environment subcommittee when he successfully challenged Congressman Richardson Preyer (D-N.C.), a respected senior member, for that panel's chairmanship in 1979. Like Gramm, he took a substantial risk, but, as entrepreneurs, both saw great potential rewards—in policy and career terms.

The value of any given position is always contingent upon a politician's skill in exploiting the opportunities. With the proliferation of party leadership slots, power committee openings, meaningful subcommittee chairs, and informal caucuses, most legislators can fold some positions into their enterprises. But individual skills remain paramount, as legislators move from one meeting to another, serving as leaders in one gathering, as part of the audience in the next.

In the end, the new politicians operate within a process where there is little predictable power, only the continuing possibility of influence, in one forum or another. These opportunities are shaped, even for top leaders, by the fact that most legislators remain insulated from serious electoral threat at home. To understand the individualism of Capitol Hill requires examining the "electoral connection" that either demands (in marginal seats) that legislators ignore party leaders or frees them (in safe seats) from responding to leaders' entreaties. In his last term as Speaker, Tip O'Neill observed that

> It's wrong when you can go out and raise a couple of million dollars. . . . What does that mean? That means that I scare anybody from running against me. Now, when you have a fellow like that, he becomes a little bit of an autocrat, thinks he's a power within himself.[37]

The independence of policy entrepreneurs often derives directly from their electoral circumstances. The congressional enterprise does not exist just in Washington or consist only of the positions and resources that the Congress provides. The enterprise is also becoming a permanent—and increasingly expensive—campaign.

8

Rust Never Sleeps: The Congressional Enterprise as Campaign

JANUARY 1987 found the campaign organization of newly elected Congressman David Price (D-N.C.) sending out thank you notes to the financial supporters of his difficult 1986 campaign, which cost more than $600,000. On Capitol Hill, Price was making the essential choices on how he would set up his office—whom he would hire, what computer system would work best, and how many staffers would remain in the district, along with dozens of other mundane, but equally important, decisions. With an eye to the future, regardless of incumbency's alleged advantages, Price knew he could not build his reelection efforts solely around his office and staff. Therefore, he kept his campaign organization intact. Scarcely a month after sending out its thank-yous, the Price campaign mailed a detailed and urgent request for funds. One of Jesse Helms's top lieutenants had announced that he would mount a 1988 challenge, and the congressman concluded there was no time to lose in warding off this serious threat. In establishing his congressional office while simultaneously retaining an active campaign unit, the Price enterprise—which began as a campaign, of course—was quickly becoming a multifaceted set of overlapping organizations.

Operating on a grander scale than his freshman House colleague, Senate Finance Committee Chair Lloyd Bentsen (D-Tex.) decided that he would exact from lobbyists (through their political action committees) $10,000 campaign contributions to attend a series of breakfasts with him—a practice begun by previous Finance Committee Chair Bob Packwood, whose charge was a mere $5,000. More than two hundred had agreed to this arrangement when the story broke in the *Washington Post.* Embarrassed but hardly chastened, Bentsen returned the money, much of which ultimately found its way back to his campaign coffers.[1] On the other hand, Senate Majority Leader Robert Byrd did not return the $10,000 contributions lobbyists had given to him under similar circumstances, but without the breakfasts.[2]

These instances, whether well-publicized (Bentsen) or obscure (Price), illustrate the difficulty of disentangling the official parts of a congressional enterprise from its campaign components. When Senator Bentsen sits down to bacon and eggs with a lobbyist, does he do so as a 1988 candidate for reelection who needs $8 million to run a Texas-size campaign? Or is he the head of the committee that will have immense impact as an "appeals court" in fine-tuning the Tax Reform Act of 1986 and in shaping a Democratic trade package? Bentsen is both candidate and chairman, of course. On a lesser scale, Congressman David Price's top district aide will play, almost by definition, simultaneous administrative and political roles within the congressman's nascent enterprise.

Such an operation is best viewed as a whole, albeit one with many faces. Indeed, the signal virtue of the enterprise concept is its capacity to aggregate—to include an array of distinct, even disparate, components into a comprehensible whole that revolves around the politician. The original formulation of Salisbury and Shepsle does not include the campaign personnel within the member's enterprise, nor does it take into account the increasingly common pattern of placing several staffers in one or more district offices. They consider only the personal office staff in Washington, committee staff under the member's control, and former employees ("alumni") in the private or public sectors.[3] Although these elements of the enterprise are significant, by no means do they represent the entire operation.

The congressional enterprise is capable of doing many different things at the same time. Thus, Senator Chris Dodd's committee staff could perform extensive research on a maternity leave policy initiative, while Dodd himself was visiting Nicaragua. Even more graphic was the division of labor for Senator Joseph Biden (D-Del.), who juggled his duties in directing the Judiciary Committee with his ill-fated presidential bid. Conversely, an enterprise can undergo total mobilization in pursuit of a specific goal—usually electoral. The most striking example here is the overnight conversion of former Congresswoman Geraldine Ferraro's (D-N.Y.) modest congressional office into the hub of a vice-presidential campaign operation.

More often, the change in the congressional enterprise from its normal, multifaceted mode to a campaign operation develops gradually and becomes complete (to its legal limits) only within marginal-seat offices. In these instances, staff members frequently take vacation time to work for the campaign or, on occasion, temporarily resign from the congressional staff to go on the campaign payroll. Especially in marginal seats or attempts for higher office, the enterprise does not just include the campaign, it eventually becomes the campaign. This notion of enterprise as campaign makes sense within at least three different contexts: the apparent growth in the power of incumbency; the actual operations of congressional offices (see chapter 6), including the working assumptions of members and staff; and the ways in which campaign funds are raised, spent, and (increasingly) banked.

Enterprises and Incumbents

Whatever the reasons, the winning margins of incumbent members of the House of Representatives have grown in the postwar era, although Gary Jacobson argues that sitting members are no more secure at present than in the 1950s.[4] Whether or not the marginals have vanished or merely have been transformed, congressional incumbents clearly hold great advantages over their challengers, both actual and prospective.

Given the apparent safety of most incumbents, the work of political scientists Jacobson and Tom Mann is especially important. Mann's mid-1970s research, presented in the aptly titled *Unsafe at Any Margin* (1978), finds that many incumbents with apparently healthy electoral cushions remain extremely concerned about their prospects for reelection.[5] Either by the example of others or the recollection of a past difficult race, sitting members can find any number of reasons for their electoral concerns. Within former Congressman Bob Edgar's enterprise, for example, everyone's point of reference was 1978—"the election Bob almost lost." In 1980, Edgar more than doubled his expenditures and subsequently increased his margin of victory in a Republican district that gave only 36 percent of its vote to Jimmy Carter. Perhaps the best strategic politicians are the most neurotic.

In any event, worried incumbents have had some good reasons to fret. Although the average margin of victory in House districts has grown from the figures of the 1960s, a modest number of incumbents continue to lose. The probability of incumbent defeat has not varied significantly since 1952; rather the range of vulnerability has increased.[6] Very narrow margins usually do indicate, at least temporarily, a competitive district, but Jacobson finds that a House incumbent is just as likely to lose in the next election with a vote total between 55 and 60 percent as between 65 and 70 percent.[7]

Nevertheless, House incumbents win. The blizzard of studies on incumbency effects notwithstanding, the fact remains that there is no scholarly consensus on how, or even if, incumbents benefit from their congressional positions and resources.[8] Despite a great deal of research on the power of incumbency, we have a lot of suspects, but no smoking gun.

Aside from tailoring their issue positions and votes to suit their constituents, incumbents attempt to solidify their hold on their districts in two related ways. First, in providing lots of service and access, legislators supposedly win the voters' support by increasing his or her familiarity and by "taking up their causes."[9] Second, incumbents seek to dissuade strong opponents from challenging them.

One problem with these prescriptions for electoral security is that neither operates in a straightforward manner. Although providing extensive services to all constituents should result in "pure profit" for a congressional office, researchers have found no clear pattern of positive electoral impact. Furthermore, high campaign expenditures by an incumbent might be considered a signal of strength, designed to discourage serious challengers. A sitting member's high expenditures, however, can appear as a sign of weakness, which may invite a subsequent challenge.[10] One clear trend is for incumbents to build large campaign accounts, which sometimes dwarf their actual expenditures, as a means of warding off serious opposition. In effect, the incumbent forces a potential opponent to ask the question, The member can spend hundreds of thousands of dollars, and raise even more, so why should I bother to make the race from such a position of disadvantage?

In the end, the legislator's talents in making effective use of official resources and in discouraging prospective challengers may be more important than any specific perquisites or accumulations of campaign funds. Such skills are difficult to assess.[11] One possibility is to examine the overall growth of the congressional enterprise, both inside the House and beyond it, as part of an unending campaign process.

OPERATING THE ENTERPRISE

In Congressman Tim Wirth's 1982 run for reelection, his campaign enterprise—even though it spent almost $750,000 at the heady rate of $35,000 per week—retained its amateur standing. The *National Journal*'s Dom Bonafede reported:

> [Wirth] estimated he spends as much as $35,000 a week on radio and television spots. "All of the work, including media liaison, campaign commercials, direct mail and scheduling, is done in-house," Wirth said. His wife, Wren, and Cary K. Caton, his administrative assistant, draft his political advertising and television scripts.[12]

With his competitive seat and progressive ambitions, Wirth was certainly an exception in not relying heavily on professional advice and services, yet his efforts illustrate the capacities that members' enterprises can exhibit, when pushed to their limits.

Although congressional operations incorporate multiple activities and serve multiple goals, thoughts of and efforts at winning reelection seldom sink far below the surface. Logically (if depressingly) enough, this begins almost at the moment of a member's initial election. The most common background for the administrative assistant is prior service as the candidate's campaign manager.[13] The trust that often characterizes relationships between candidate and campaign manager closely resembles the most productive working arrangements between member and AA. Much as the best candidates allow others to manage their campaigns, so too do many effective members delegate a great deal of operational responsibility to their staff, especially to a strong AA, as Wirth did with his veteran aide, Cary Caton, both in Washington and in pursuit of reelection.

This does not mean that all campaign managers make good AAs, or vice-versa. Far from it; many expert campaign aides cannot adapt to Washington, the frustrations of congressional life, and the pace of life with a relatively powerless freshman legislator. Nevertheless, the AA and campaign manager jobs are similar, although the political tasks of a typical administrative aide represent only a fraction of his or her duties. Moreover, to the extent that legislative enterprises have a political core, the AA ordinarily takes responsibility by managing the overall operation and thus integrating campaign efforts with those of the congressional office.

However much AAs see themselves as part-time directors of reelection efforts, press secretaries are, if anything, even more electorally inclined. As David Mayhew has theorized and most legislators admit, members of Congress are continually engaged in advertising activities.[14] Most of their efforts are directed straight back to the district, either through press releases or, increasingly, satellite-based local television reporting.

In addition, the trend toward locating increasing numbers of aides in district offices contributes mightily to the perceptions of both staff and constituents that the congressional office and the campaign are virtually interchangeable. In 1974, all House enterprises located an average of 3.5 staffers in their district units. By 1986 this had almost doubled to 6.7 non-D.C. staff aides per member.[15] Although political scientists may not have found convincingly strong relationships between district staffing levels and electoral outcomes, the legislators and their staff do not doubt the power of a sustained local presence. One California congressman's field representative flatly observed:

> I'm never through campaigning—except for one evening every two years. Election night there's no campaign. We have a victory party, I drink a lot of champagne, and I go home and go to bed. Next morning I begin campaigning all over again.[16]

Despite formal constraints and limitations, the combining of campaign and constituency service functions is almost complete. A district representative who is handling a social security case one minute is arranging the details of a campaign fund-raiser the next. Political scientist John McCartney, a close observer of congressional enterprises' local arms, concludes:

> No matter how dazzling a campaign organization a challenger puts together, it will always be an ad hoc group, unfamiliar with the territory and with each other, while the incumbent fields a publicly paid team of experienced veterans to do a task they have succeeded in before, perhaps many times before, and which differs very little from their everyday jobs.[17]

Campaign Cash: The Bonds That Tie

Since the 1970s, campaign expenditures have risen sharply, and these funds have increasingly come from political action committees. In addition, incumbents' campaign organizations have retained large amounts of cash on hand. Combined with the growing tendency for individual legislators to form their own political action committees, these developments have radically changed and expanded the role of the campaign within the congressional enterprise. Some basic figures help to sketch out the changes.

In 1974, an average campaign for the House of Representatives cost approximately $54,000; in 1986, this figure stood at $244,000. In 1974, average Senate campaign expenses were $437,000; in 1986, the mean was $2,631,000.[18] At the dawn of the age of political action committees, 1974, virtually no candidates for the House received more than half their campaign funds from these groups. By 1978, the number of representatives who obtained such support was 63 and by 1986 the number had risen to 194. In this same 1978–86 period, Senate candidates' PAC contributions rose from about $82,000 per campaign to an average of more than $692,000. Finally, although figures are sketchy, average cash on hand for incumbent House members has risen from a few thousand dollars in the mid-1970s to about $55,000 in 1982 and to more than $122,000 at the end of 1986.[19]

Despite the rhetoric of reform, incumbent legislators have created a campaign finance system that serves them exceedingly well. This minor item from the *National Journal* speaks volumes about how the campaign finance works to maintain a congressional enterprise.

> There's a tidy symmetry to [1987] fund raising of Rep. Jim Moody, D-Wis. More than four dozen business lobbyists paid $350 each to breakfast with the Milwaukee liberal—a new Ways and Means Committeeman—on February 25. Labor's chance comes on March 10—same buffet, same price, same Capitol Hill Club. Twin fund raisers aren't all that uncommon, but Moody's timing is. He used to wait until late spring; his campaign coffers are nearly bare, though, and he intends to use his breakfast booty—$20,000 or more—to foot a half-year's worth of political expenditures.[20]

Moody, unopposed in 1986, had almost $59,000 in campaign cash on hand in mid-October, but his enterprise fell far short of the average incumbent's postelection cash balance of $122,000.[21]

Although incumbents have generally increased their campaign spending, the cash-on-hand figures are striking, especially when members really work at accumulating a surplus. In 1980, only three House members held a post-election balance of more than $250,000, with none of these hitting $300,000, and in 1982, only seven representatives retained more than $300,000.[22] After the 1983–84 election cycle, twenty-three House members had accumulated more than $300,000. During the 1985–86 cycle, this number rose to thirty-eight, and fifty-four congressmen had at least $250,000 in the bank. The retention of funds can serve any number of purposes; for example, of the twenty members who have accumulated more than $400,000 cash on hand, sixteen are eligible to convert the funds to personal use upon retirement. Judging from the 1983–84 figures, one common use is to provide the base for a subsequent Senate campaign. Of the twenty-one House members with the largest amounts of cash on hand after the 1984 elections, five ran for the Senate in 1986.[23]

Beyond the accumulation of rising cash balances, the totals of funds spent and retained have risen steadily. In fact, this may be the truest measure of the campaign enterprise. Thus, in 1986 the average House incumbent had spent almost $310,000 and retained more than $122,000 cash on hand—a sum of more than $432,000, which represents a rise of $85,000 from 1984 totals.[24]

Members of Congress have proven themselves remarkably adaptable when it comes to balancing the books of their operations. Regardless of increasingly tough official expense regulations, Federal Election Commission standards, and PAC limits, the fact remains that both senators and congressmen have found avenues to channel election contributions into a wide range of their activities. Although some of these expenditures are broadly political (for example, contributions to other members' campaigns or even Christmas cards to 40,000 close friends), many strain the limits of the broadest interpretation of political purposes. In 1977 the House formally abolished "unofficial office accounts," or, less elegantly, "slush funds." But current campaign accounts are little different in practice. Moreover, despite the appearance of post-Watergate reform, the Senate allows its Democratic and Republican committees to channel funds to defray senators' "official expenditures," which can range from expensive meals to interior decorating advice to driving lessons.[25] The Congress is no better at removing its slush than is the District of Columbia government at cleaning up after a February snowstorm.

Recent House reports have shown expenses such as $665 for a forty-foot church flagpole (Congressman Carroll Hubbard) or "thousands of dollars [of] gifts for 'constituent hospitality'" (former Congressman Sam Hall, D-Tex.).[26] Expenditures more often help supplement members' official budgets. For example, many legislators use campaign funds to lease automobiles for use in the district throughout their entire two-year terms. And in 1986 Congressman Robert Badham (R-Calif.) paid $617 for his wife's outfits to attend various functions.[27]

As campaign surpluses mount, the tendency will increase to use more funds for more questionable purposes.[28] The House, through its Ethics Committee and the practices of its individual members, becomes the final arbiter. As former Congressman William Boner (D-Tenn.) wrote, in response to a Common Cause exposé of his political expenditures:

> There is no specific definition of "bona fide campaign purpose" provided in the [House] rules. As a result, what would be considered a legitimate or bona fide political and campaign expense, is dependent on the particularized facts of a specific situation.
>
> In fact, the history of the interpretations of this rule, both in debate and elsewhere, have left the definition up to the Member, with the guidance of the House ethics committee.[29]

The pattern of legislators maintaining large amounts of campaign cash on hand is not a recent phenomenon. Large accumulations of campaign funds have sometimes served as retirement accounts. Although this practice is currently prohibited, members who were serving as of January 8, 1980, can legally convert campaign monies to personal use at the end of their legislative careers, as long as they pay taxes on the funds. In 1985, the 251 congressmen allowed this privilege had an average of almost $107,000 cash on hand, while their less senior colleagues averaged $50,000.[30] Still, the campaign funds are more often used to pursue influence within the House, to ward off challengers, or to run for higher office. Indeed, in the 100th Congress the single largest House war chest—almost a million dollars—belongs to Congressman David Dreier (R-Calif.), who was first elected in 1983 and thus not eligible to keep the funds.[31]

CAMPAIGN CONTRIBUTIONS: INVESTMENTS IN THE FUTURE

With so much money accumulated and earning interest, policy entrepreneurs are more than willing to make contributions to the campaigns of other politicians, both within the Congress and back home in their districts. Although at least thirty members of Congress have established their own political action committees, no such mechanism is necessary for them to provide campaign assistance to other congressional candidates. In 1986 Majority Leader (and Speaker-in-waiting) Jim Wright spent more than $1,174,000 in personal campaign funds, some on his own campaign, but most in assisting Democratic House candidates.[32] Party leaders have traditionally played this role, but the growth of rank-and-file members' cash accounts has made this a practice that many members can and do engage in. For example, Congressman Solarz gave almost $61,000 to the 1982 campaigns of state and local candidates in New York, as well as to twenty-three of his fellow House members.[33]

Solarz may use campaign funds to give himself some breathing room in the House, where his publicity-conscious behavior often puts him at odds with his fellow legislators. He concludes that "people will be grateful and my presumptive influence will be enhanced."[34] Ironically, the Solarz enterprise, which ended the 1986 campaign with more than $800,000 in cash on hand, grew geometrically in the early 1980s, as it responded to a potential redistricting scheme that would have pitted the congressman against another incumbent. Once this threat evaporated, Solarz kept raising money, parceling it out, and increasing his cash on hand. The uses for the money may have changed, but the enterprise, given its liquidity, never missed a beat.

In the Senate, similar practices occur, both with campaign funds and personal political action committees. Increasingly, key legislators function as brokers who can direct contributions from large donors and PACs to specific candidates. This is often the province of current or prospective leaders. Senator Bennett Johnson (D-La.), who was seriously considering a challenge to Majority Leader Robert Byrd, arranged in 1986 to raise or funnel funds into the campaigns of several Democratic incumbents and challengers. PACs and individuals "give the contributions to me," Johnson said, "and I give it to the other guys. . . . It is very clear that they are giving to my leadership race," which he eventually abandoned.[35] In campaigning for the Democratic whip position in the House, Congressman Tony Coelho and Charles Rangel (D-N.Y.) adopted similar tactics, although they both channeled their funds—$567,000 for the victorious Coelho and $225,000 for Rangel—through their own political action committees.[36]

The ambitious and aggressive policy entrepreneurs are most likely to organize their own political action committees. Indeed, of thirty such committees operating in 1987, almost all represented either presidential candidates, past or present (nine), top congressional party leaders (eleven), or major policy entrepreneurs. Of course, there is considerable overlap among these three categories: Dick Gephardt and Bob Dole qualify on all counts.

Member-based PACs, while growing in importance, are much less common parts of congressional enterprises than are continuing regular campaign operations that maintain increasingly hefty cash balances. The average House member's cash reserves of more than $122,000 far surpassed all House member PACs in 1986 save for those of Ways and Means chair Rostenkowski ($701,000), Whip candidates Coelho ($567,000) and Rangel ($225,000), Majority Leader Wright ($317,000) and Waxman ($192,000), one of the most aggressive policy entrepreneurs on Capitol Hill, whose distribution of PAC funds was central to his success in obtaining a key Energy and Commerce subcommittee chair in 1978–79.[37] As clearly as any other contemporary member of Congress, Waxman understands the relationship between the campaign enterprise and the role of the legislative activist, observing that

> one of the fundamental rules of my politics is there is no clear distinction between the political process and the legislative process. . . . It is important to get people into office to get things done I believe in. It's not enough just to make the most of those natural allies already there.[38]

As more legislators increase their cash balances and organize PACs, congressional "warlordism" may prevail, much like that of the California legislature, where Waxman cut his political teeth.[39] As Congressman Charles Rangel discovered, when he reluctantly established his political action committee, such a situation encourages, even demands, that party leaders, policy entrepreneurs, prospective senators, and presidential candidates all use the current campaign finance system to enhance their individual opportunities.

THE SUPPLY OF AND DEMAND FOR CAMPAIGN FUNDS

The development of what Sidney Blumenthal has labeled the "permanent campaign" at the presidential level has filtered down, with appropriate modifications, to congressional politics. Blumenthal notes:

> The permanent campaign is the political ideology of our age. It combines image-making with strategic calculation. Under the permanent campaign governing is turned into perpetual campaign. Moreover, it remakes government into an instrument designed to sustain an elected official's public popularity.[40]

Most legislators have continuing campaign organizations and treasuries that help them ward off prospective challenges as well as grease the wheels of their overall operations. The growth of the enterprise as campaign is rooted thoroughly in the expansion of congressional resources. Equally important, however, is the availability of campaign funds (to incumbents) and the almost endless uses for these monies.

From a supply-side perspective, congressional enterprises can attract major contributions because so many well-heeled donors are available and approachable, both as individuals (for example, the Jewish community for Solarz) or as representatives of PACs (the trade and financial communities for Bentsen). At the same time, the demands of congressional enterprises have grown over time as the cost of deterring challenges has increased. Perhaps more significantly, many members' spending for "political" expenses have risen steadily, so that their enterprises require continuing high levels of contributions, even when the legislators find themselves in no serious electoral danger.

An additional consequence of this trend is that members are becoming more actively involved in fund-raising for themselves as well as for others. This is especially true of House members running for the Senate. By one estimate, in 1986 these candidates spent well over half their time soliciting campaign funds. As one lobbyist noted, "It's very hard to say 'no' to a Senator or Congressman."[41] At the same time, with more than $200,000 in campaign expenditures and rising cash balances, the average House member must keep a close eye on the till. Therefore members not only do more fund-raising personally, particularly where large donors are concerned, but party leaders and other notables especially can do their colleagues a favor merely by appearing briefly at receptions or other events. Politics remains a series of exchanges, regardless of what serves as the medium of barter. In many ways, the members of the class of '74 have demonstrated how well this game can be played.

The Total Operation as Campaign: The Class of 1974

In the 1974 elections, the ratio of House seats that went to new members was one in five for the 94th Congress (1975–76). The great majority (seventy-five of ninety-two) of these freshmen were Democrats, and they have survived at rates that few would have predicted. Of the ninety-two original members, thirty remain in the House, and only twenty-three have lost reelection bids through 1986, despite the fact that the Democrats captured forty-nine previously Republican seats in 1974. In contrast, of eighty-four first-term representatives elected in 1964, another high-turnover year, twenty-four lost their initial reelection contest.

No single explanation for the 1974 group's success stands out,[42] but Congressman Richard Cheney speaks for many of his colleagues in his observation that "the Watergate babies [have] expanded the hell out of the powers of incumbency."[43] Perhaps, but most analyses do not permit the easy acceptance of this simple explanation.

THE CAMPAIGN: ON ITS OWN

Campaign organizations certainly merit discussions in terms other than their financial condition. For example, class of '74 members such as Senator Tom Harkin and former Congressman Bob Edgar developed extensive canvassing operations that incorporated large numbers of volunteers. Edgar learned from Harkin's success and went so far as to hire Theresa Vilamin, Harkin's campaign manager, to direct his own operation.[44] Nevertheless, emphasizing the financial side of campaign-enterprises does allow for general comparison (see table 8.1).

Campaign enterprises are becoming more costly, even when inflation is taken into account. This has occurred in the face of the growing electoral strength of the class of '74. By 1986 most marginal-district members had either made their seats relatively safe (for example, Congressman Tom Downey), had

TABLE 8.1

Campaign Expenditures and Cash-on-Hand, 1974–86
Class of 1974 (mean figures, in thousands)

Year	Expenditures	Cash-on-hand, after election	Expenditures plus Cash-on-hand
1974	$102	—	—
1976	105	$ 12	$117
1978	131	15	146
1980	169	23	192
1982	242	42	284
1984	271	106	377
1986	222	177	399

SOURCES: Compiled by author from Common Cause reports (Washington, D.C.): April 7, 1987; February 13, 1987; April 12, 1985; March 14, 1985; March 20, 1984; and February 1, 1983.

lost, or had sought higher office (Bob Edgar). Of the Watergate babies, no more than two or three were in electorally precarious districts. Nonetheless, their campaign enterprises keep growing, although they fall a bit short of the average House campaign as total operations. In addition, despite declining expenditures from 1982 to 1986, their levels of retained cash quadrupled in these four years.[45]

For some members, like Downey, raising large sums of campaign funds is the rational act of a strategic politician who wishes to discourage strong opposition. For most, however, campaign contributions help these policy activists build larger overall enterprises, and the payoffs come within the House, in subsequent bids for higher office, or perhaps upon retirement—if they choose to take the money and not run, so to speak. Although all members of the class of '74 are eligible to retain campaign funds for personal use when they retire, most of these legislative careerists are relatively young; their attention is on accumulating influence within the House.

THE FULL-TIME CAMPAIGN

Despite growing campaign treasuries and large district staffs, political scientist Gary Jacobson observes that

> congressional campaign organizations are personal, temporary, and, for the most part, staffed with volunteers. . . . To be sure, candidates who conduct more than one campaign—notably incumbents—gain useful experience and develop a core of experienced campaign workers. . . . Still, organizations usually have to be put together anew each time.[46]

Such a characterization has been accurate historically, but the dual trends of district staff growth and large sums of retained cash lead to more opportunities for continuity inside the campaign. With a major professional presence in the district and (often) $200,000 in the bank, a legislator can monitor local politics and act in timely, flexible ways, even if a campaign is not under way. Moreover, as Glenn Parker notes, increasing numbers of senior incumbents continue to return regularly to their districts and thus monitor both their staffs and the local use of their political funds.[47] In short, the contemporary congressional enterprise does not just occasionally act as a campaign. Combining official resources and substantial amounts of cash, it continues to function as a campaign throughout the two-year electoral cycle (or six-year for senators, who have become increasingly active fund-raisers early in their term of office).

Regardless of the measure, the size of overall House enterprises for the class of '74 approximately doubled in the 1978–86 period (see table 8.2). This does not mean that incumbents

TABLE 8.2

Enterprise as Campaign for Class of 1974: Three Versions (averages in thousands of dollars)

	1978	1986
Campaign Expenditures plus Cash-on-hand	$146	$399
District Office Staff Value[a]	87	151
Total	$233	$550
Campaign Expenditures plus Cash-on-hand	$146	$399
Total Personal Office Expense	340	507
Total	$486	$906
Campaign Expenditures plus Cash-on-hand plus Personal Office	$486	$906
(Sub)Committee Staff Salaries[b]	17	205
Total	$503	$1111

SOURCES: Ira Chaleff, *Congressional Management Foundation 1987 Salary Survey* (Washington, D.C.: Congressional Management Foundation, 1987); *Report of the Clerk of the House* (Washington, D.C.: U.S. Government Printing Office, 1978), House Documents 95-88, 95-204, 95-265, 95-298; and *Report of the Clerk of the House* (Washington, D.C.: U.S. Government Printing Office, 1986), House Documents 99-236, 99-255, 100-15, 100-35.

NOTE: Figures are for annual official expenditures and for election cycles.

[a]Valued at $15,000 per aide in 1978; $20,000 in 1986.

[b]Valued at $35,000 per aide.

incorporate all these resources, from personal and committee offices, into their campaigns, but their bases are continually expanding. In addition, there is considerable movement within the overall enterprise. For example, incumbents use official staff as their campaign managers over half the time.[48]

However great the increase in the cumulative resources of House enterprises, the resulting benefits that accrue to the campaign remain an open question. In fact, simply describing the growth in the enterprise's campaign-oriented dimensions poses a real problem. David Mayhew noted in an earlier era:

> The Hill office is a vitally important political unit, part campaign management firm and part political machine. The availability of its staff members for election work in and out of season gives it some of the properties of the former; its casework capabilities, some of the latter. And there is the franking privilege for use on office emanations. The dollar value of this array of resources in an election campaign is difficult to estimate. Leuthold gives a 1962 value of $25,000 for House members (including a sum for member salary). In 1971 a House member put it at $100,000 (including a sum for general media exposure). The value has certainly increased over the last decade [1964–74].[49]

The value has risen even more in succeeding years. Still, how much?

In 1978, incumbents from the class of '74 put together campaign enterprises worth an average of $146,000, but when office expenditures and franking costs are included, the value shoots up to more than $376,000 (see table 8.3). In 1986, using the same measures, the campaign elements totaled $399,000, with another $401,000 coming from official expenses. Campaign expenses and office resources are increasing, but the former are rising considerably more quickly than the latter, both in absolute terms and in their percentage of the total enterprise.

TABLE 8.3

The Changing Campaign Enterprise: Average Figures, 1978 and 1986 (Members of the Class of 1974)

Year	Campaign Expenditures, Plus Cash-on-Hand		50% of Office Budget		50% of Average Franking		District Aide "Bonus"[a]		Total
1978	$146,000	+	$170,000	+	$ 37,000	+	$23,400	=	$376,400
1986	$399,000	+	$253,500	+	$110,000	+	$37,500	=	$800,000

SOURCES: Calculated from *Report of the Clerk of the House* (Washington, D.C.: U.S. Government Printing Office, 1978, 1986), and from table 8.1; also Alan Ehrenhalt, ed., *Politics of Congress, 1982* (Washington, D.C.: CQ Press, 1981); Alan Ehrenhalt, ed., *Politics of Congress, 1988* (Washington, D.C.: CQ Press, 1987); Norman J. Ornstein, Thomas E. Mann, and Michael J. Malbin, *Vital Statistics on Congress, 1987–1988* (Washington, D.C.: Congressional Quarterly Inc., 1987), p. 153.

NOTE: In calculating the approximate overall worth of campaign resources, I have taken the 1978 and 1986 figures for election expenditures and retained cash on hand and added to these 50 percent of both overall office expenditures and franking costs, as well as a small bonus for each staff member working in the district. These figures include neither members' salaries nor any general media exposure value. Excluding salaries was simply an attempt to be somewhat conservative in making admittedly inexact estimates, and the variations in media exposure make attaching any figures almost completely arbitrary.

At the same time, using a 50 percent figure for the campaign portion of office expenditures (staff salaries, computers) and franking is equally arbitrary. Given the consistency in the assessments, however, the trends should be clear, even if the dollar figures are a bit off base. Finally, there are no corrections for inflation, save for a slight increase in the value of a district aide between 1978 and 1986, given the salary increases that such staffers have received.

[a]$4,000 per aide in 1978; $5,000 per aide in 1986.

The implications of these patterns may be felt more on Capitol Hill than out on the hustings.

WINNERS AND LOSERS: THE IMPORTANCE OF THE ENTERPRISE

Without question, the class of '74 set new standards in exploiting their congressional office resources. For a while—at least through 1976—this seemed enough to retain their seats. The elections of 1978 and especially 1980 demonstrated, however, that official resources were not enough. Although enhanced service to constituents may have been a necessary condition for electoral survival, it was not sufficient. The campaign elements within the enterprise required attention, and this has meant fund-raising on a scale unimagined by the 1974 group when they entered the House.

As with their publicity and policy efforts, the Watergate babies did not invent many new ways to employ their office resources and raise large campaign war chests. Rather they adopted en masse a series of tactics previously used by only a few legislators. From liberal Gerry Studds (D-Mass.), for example, the Democratic newcomers quickly learned the value of holding regular "town meetings" throughout their relatively conservative districts. They rented mobile vans and engaged in all possible outreach efforts to generate personal contact with voters as well as to establish high levels of name identification. Relentlessly, they traveled back to their districts; some Californians returned almost every week, catching the Sunday evening "red-eye" flight back to the capital. All this activity seemed to work. Despite the defeat of seven relatively weak class of '74 members in 1978, the political machine aspects of the congressional enterprise appeared to protect even the most visible (some would say obnoxious) liberals like Michigan's Bob Carr and New Jersey's Andy Maguire from defeat.

Then came 1980, and the popularity of Ronald Reagan at the top of the ticket served to demonstrate the limited powers of even the most sophisticated district operations in hostile environments. Carr and Maguire lost their seats, as did seven more of the fifty-six freshmen from the class of '74 running for reelection. Constituency service and intense personal involvement could not overcome the twin problems of being both liberal and highly visible. The activist style that Carr and Maguire practiced in Washington could not be completely toned down in the districts.[50] The congressional enterprise is essentially indivisible, and district outreach consisted of the presentation of the legislators' basic, aggressive styles. As Carr supporter John Swain concluded, "Doing this [constituency] stuff keeps your head above water, is all."[51] The remainder of the enterprise—the overall style, the voting record—remains significant.

What the class of '74 did was to set a high standard of constituency service, against which their colleagues and successors could be measured. Congressman John Murtha's five district offices would become the basic number in his geographically difficult constituency. Congressman Downey noted that "I had the first mobile office on Long Island, but now everybody has one. . . . All these frills can quickly be forgotten."[52] In fact, mobile offices have gone out of style in all but a few districts. The standard of service remains, however, a given. It's a classic instance of the constituent's perennial question: what have you done for me lately? Congresswoman Marge Roukema (R-N.J.) answered the only way she could have in 1980, when she defeated Andy Maguire. She pledged to run an outreach program that an aide described as, "even better than Maguire's."[53]

Although money may not be everything, fund-raising capabilities do separate the successful new pols from their defeated brethren, at least within the class of '74. Former Congressman Jerome Ambro, who lost in 1980, concludes: "It was always the same. I could never raise any money. The last time I thought I was doing well—I raised $125,000." His opponent, challenger Gregory Carmen (R-N.Y.), spent more than $300,000 in squeezing out a 3400-vote victory.[54]

Raising such sums becomes easier as legislators gain seniority and positions of influence, but in 1978 and 1980 the class of '74 was only beginning its climb up the congressional ladder. For many, their very marginality could serve as an asset in appealing for assistance, especially when they could come to count on support from specific groups, such as environmentalists (Edgar) and arms control advocates (Downey). However, much of their support has been drawn directly from their constituents—often crossing party lines. Both Edgar and McHugh appealed to moderate Republicans with their low-key demeanor, diligent constituent services, and district-oriented policy emphasis—with satisfactory results. Edgar's personal circle of backers far surpassed the local Democratic base of supporters. And McHugh observes:

> My friends come to my assistance. I have a lot of good friends [smiles]. We try to raise as much in the district as possible [about two-thirds of $400,000 budgets]. . . . We have developed long lists of contributors, it's taken a lot of work over the years.

In examining those who have won over the years and those who have lost, the key difference does not come in the use of official resources but in success at raising campaign funds. Of the twenty-one class members who lost to a challenger in a general election contest, only two managed to outspend their opponents.

The failure to raise large amounts of campaign funds may not be fatal in itself. Rather, for these marginal-seat legislators it may reflect some more substantial weakness in adjusting to the requirements of contemporary electoral politics. Large-scale campaign enterprises quickly became a requirement for these legislators, especially for the Bob Edgars or Joe Fishers of the Congress who rarely "shaved" a vote (Fisher's term) to please a key group of constituents. Both played this part of the game well, although Edgar squeaked through, while Fisher did not, losing in 1980, despite spending more than $270,000.[55] Many of their colleagues, however, either could not or would not build campaign enterprises capable of withstanding tough competition.

Winning challengers have outspent incumbents substantially (see table 8.4), which is not unexpected. More significant, however, is the behavior of the control group of successful marginal seat incumbents (Congressmen Downey, Edgar, McHugh, Sharp, Wirth), who reacted to their status by raising large sums, a practice that continued into the 1980s. Edgar, for

TABLE 8.4

Campaign Spending and Election Results: Marginal Seat Democrats Class of 1974 (1976–1984)(in thousands of dollars)

	Losers			Winners[a]		
Year	Own Money	Opponent's Money	Advantage/ Disadvantage[b]	Own Money	Opponent's Money	Advantage/ Disadvantage
1976	$ 71	$145	−51%	$142	$133	+7%
1978	171	259	−34%	199	215	−7%
1980	204	327	−37%	297	200	+49%
1982	—[c]	—	—	475	200	+138%
1984	503	661	−24%	499	254	+96%

Sources: Michael Barone, Grant Ujifusa, and Douglas Matthews, eds., *The Almanac of American Politics 1978* (New York: E. P. Dutton, 1977); Alan Ehrenhalt, ed., *Politics in America 1982* (Washington, D.C.: CQ Press, 1981); Alan Ehrenhalt, ed., *Politics in America 1986* (Washington, D.C.: CQ Press, 1985).
[a]Includes five marginal members who won five consecutive House races (Downey, Edgar, McHugh, Sharp, Wirth).
[b]Incumbent's spending, divided by challenger's.
[c]Congressman Leo Zeferretti (D-N.Y.) lost to fellow incumbent, after redistricting.

example, responded to a severe challenge in 1978 by more than doubling his 1980 campaign spending, from $142,000 to $295,000.[56] In 1984, as he withstood another difficult challenge and anticipated a subsequent Senate race, he spent $625,000—and kept $100,000 in the bank, even though his House contest was excruciatingly close. As former Congressman Floyd Fithian commented, in awe of such restraint, "Bob must have ice water in his veins. If that had been my campaign, I'd have spent every cent. I know I would have." Edgar could not have known that he would win his 1984 race by a mere 412 votes, but his tactic did allow him to transform his enterprise into a Senate campaign with a modest financial base.

As Table 8.4 illustrates, incumbents' campaign enterprises have expanded greatly over the course of the 1974–86 period. So too have their official resources—their campaigns' cash balances. In the 1970s these enterprises could be described accurately as "small businesses."[57] For most contemporary House members, such a label seems far too modest.

The Campaign as Enterprise: Elections and Beyond

Both the campaign and office-related parts of congressional enterprises have grown steadily since the early 1970s, and in the 1984 and 1986 elections at least, few incumbents (even by historical standards) fell by the wayside. It may be that young, energetic, well-financed incumbents can hold off challengers under almost all circumstances. In any event, rising campaign costs and permissive interpretations of appropriate political expenses have prompted many House members to raise funds with a vengeance. There's no substitute for cash in allowing legislators maximum flexibility to cope with an unstable political environment.

Indeed, the ability to adjust stands as a hallmark of the entire congressional enterprise. Official House office accounts have become increasingly flexible in recent years, and members can weigh the trade-offs of paying higher salaries as opposed to adopting a more costly (and powerful) computer system. To increase his influence a Congressman Stephen Solarz can combine his chairmanship of a Foreign Affairs subcommittee, his policy and publicity-oriented personal office, and his ability to wring campaign contributions from the Jewish community. Likewise, Congressman Henry Waxman can use his affluent Hollywood/Beverly Hills constituency to provide the funds for congressional allies in California and on the Energy and Commerce Committee.

To the extent that Waxman, together with Congressman Howard Berman and his California political consultant partners, has produced a new kind of enterprise, it is a "machine . . . built around issues, personal activism, and a carefully constructed network of campaign contributors."[58] The Waxman "alliance" of progressives provides no patronage beyond the standard constituency services that virtually all incumbents can bestow. Rather, what Waxman and his friends can "deliver" is an enhanced opportunity to influence national policy. In many ways, the Waxman enterprise gives its supporters the kind of issue-oriented benefits that an interest group entrepreneur often provides.[59]

At the same time, expensive, expansive enterprises furnish House members with a strong base in running for the Senate, especially in smaller states. Congressman Tim Wirth's $700,000 campaigns and his subcommittee's well-publicized tussles with AT&T gave him great visibility in a state with a single media hub. This is also true for the progressions from House to Senate for a Charles Grassley or a Tom Harkin in Iowa. Within a Congress where career patterns have become increasingly fluid and opportunities for influence exist for almost every legislator, building one's enterprise can provide many members with some much needed focus. Official resources are limited, but they are more available as members gain seniority. Campaign resources, however, can be acquired with relative ease by most incumbents, although a Ways and Means chair can hope for a better return than can a minority party freshman on Science and Technology.

In the end, campaign enterprises grow for many of the same reasons that legislators seek publicity. Some, like Waxman, have policy goals; others, like Wirth or Louisiana's Republican Henson Moore, have harbored ambitions for higher office. Many others, however, raise the money because it's there, because a hefty campaign account, like thirty seconds on the "Nightly News" or an op-ed piece in the *New York Times,* gives some temporary reassurance that even a junior member of the House is a force to be reckoned with.

Among various implications of the growth of enterprises, two stand out. First, as Jacobson points out, the flow of money to incumbents tends to underfund challengers who have a real chance, especially for Democrats.[60] Thus, in 1982, Democrats gained fewer seats than national conditions warranted. Second, the growth of independent enterprises makes the job of the leadership all the more difficult. In this context it makes sense for a Jim Wright, a Tony Coelho, and a Dan Rostenkowski to spread campaign monies around. Nevertheless, most leaders would gladly trade their financial leverage for firm power to build majorities without having to negotiate time and again for the votes of their own partisans. In an era of congressional individualism, strong and growing enterprises are more likely to stand in the way of majority-building than to foster it.

9

Ambition: A New Era, a Timeless Drive

IT IS a hot summer day in 1984, and in the lobby of the Rayburn Office Building, Congressman Tom Harkin scurries by, an aide at his side, as he maps out his (ultimately successful) campaign for an Iowa Senate seat. He has that familiar look of a candidate with so much to do—and so little time. A moment later, Congressman Tom Downey strolls past, joking with a fellow member, as he heads for a midafternoon basketball game.

By any measure, Downey is as driven and ambitious as is Harkin, his 1974 classmate. Both are serious policy entrepreneurs who desire a national audience, and in 1984 each played to his own strengths. Harkin, as one of six House members from Iowa, was by definition a major political figure in a state with a tradition of defeating single-term Senate incumbents. The rewards he could hope to reap from a successful race—a national platform, a seat on the Appropriations Committee—made it reasonable for him to risk his position as a middle management House member, who chaired an Agriculture subcommittee very important to his Iowa constituents.

Downey's more leisurely stroll toward the House gym made just as much sense. Given his seats on the Budget and Ways and Means committees, Downey's ability to play the game within the House was assured, and an arms-control working group of members and outside activists continued to provide him with a forum for influencing this policy debate. Beyond that, Downey's youth and residence worked against running for higher office. At age thirty-five, with ten years of seniority under his belt, Downey had the luxuries of time and choice in planning career moves. At the same time, his status as one New York representative from a delegation of thirty-four has worked against any attempt to win a Senate seat. Among the more than twenty class of '74 colleagues who have run for the Senate, only Paul Simon has won election in a state with a population of over five million. With youth and his House positions on his side, Downey could afford an afternoon session of basketball, while Harkin pressed on, playing for higher stakes.

Ambition: The Rock of Political Salvation

To examine national politics, whether in 1787 or 1987, requires that ambition be placed center stage. The framers incorporated their insights on human nature into the Constitution, which has shaped the overall structure of political opportunities for two hundred years. Mincing no words, Patrick Henry raised the question of political motives:

> Will not the members of Congress have the same passions which other rulers have had? They will not be superior to the frailties of human nature. Tell me not of checks on

> paper; but tell me of checks founded on self-love. . . . The real rock of political salvation is self-love.[1]

Henry's views were echoed by almost all his peers. Michael Malbin concludes that "if there were any one point on which Federalists and anti-Federalists seemed all but unanimous, it would be that selfishness is an unchanging feature of human nature, the constant bedrock from which all else must begin."[2]

The framers directed this selfishness toward the achievement of honor and glory in public life. The "guiding beacon" of the presidency, Malbin notes, would lead ambitious politicians toward congressional behavior that would enhance their reputations for leadership.[3] Still, many representatives and senators could not realistically aspire to the presidency. The question thus became: how to channel the self-interest of such important officeholders? The answer soon came forward, not in the wisdom of the framers, but in the practices of legislators.

Rewards such as glory and a chance for the presidency were supplemented by internal rewards, provided first by leaders within the legislature and later by the members themselves, as they wrote the rules and established the folkways. For more than 175 years, the congressional chambers created their own sets of internal rewards and, especially in the House, an elaborate combination of formal organizations (committees) and informal practices (seniority, apprenticeship) to maintain these incentives.[4]

In the 1970s, however, much of this structure crumbled. Writing in 1982, congressional scholar Norman Ornstein observed that

> Congress has become an open system. External incentives and rewards now compare with the internal for members' time, attention and behavior. The internal rewards . . . have been democratized . . . [and] come automatically. . . . Moreover, what would have been defined as aberrant or maverick behavior in the past . . . is no longer grounds for chastisement.[5]

In this context, ambitious self-promoters could seek publicity, pursue their own agendas, and ignore many internal constraints. For example, consider one staff aide's assessment of the House Democrats' industrial policy task force headed by Richard Gephardt and Tim Wirth, and "assembled by a Caucus Chairman with a keen eye for up-and-coming young Democrats":

> I think of it as a ride for them, in terms of their political careers. . . . it gave [the Committee members] an excuse to have the exposure and to sit down with the editorial board of the *New York Times* and they were saying, in effect, "Hey look me over. Maybe I'm the one to lead the party out of this." . . . Industrial policy sort of gave them the hook to get in on all these things. But the real agenda was, "Hey, look me over, maybe I'm the one."[6]

Political careers are necessarily tied to issues, and this is probably more significant in the 1980s than at any previous time in the twentieth century. Demonstrating policy competence is a first step toward a politician's influence or advancement. At the same time, publicity has surely become equally important. The missing piece of the puzzle, beyond expertise and visibility, is accomplishment. A political system that works well will find ways to reward skilled, ambitious politicians. The old, seniority-based politics of Congress broke down by the 1970s precisely because such rewards—public acclaim, internal recognition, or a personal sense of achievement—were not forthcoming for most legislators.

THE CHANGING STRUCTURE OF OPPORTUNITIES

Contemporary politicians are probably no more or no less ambitious than their predecessors, but the context for their ambitions has changed, especially within the Congress. From 1910 through 1970, approximately, the committee-based seniority system grew increasingly rigid, and well-qualified Southerners continued to be excluded from serious consideration for the presidency (as with Georgia's Democratic Senator Richard Russell). These political facts of life served to create a well-defined "structure of opportunities" for national politicians.[7] By the 1950s, this structure had become thoroughly institutionalized; a few basic but unwritten rules governed promotion among members of Congress, including:

- For almost all House members, internal advancement depended upon length of continuous tenure on a single committee (the seniority system).
- Top party leaders in the House rose on a leadership ladder (whip, majority leader, Speaker) that typically took more than twenty-five years to ascend.
- Representatives were not, in practical terms, eligible to run for president.
- Representatives who sought to fulfill their ambitions in the Senate should run for that seat within their first three-to-five terms in the House.[8]
- Senators constituted the most obvious pool of presidential contenders, although the vice presidency was often the reward of those who sought the highest office.[9]
- The seniority system also operated for senators, but was less important in that body.
- Aspiring to and winning Senate party leadership positions required neither long tenure nor a climb up a specified career ladder.
- Although Senate party leadership positions could act as stepping-stones to presidential bids, similar House positions were career pinnacles.

Through the 1970s and into the 1980s, some of these rules continue to hold true (for example Jim Wright had served thirty-two years in the House before becoming Speaker in 1987), but others have been greatly modified, often by changes in congressional life. Briefly put, the structure of opportunities is much more open and considerably less predictable than it was a generation ago, when Senators Kennedy, Johnson, and Goldwater sought to occupy the White House and congressional committee chairs could afford to be unresponsive to peers and presidents alike.

The breakdown of a rigid structure of opportunities has contributed directly to the development of the entrepreneurial style, which flourishes within a context that does not unduly restrict the actions of most legislators. The fluidity of activity in the Congress, and especially the House, suggests pools of opportunities rather than any clear structure. Some pools are exclusive—subcommittees, committees, top leadership groupings, a few informal caucuses—but many are open to all, as with various caucuses and the floor itself. Most important to the emerging organization of the House are the pools available to party members, such as the whip organization, task forces, and some caucuses. In every era, in Richard Fenno's words, "we get the Congress that the members give us,"[10] but the contemporary House is exceptional in that the junior members have played major roles in forging the opportunities they and their peers have subsequently taken advantage of.

UNDIFFERENTIATED AMBITION

In a House with a clear, seniority-based structure of opportunities and few chances for visibility outside the chamber, legislators were faced with the stark career choice between the more glamorous Senate and the distant, but automatic, goal of a House committee chairmanship. Running for the Senate remains an important possibility, but House members have many more options in shaping their careers. Congressmen Les Aspin, Tony Coelho, and Richard Gephardt, and Senator Tim Wirth, four archetype "new breed" Democrats, demonstrate the range of career paths offered by ambition flowing in less structured ways.

These four new pols entered the House during the 1970s, although only Wirth is a class of '74 member. As of 1988, all are in their forties, but none are baby boomers, having been born before or during the early days of World War II. All are unapologetically ambitious and willing to seek publicity, but none, not even presidential aspirant Gephardt, has become a truly familiar national figure. Beyond these similarities, the common threads running through their careers are the dispatch and innovative ways these still-young politicians have found to accumulate power, affect policy, and advance to important formal positions. They have expressed their ambitions imaginatively and across a wide range of actions, before moving toward more structured career paths. Such undifferentiated ambition exudes from many younger members as they move from one pool of opportunity to another; there may be a long-term goal, but no path emerges as the single best avenue for its pursuit.

In many ways, Senator Tim Wirth has experienced the most conventional career progress among these politicians. After serving twelve years in the House and chairing a subcommittee for three terms, Wirth ran for the Senate in 1986 when Gary Hart gave up his seat to seek the presidency. Beneath this normal progression lies the story of an impatient activist, who sought to maximize his influence from the days immediately after his 1974 election, when he put together the class organization (see chapter 2). Wirth served on, but did not chair, several party task forces in the late 1970s. As the organizing member of the Budget Committee's gang of four in 1980, Wirth focused attention on a need to reorient Democratic economic priorities toward more investment. He followed this train of thought in cochairing the Caucus's 1982 task force on long-range economic planning and writing the yellow book that laid out its conclusions.

Most important, in 1981 Wirth took over the Telecommunications subcommittee of Energy and Commerce, which placed him firmly in the midst of volatile, complex policy making on the cable television industry and the break up of AT&T.

For a policy entrepreneur like Wirth, this chairmanship was a perfect middle management position, offering visibility and the real potential for impact. At the same time, Wirth was widely, and correctly, regarded as intensely ambitious. Still, as one veteran party staffer observed "if you're not running for anything—if you are just generally ambitious, I don't think that hurts." When the Senate opportunity arose in 1986, Wirth was well prepared—both as a veteran policy entrepreneur and as a marginal-seat congressman who had grown accustomed to raising more than $500,000 every two years for his campaign enterprise.

At a glance, Les Aspin's career looks like a throwback to an earlier congressional age. As the previous discussion of Aspin's talents at obtaining publicity demonstrates (see chapter 4), nothing could be further from the truth. Undeniably, Aspin has made his reputation by sitting on one committee, Armed Services, since entering the House in 1971. Nevertheless, the *Almanac of American Politics* notes that "by 1983 Aspin had become the de facto leader of the House on military issues."[11] That same year he rose to chair a subcommittee and immediately demonstrated his skills as an inside player by slipping major cost-saving provisions into legislation on military pensions. Finally, in 1985 Aspin successfully challenged the aging Congressman Mel Price (D-Ill.) as chair of the Armed Services Committee, leap-frogging six more senior members and overcoming the opposition of Democratic leaders, including Speaker O'Neill.

Aspin's subsequent rejection and ultimate retention as committee chair in 1987 caucus votes does illustrate the tensions between old and new breeds on Capitol Hill, but the reality of the episode is considerably more complex. Regular allies became serious opponents. Among members of the class of '74, George Miller, an Aspin opponent, worked against his friend Tom Downey, a supporter. Issues, ideologies, personal loyalties, and the backing of various top leaders all came into play. Ironically, in defeating an even less senior colleague, the outsider Aspin benefited in part from his seniority, although Aspin's personal contrition, ideological acceptability, and policy skills were more important factors in saving his position. Whatever else, Aspin's halting progress has demonstrated how the democratized House has opened up the process of achieving leadership positions, all the while making advancement difficult to predict.

Among these four members of Congress, Richard Gephardt has stretched the possibilities of the new opportunity structure the farthest. Indeed, only a very few others, such as Senator Phil Gramm, have been his equal in rewriting the rules. At the same time, Gephardt demonstrates the age-old value of having a powerful mentor (or two). Early on, Tip O'Neill certainly favored Gephardt, who, in 1977–80, chaired six of the Speaker's twenty task forces and subsequently became the deputy whip in charge of task forces. Even more important was the role of Congressman Richard Bolling, who helped his fellow Missourian obtain a plum committee assignment (Ways and Means) as a freshman. From his position as a senior Rules Committee member, Bolling further assisted Gephardt by bringing him into the party leadership. A senior leader commented:

> Dick Gephardt has a sponsor in Dick Bolling. He's been of considerable help. I think he looks at him sort of like a son, or an adopted son. Like the older athlete who now has his son to compete for the medals. [Q. That he never won?] Yeah.

Beyond a power committee position and party leadership roles, Gephardt also won a seat on the Budget Committee and acted, with the gang of four, to reorient budget priorities and to produce the Democrats' yellow book initiative on industrial policy. Their participation on this latter project emphasizes differences in how ambitious politicians use policies. A party staff member observed:

> Gephardt . . . had this perception that you couldn't beat something with nothing and the Democrats didn't have anything. . . . I think Wirth had a more substantive interest. I mean, Wirth had given [industrial policy] a lot more thought. . . . Gephardt's call is always on politics. Wirth's call is on both. Is it good politics and good economics?[12]

Gephardt won the Democratic Caucus chairmanship in 1984, and he began to receive a lot of attention as the cosponsor of the Gephardt-Bradley tax reform proposal. Gephardt abandoned active support for this legislation, just as he had earlier abandoned industrial policy, moving his emphasis to trade, while Bradley slogged it out, winning great credit for his ultimate success on tax reform.[13]

Equally important to what Gephardt did in this period is what he didn't do. He did not run for the Senate from Missouri, even though he had an open seat opportunity in the strongly Democratic year of 1986. At some point Gephardt had decided to pursue the presidency from the House. Unlike conservative Congressman Jack Kemp, whose presidential efforts relied most heavily on his support outside the Congress, Gephardt initially based much of his campaign on the policy entrepreneur style that he developed within the House. Gephardt's one-on-one skills, his ability to tie policies to politics, and his uncanny capacity to find the center of most issue controversies are talents that have served him well in the House. Indeed, Gephardt built much of his campaign upon the support of dozens of his House colleagues, who have seen him work effectively since he set foot on Capitol Hill. Much of this support has been much deeper than that dictated by simple institutional loyalty, especially to the extent that members have used their own enterprises to raise funds for Gephardt.

To transfer the congressional policy entrepreneur style to presidential politics is extremely difficult. Other entrepreneurs, like Jack Kemp or Gary Hart, while issue oriented, have been congressional outsiders playing more to the media than to their peers. Gephardt faced the difficult task of balancing the need for public attention with the long-term ties he has created in the Congress. David Broder notes with extreme skepticism Gephardt's denial that his increasingly tough stand on trade has had any political motivations, observing that "the credibility Gephardt has earned with his colleagues over ten years of hard work is a great asset—one which he would be foolish to jeopardize."[14]

In the end, Gephardt, the consummate political insider, failed to transform himself into a credible populist outsider. Both the press and the opposing candidates hit upon Gephardt's dramatic changes on issues and in his overall style. Gephardt did hew to the policy entrepreneur approach in hitching his fate to trade policy, but such an issue played well only in a few locales, including Iowa, where Gephardt won after abandoning his insider, "retail" campaign style.

Gephardt did become a much stronger media presence over the course of the 1988 primaries. His transformation, however, was not enough to overcome the contradiction between his established style and the image he wished to convey. As National Public Radio's Linda Wertheimer noted, "It was the difference between what Gephardt is and what he claimed to be. That was clearly a problem."[15]

One mark of the fluidity of contemporary political opportunities is that had Dick Gephardt not decided to run for president, his logical target for advancement would have been the Democratic whip position in the House. As chair of the Democratic Caucus, he would have made a very strong candidate for an office that would have put him on the "escalator" toward eventual service as Speaker.[16] In any event, Gephardt chose a different path, and Californian Tony Coelho ran away with the caucus election for the whip slot, despite having served in the House for less than eight years.

It speaks volumes that a House full of policy entrepreneurs would select a colleague with virtually no substantive policy record as a major party leader. Rather, as the chair of the Democratic Congressional Campaign Committee between 1981 and 1986, Coelho brought the House Democrats into the modern age of fund-raising and campaigning. Not only did he help the party retain control of the chamber and its myriad positions, Coelho also provided the know-how and financial wherewithal for members to build their enterprises. In return, by directing campaign contributions to most incumbents and honoraria to various members for a speech here or an appearance there, Coelho built his base for moving into the top echelons of the party leadership.

Coelho's driven style, with an obsessive attention to the detailed mechanics of politics, distinguishes him from most of his colleagues, who have emphasized ideas and agenda setting. His separation from policy during his first eight years in Congress is the exception that proves the rule. Congressman George Miller, a fellow Californian, explains,

> You've got to remember that with Tony we gave him a charge—that he was to carry out, and which he did. He'd come into a hearing and make a statement and he'd be gone. He didn't have the opportunity to do policy. In fact, when he was here, we'd say, "Why aren't you in Omaha?" Or Albuquerque. Or wherever. He wasn't supposed to be here.

Like his peers, Coelho demonstrated the cardinal virtues of hard work and expertise. It was just that his skills came in fund-raising, campaigning, and recruiting candidates, not setting the policy agenda or building legislative coalitions.

In many ways, Coelho is simultaneously the most and least traditional of these new pols. He has the time-honored understanding of how to transfer funds from contributors' pockets into the right campaign coffers; no one compares more favorably to Coelho than Lyndon Johnson, when, as chair of the House campaign committee in 1940, he routed independent oilmen's money to a host of Democratic candidates, across the nation.[17] At the same time, Coelho has few peers, especially among elected officials, in understanding the technology, tactics, and organization of contemporary electoral politics. Even more than Senator George Mitchell (D-Maine), former chair of the Senate campaign committee, Coelho has demonstrated his entrepreneurial capacities outside the realm of policy making.

A few general implications can be drawn from these political careers in progress. First, the structure of opportunities is extremely loose for those beginning their careers as national politicians. This does not mean later on, as seniority and movement up the leadership "escalator" come into play, that structure will not become extremely important. For example, aside from Les Aspin, all the committee chairs in the 100th Congress—House and Senate—are their panels' most senior eligible members. Nevertheless, ambition can push activist politicians in many directions.

Second, the role of party has grown, as committee chairmanships have been somewhat devalued. Whether within the party leadership, task forces, the campaign committee, or the party caucus, key decisions are made and opportunities offered within a partisan context. This has especially serious implications for Republicans in the House, who can realistically see little chance of becoming a majority party. It is no wonder that a talented and effective legislator such as Republican Whip Trent Lott (R-Miss.) would seriously consider a Senate race, despite his status as heir apparent to minority leader Congressman Bob Michel (R-Ill.). Lott could expect to wield more immediate influence as an individual senator and harbor some real hopes of eventually serving as a member of a majority.

Third, career patterns continue to solidify in a politician's forties. Regardless of political era, individuals' patterns become more constrained over time, as choices are made, opportunities bypassed.[18] Although one could certainly see a Wirth candidacy for president or an Aspin tenure as secretary of defense, the futures for these two legislators and Coelho are reasonably predictable. Even Gephardt's presidential bid had limited risks, in that he will retain his House seat. Congressman Morris Udall was not hurt by his 1976 flirtation with the Democratic nomination, and Gephardt's energies and skills would serve him well in the House, where he might easily rise to chair the Ways and Means Committee. Conversely, he may make the decision that typifies how many House activists approach the Senate—up or out (of the Congress).

POLICY ENTREPRENEURS AND THE SENATE: A NATURAL MATCH

Ambitious House members have always sought Senate seats. Even in the heyday of the seniority system in the House and the "inner club" of the Senate, during the early 1950s, it was more pleasant to be treated like dirt as a senator than as a representative. Six-year terms and a smaller number of players have long proven attractive to House members. In the 1970s and 1980s, however, the Senate attraction proved even stronger. Senator Tom Harkin notes, "In the House you have a few chiefs and a lot of Indians. In the Senate, they're all chiefs."[19] Harkin's senatorial colleague, Charles Grassley, states, "I wanted my fingers in as many pies as I could get them in because I think I can be a more effective legislator."[20] Within the class of '74, only three individuals have sought governorships, while twenty-four have made serious runs for Senate seats. And two of those seeking a statehouse, Jim Florio in New Jersey and Carroll Hubbard in Kentucky, did so in odd-numbered years, which allowed them to retain their House seats.

The large number of Senate candidacies has derived to a great extent from the nature of the congressional job as it has developed since the 1970s. "The Senate is an ideal job," notes former senator Paul Tsongas, ". . . if you like issues and [are] not into the responsibility of being president or vice-president. This is the best political job in the country, I think."[21] To the extent that this is the case, the deference accorded individual legislators makes it so. Senator William Armstrong observes,

"It's possible for even a brand new member to jump right in. If you have the expertise and the grit to get out in front on it, you can get the Senate to pay attention to an issue you want attention paid to."[22]

Expertise and the "grit" of hard work are the same characteristics that House policy entrepreneurs value most. Indeed, senators with previous House experience generally agree that the two bodies are becoming increasingly alike.[23] Thus, growing numbers of legislators may be spending their House careers in active apprenticeships for their subsequent Senate service, when they will enjoy much larger enterprises and have the capacity to affect many more issues, both in committee and on the floor. As a result, former Congressman Floyd Fithian, who serves as administrative assistant to Senator Paul Simon, points out, "one major difference [between the two houses] is the extraordinary pressure of time. I thought that I was busy as a person could be in the House. But Paul [Simon] is five times as busy as he or I was in the House."

Individualism also dictates that Senate majority party status makes much less difference in pressing one's policy agenda than in the House. As one Senate administrative assistant noted:

> The Senate is a body that emphasizes personality—it exaggerates personality. It's the sheer numbers on a subcommittee. If you can convince two members to vote with you, even if you're a minority member. . . . The emphasis is on personal relations.

Even good personal relations are unnecessary for some thick-skinned entrepreneurs. As Senators Phil Gramm and Howard Metzenbaum have demonstrated, an absence of cordial relations has not hindered them in making the Senate's respect for the individual legislator work to their advantage.

Most House members do, of course, remain in their own chamber. The class of '74 illustrates two trends in not running for the Senate. First, many House members harbor no senatorial ambitions; in a 1980 survey of class members, only one-half expressed the desire to run for higher office. A senior staff aide noted that Congressman Phil Sharp had rejected entreaties to run for the Senate:

> You've got to be somewhat excessive. Phil's just not like that at all. . . . I think there are House types and Senate types. If you're in the Senate, you have to be willing to turn everything over to staff; it helps to be able to make the short, outrageous statement that gets attention. You need to have a position on everything and sit on nine or ten subcommittees.

Sharp's more controlled, specialized style simply fits the House better than it would the Senate, although a 1974 colleague, Montana's Senator Max Baucus, has maintained a House-like style in the Senate, while a Steve Solarz or a George Miller acts a good deal like a senator. Even though the House and Senate styles have converged, some major differences in the basic jobs certainly remain.

Second, within the class of '74, the members who are building the strongest careers within the House come from the most populous states—namely New York and California. Part of this is happenstance, but since 1970, neither New York nor California has elected a House member to the Senate, even though there have been numerous candidacies and substantial senatorial turnover. Just as southern states often encouraged long congressional careers, it may now be the turn of large states. Among the Watergate babies, Californians Miller, Mineta, and Waxman, and New Yorkers Downey, McHugh, and Solarz have distinguished themselves as major forces in the House. Conversely, small-state representatives have been more successful in reaching the Senate (for example, within the class of '74, Iowans Grassley and Harkin, South Dakota's Pressler,

Montana's Baucus, Colorado's Wirth, and Connecticut's Dodd).

A NEW HOUSE CAREERISM: INDIVIDUAL AND INSTITUTIONAL ADAPTATION

During the 1970s, a decade marked in Congress by structural overhaul, greatly increased workloads, and rampant free-lancing, many legislators retired, choosing to take their recently enhanced pensions and avoid the maelstrom of the changing House.[24] Most of the retirees were senior members, but a scattering of talented junior representatives, such as Barbara Jordan (D-Tex.) and John Cavanaugh (D-Nebr.), joined them. The conventional wisdom ran that the House job had become too demanding, too costly, and too frustrating. In reality, a fragmented and fractious House made life there unpleasant, which led to retirements and even less continuity. As Aaron Wildavsky observed in 1975, "The decline of seniority in Congress may permit talent to be substituted for age; it also guarantees that Congress will provide less attractive careers."[25]

Drawing on late-1970s' interviews with retiring House members, political scientist John Hibbing concluded that in the future "careerism will not be prevalent, and, in fact, will probably be as rare as it was in the 1930s and 1940s . . . And the major reason given for retirements will be the hectic pace and associated demands of service in the U.S. House."[26] Of ninety-two House members first elected in 1974, only five have retired as of 1988. Some representatives have expressed their dissatisfaction with the House by running for the Senate. Others simply have grumbled, but voluntary retirement has not thinned their ranks in the post-1974 Congress. This has led to an institution with a very stable membership during the mid-1980s. Only forty-four new representatives took office in 1984, and just fifty in 1986.

Why no wave of retirements? Members of the class of '74

express great satisfaction with their current status in the House and their unfolding careers. Even though House rules forced him to rotate off the Budget Committee in 1985, and away from this center of House activity, Congressman Norman Mineta, an older, savvy legislator, voices a "freshman-like love for the House. . . . Its history, lore, rules, and traditions thrill me. I'm here to stay as long as my constituents want me." Mineta does not sound much like a skeptical reformist of 1974; rather, one hears the refrain of institutional patriotism, most notable for its absence in the late 1970s and early 1980s.

Mineta's California colleagues, Henry Waxman and George Miller, two major entrepreneurs, express their satisfaction in more policy-oriented terms. Waxman observed in 1987 that

> regardless of position, I'll still push the issues that I'm interested in, and if things go well, if I become subcommittee [sic], full committee chairman, speaker, whatever. Who knows what the future will bring. I'm happy here. [Q. Is it fun?] Sure it's fun. That's why I came here—to pass legislation, to make policies.

Miller strikes a similar note, as he emphasizes the challenge of making policy. "This place is a mosaic. Putting the pieces together is what's so interesting. . . . No matter what the frustrations—how late the hours, how screwed up the schedule, you enjoy it. It's a great job."

Part of the cost-benefit calculations in deciding whether to remain in the House is the expense of staying. Congressman Butler Derrick commented in a 1976 interview that one major surprise in his first term was "the cost." He continued, "My net worth has declined since I've been here. And you've caught me on a bad day. I was on the phone about three hours ago, authorizing the sale of some land I swore I'd never sell."

Although Derrick subsequently considered running for the Senate and contemplated retirement, the potential of a House job that included service on both the Rules and Budget committees was attractive enough for him to stay. In 1984 Derrick still felt the financial pinch, but viewed the issue much differently than he had eight years earlier. "It's hard to plead 'poor' when you're making $70,000 a year, but it has been hard—two kids in school, two houses, two cars. But I've never regretted what I've done. If it had taken everything I've got, I'd stay."

Much of the surviving class of '74 members' contentment derives from a real ability to influence policy and an increasing sense that they play an integral role in running the institution. This group may have had little institutional loyalty to the House of the late 1970s, but they appear much more attached to this body in the 1980s. After all, the House of this era is the institution that they have helped to create. And an institution that begins to work better for policy-oriented individuals may well work better for everyone.

In fact, the actions and sentiments of many House members in the 1980s may present a mirror image of what Richard Fenno found in the 1970s: the ubiquitous strategy of members' "running *against* Congress," through which "the institution bleeds from 435 separate cuts." Fenno suggests with understatement, "In the long run, therefore, somebody may lose."[27] Conversely, starting with modest levels of satisfaction and pride in individual achievements, members may desire to build a stronger institution. To stand Fenno on his head: somebody may win. In fact, the institution as a whole may come out the winner as these new careerists continue to construct the institution in which they want to make policy. As Butler Derrick notes, "I don't want to say that 'the enemy is us,' but the Democratic party [in the House] is us," and it is that group that has determined the nature of the House since 1955 and will continue to do so for the foreseeable future.

The questions that remain revolve around whether participation can affect policy enough to keep members satisfied and whether the legislators can keep up the levels of activity required to make this consultative system of leadership work.

This, in itself, may induce higher turnover, and more Senate candidacies. Congressman Matt McHugh notes: "Some people run for the Senate because they would enjoy it, but not the House anymore. . . . Since you like Congress and the work, you opt for the Senate . . . If you lose, then you've made your commitment."

THE PERSONAL COSTS OF SERVICE

In a 1984 column, Ellen Goodman captured the difficulty faced by politicians who seek to maintain normal family ties:

> I met Paul Tsongas once on a late-afternoon flight from Washington to Boston. The senator from Massachusetts was traveling light that day. No bags, no briefcase, no aides. All he had with him was a daughter.[28]

No matter how satisfied members may be with their legislative life, the costs of staying in the game remain high. Congressman Dick Gephardt, when a mere House activist, not a presidential candidate, almost never ate at home with his family.[29] Nor do most House members. Stories of marital discord and neglected children are so commonplace that they would become trite were it not for their poignancy. Even parents can get short shrift. Democratic Congressman Jim Slattery, a rural Kansas native, recalls a brief airport phone call made to his father, who was soon to die. "I should have been home talking to my dad instead of rushing back to Washington. There are joys to this job and rewards, but I won't forget the price."[30]

Although this is not the place for any complete accounting, the potential costs of ambition and accomplishment are worth examining. Both families and politicians bear the scars; the congressional job continues to take its toll.

Given his continuing battle with cancer, Paul Tsongas may be the most introspective member of the class of '74. He has expressed his sentiments eloquently on the significance of family relationships for public officials, although others, like Congressmen Phil Sharp and Matt McHugh, evince great sensitivity in these matters. With only a hint of irony, Tsongas commented that the Congress "is the place to be if you don't love your wife, your kids are grown, and you don't like the state you come from."[31]

Like Tsongas, Sharp and McHugh have taken the offensive, as much as possible, in protecting their family lives. Even so, they cannot control the legislative schedule, which frustrates members and families alike. Near the end of an hour-long interview, Congressman Sharp, a low-key politician, exploded (for him, at least) and blamed the leadership for too many wasted evenings. "It's my biggest gripe," he said. "The Speaker could do a lot better job. It would be a lot fairer to us and to our families."[32] Nevertheless, Phil Sharp has tried to minimize the impact of his position and the ever-present demands of his historically marginal seat. Former Congressman Floyd Fithian, also from Indiana, acknowledged that Sharp had "protected his family relationship" far more than he had over the years. Fithian, who lost a 1982 Senate race, ultimately shied away from a second Senate attempt, partially because the election "was harder on [my wife] than on me."

Reflecting on the costs of his House career, Congressman McHugh concluded that "the greatest price is the time you don't spend with your family. I don't get home to have dinner with my children. I get home at eight or so; sometimes my wife waits for me, sometimes not." For McHugh, who lives in Washington, there's the additional time spent in his predominantly Republican, upstate New York district.

> I spend every other weekend in the district. It's tough to leave here on Friday afternoon, headed for a full weekend there. If you're paying that heavy a price, you question whether you're doing it for yourself and ego gratification.

McHugh, as an Appropriations Committee member and a key broker for liberal forces within the House, continues to seek reelection. He states firmly that this decision involves the entire family and requires a real reexamination every two years. McHugh spontaneously observes that his wife is "an essential partner in this enterprise." As Paul Simon advanced from the House to the Senate and subsequently became a presidential candidate, his strongest support came from his wife, Jeanne, described by one reporter as "more enthusiastic about [a presidential race] than he is."[33]

The other side of the coin for political marriages is discord and dissolution. After their initial election, many class of '74 members faced a particularly difficult situation, having had no real expectations of winning. Life in Congress and in Washington came as a complete shock to the entire family, especially when combined with their early activities and acclaim. Paul Tsongas and his wife, Nicki, entered this arena with a nine-month-old daughter. As a member of Congress, Tsongas soon had a Washington niche; Nicki Tsongas notes, "I felt very irritated sometimes that he was gone and that I had this baby and was in a city where I didn't know anybody, really."[34]

At the extreme, the personal costs of marital discord can have political repercussions, as Gary Hart discovered in his 1988 presidential campaign. Although the pressures on politicians' relationships may be no greater than those on investment bankers, chief executive officers, or high-powered lawyers, the public nature of politics exacerbates all tensions.

Given the travel resources now available to members of Congress, virtually all can choose a different, if equally unattractive, answer to family arrangements. Almost any legislator can become a part of the Tuesday-to-Thursday contingent, whose families remain at home. This situation places its own kind of strain on relationships (and the always airborne politicians), but it can solve many logistical problems. At the same time, the strain of a long round trip every weekend (often returning on the late night "red-eye") creates its own problems for members who stumble off the plane almost every Tuesday morning. Time remains the activist politician's most implacable foe, whether in the House or the more hectic Senate. Domestic life, in Washington or at home, must compete with the district's needs, Capitol Hill's demands, and ambition's distinctive drumbeat. In the end, there are few satisfactory answers, only temporary compromises, always subject to renegotiation or breakdown.

The New Political Style and the Glue of Ambition

A fragmented, democratized Congress full of policy entrepreneurs poses great organizational problems for its leaders. The House, especially, has responded by becoming increasingly partisan—in rhetoric, procedural arrangements, and voting. Congressman Richard Cheney, ordinarily a low-key, genial leader, emotionally argues that, given Speaker Jim Wright's heavy-handed willingness to "do anything he can to win at any price . . . there is no sense of comity left. Why should a Republican . . . think of a Democrat as a colleague? They aren't colleagues."[35]

Partisanship clearly disadvantages minority Republicans, but it also makes the Congress a less pleasant place for all legislators intent on building a career. Nevertheless, ambition as much as anything bonds the Congress together. The expansion of party leadership slots, subcommittee chairs, and caucus positions provides well over three hundred positions entrepreneurs can aspire to and operate from. In addition, the House increasingly offers lessons in free-lancing that may encourage more Senate candidacies from its ranks.

The very fragmentation of the Congress allows ambitious politicians to strive, almost continually, for one new position or another. Like building enterprises or seeking publicity, moving up, even incrementally, offers politicians the sense that they are accomplishing something, in the absence of more concrete evidence. Again, the entrepreneurial style often invites talented politicians to turn away from substantive accomplishment in pursuit of more accessible goals.

10

The Substance of a New Style

THE SHAPE of national politics has changed greatly over the past two decades. Nowhere have those changes been more pronounced than within the Congress, where a new generation of legislators operates under different sets of formal rules and informal expectations than did their predecessors. Most notably, the individual congressmen and senators have much greater latitude in approaching their institutions and careers. A long, passive apprenticeship is a thing of the past. The seniority system remains, but in a weakened state. The admonition that junior members should be seen and not heard is observed in the breech. The structure of opportunities allows a House member to mount a realistic campaign for the presidency. Although it is true that the class of '74 and its successors have taken advantage of the reforms put in place by previous generations of congressional activists, it is also a fact that the new-breed politicians have shaped the Congress to suit themselves. They have created an institution that encourages entrepreneurial activity and the building of large personal enterprises, both driven by an almost unrestricted flow of ambition.

The results are often not a pretty sight. The Congress gives us annual budget battles, $600 billion appropriations bills that defy comprehension, and procedural deadlock over important problems such as acid rain. At an individual level, we get government by press release, as scores of congressmen adopt a free-lancing style most appropriate to senators. Nevertheless, at no time in the twentieth century has the Congress encouraged more meaningful activity from all its members. Legislators hone their political skills not by observation but through participation. This has led to some important policy changes, most notably sweeping tax and immigration reforms. From a long-term perspective, the Congress is filled with politicians who have practical experience in crafting national legislation.

At the heart of the evolution of congressional politics stands the class of '74, whose members have combined luck and skill to serve as models for many of their junior colleagues. As they move toward the upper echelons of House leadership, toward the Senate, and, haltingly, toward the presidency, these new pols and their colleagues continue to redefine the nature of national politics.

The New Style Redux

In the end, the entrepreneurial style boils down to an emphasis on the individual as captain of his or her own political fate. Democratization has led to a leveling within the Congress, with less formal hierarchy. House members act a lot like senators. Resources are spread around. Opportunities to participate are nearly unrestricted, although participation does not guarantee success.

What drives participation? An attention to issues, the desire for publicity, ambition, and the ability to accumulate resources within an overall enterprise. Expertise provides the ticket to enter the game, especially in the House. One senior Democratic aide noted, "If you have the ability, if you're energetic, it's inevitable that you're going to have influence." In many ways Congress has become a meritocracy, where the most valued attributes are hard work and expertise. In the past, legislators demonstrated these qualities in the private arenas of committee meetings. Today, most perform both within the Congress and for the press.

When assessing the actions of policy entrepreneurs, whether or not publicity actually drives policy becomes a meaningless question. Legislators, reporters, lobbyists, and other players generally see media attention as an important force within the policy process. Many legislators could offer no concrete example of media coverage affecting policy results, although some, like Henry Waxman or Paul Simon, did (orphan drugs and foreign language aid, respectively). Even so, the broad outlines of how press attention shapes policy debates are reasonably clear. Congressman Norman Mineta makes the point that the best issue activists

> don't do things for publicity reasons. . . . Rather, they want to pass legislation, but they do think in publicity terms. . . . I'm not likely to pay much attention to someone's bill unless I've heard about it from someone else—either a constituent or another member. Publicity does that for you.

The closer members get to voting, the less difference mere publicity can make. But in setting the agenda, virtually everyone believes that it makes a difference.

The importance of issues and publicity ties directly into the third major entrepreneurial trait—ambition. This goes far beyond merely noting the spate of Senate candidacies from class of '74 House members and their colleagues. Rather, congressional leaders can take advantage of the ambition-fueled energies of their colleagues to create opportunities for them to take on responsibilities and demonstrate their capacities. Adding more leadership positions makes good sense, both for the core leaders and for their eager lieutenants. As Congressman Tom Foley noted during his tenure as Democratic whip:

> You've got to ask yourself, "Do you want to sit on the heating and ventilating subcommittee or do you want to become a whip?" There may be some members who don't want to move up. . . . But most of the people around here are not like that.

Ambition is expected, taken into account, and accepted as a motivating force—whether in obtaining publicity or seeking internal power. By the same token, losing a bid to advance is no disgrace, although one's reputation cannot absorb too many rebuffs. Many successful entrepreneurs have learned important lessons from defeat, either about the process or themselves.

For example, Matt McHugh, who desired to have an impact on a broad range of issues, noted his tactical error in making a 1980 race for the Democratic Caucus chair against the late Gillis Long (D-La.). In 1984 McHugh concluded unapologetically, "Gillis is a good man. He'd lined up a lot of support. In hindsight I probably shouldn't have done it." Subsequently, McHugh won the chairmanship of the Democratic Study Group, which provided him with a position for speaking out and building coalitions on a range of policies, most notably the budget.

McHugh found another avenue to influence within the House, but Paul Simon reacted to a similar rejection by channeling his ambitions toward higher office. After finishing a weak third in an attempt to win the Budget Committee chair, Gene Callahan, a friend and aide, notes that Simon "decided he wasn't going to be in the House very long. He knew he could never be part of the leadership. It was up or out for him."[1]

Finally, members of the class of '74 and their legislative

colleagues have demonstrated consistent skills in building their enterprises. Although electoral considerations are important here, many of their efforts derive directly from their almost instantaneous involvement in the congressional policy-making process. This occurred in dramatic, "Future Shock" fashion for the 1974 entrants, as many went from obscure, underfunded congressional challengers to king-makers within a two-month span. Most members of the class of '74 were ill prepared for such a transition, never having administered anything larger than their campaign for Congress. As one stunned newcomer put it, "You've never been told you have to operate a big business." Still, as their constituency service has demonstrated, they learned quickly (see chapters 6 and 8).

From the beginning, the new pols have grasped that entrepreneurs need both physical resources, such as staff, and political capital, based on a combination of skills, effort, and reputation.

Where's the Beef?

Responding to a question of whether the members of the class of '74 were really different, NPR's Cokie Roberts responded, "Sure they are. Look at their hair." At a time when Senator Paul Simon is given high marks by advertising types for not looking "blow-dried," Roberts's comment seems flip, which it is, of course. Nevertheless, the "blow-dried" notion gets us back to the essential questions of change. Do we, in Richard Bolling's words, have something genuinely different—"a new breed of cat," or do we have a post-Watergate politician who differs from previous generations only because of a twenty-dollar haircut and the ability to speak in fifteen-second sound bites? The answer lies somewhere between these extremes. Substance is always tied to context and style, whether in the contemporary era of Congressman Dick Gephardt and Senator Chris Dodd or that of powerful Democratic oligarchs like Arkansas's Congressman Wilbur Mills and Georgia's Senator Richard Russell, circa 1960.

Those who entered the Congress in the 1974–82 period have brought with them a new style—one that goes far beyond knowing where to plug in a hair dryer. The entire entrepreneurial approach, while not invented by these new members, has become dominant. Still, does a new generation or a new style lead inexorably to a new breed of politicians who are categorically different from their predecessors? Hardly. Rather, these politicians mix their styles with the continuing requirements of the Congress, those of other institutions, and the demands of the public. The "new Congress" is new, but in degree.[2] The classic organizing tensions of committees, party, and constituencies remain. Likewise, the essential responsibilities of legislators have stayed roughly the same. And policy making has never come easily. In the 1950s, ideas bubbled up through a very different congressional committee system, encountered difficult obstacles, and finally came to fruition in the legislation of the mid-1960s.[3]

The entrepreneurial style does have some severe limitations, both for individual politicians and their institutions. The most important problem is the lure of focusing exclusively on proximate goals. Compared to achieving full-blown policy successes, legislators can much more easily attend to the chores of gaining publicity, setting the congressional agenda, participating in the process, and building their enterprises. The most successful entrepreneurs do these things, of course, but their actions are taken in pursuit of some ultimate policy objectives.

To the extent that obtaining publicity or building a strong campaign base becomes an end in itself, entrepreneurial efforts are empty of substance. The temptation is great to regard a few seconds of time on the national news or a successful fund-raiser as a substantive accomplishment, especially when real policy victories are few and far between.

Seeking higher office is an especially powerful proximate goal, as the entrepreneurial style builds upon behaviors such as fund-raising and publicity seeking, which directly serve ambition. Aspiring to the Senate is one way to focus frustrations with the House, albeit that there is little greater satisfaction among senators with the pace and possibilities of their chamber. The 1988 retirements of Lawton Chiles (D-Fla.), William Proxmire, Paul Trible (R-Va.), and Dan Evans (R-Wash.) may indicate that the costs of service have outstripped the benefits offered by the Senate for many of its members.

In addition to the temptation to pursue proximate goals, the entrepreneurial style has some other, built-in limitations. Most of these revolve around the mix of skills demanded. Agenda setting requires the ability to draw attention to problems and proposals, while building coalitions calls for the one-on-one insider abilities of retail politics. Even though the ability to deal with issues lies at the heart of both pushing items onto the agenda and creating majorities to pass legislation, these activities emphasize talents that are not necessarily complementary. To pick up the basketball analogy (see chapter 5), many entrepreneurs are one-dimensional players. The problems of reconciling the public and private sides of this style come into sharp focus when new pols have sought the presidency. The consummate retail politician, Congressman Richard Gephardt, made little headway in the Iowa caucuses, where his one-on-one approach should have been most effective, until he discarded this style. On the other hand, Gary Hart's broad, agenda-setting approach was somewhat more successful, at least in 1984, but as a senator Hart eschewed the mundane, time-consuming task of building sturdy coalitions, and he proved little different as a presidential candidate.

To the extent that most members of this political generation take their roles as policy entrepreneurs seriously within the Congress, they may make the job of running for president increasingly difficult. Having slogged through years of budget negotiations and endless series of party task forces on specific policy initiatives, many legislators have a breadth of understanding that qualifies them for higher office. At the same time, their congressional experience leads them to think in terms of grays, not blacks and whites, in terms of intricate legislative packages, not sweeping changes. For all the talk of telegenic politicians, the entrepreneurial style emphasizes competence on the issues before all else. Albert Gore and Richard Gephardt, regardless of their immaculate coiffures, possess styles that have been shaped by years of hard work in the policy trenches. That such experience and style need to be overcome for these leaders to emerge as successful presidential candidates is ironic at best.

One further, but profound, limitation on congressional policy entrepreneurs, at least among Democrats, has been the Reagan presidency. Divided government almost always poses obstacles for policy changes to emerge from the Congress, but the 1981–88 period has been an especially difficult time, given a conservative executive and a series of high budget deficits. In such a context, the legislative successes in tax reform and immigration policy were especially important, giving hope, as they did, to many entrepreneurs that fundamental changes could still occur.

New Politicians in Mid-Career: Exit, Voice, and Loyalty

Veteran congressional observer Alan Ehrenhalt concludes:

> A congressional career these days is not everyone's cup of tea. But people don't stumble into it any more. The ones who make it to Washington are nearly all there because politics interests them more than anything else they can do with their waking hours, including the accumulation of money.[4]

Many members of the class of '74 did "stumble" into the Congress, but after a decade, there were no amateurs left within their ranks. Since the 1970s, in part due to increased publicity, the nature of the congressional job is no secret. The hours are long, the salary less than what the private sector would afford, and the frustrations continual. Despite myriad complaints, few legislators retire, and most stay to play the endless game. In making their plans, they must choose among the options afforded all members of all organizations—exit, voice, and loyalty.[5]

EXIT: THE ROAD LEAST TAKEN

Although it remains uncertain exactly how contemporary congressional careers will play out, what has become clear is that few legislators—especially House members—voluntarily retire from politics at an early age. When a young, attractive House member, such as a John Cavanaugh or a William Brodhead, calls it quits, there is immediate hand wringing about the job driving good people away. In truth, most "de-recruitment" comes when a prospective candidate decides to run (or not) for the Congress.[6]

Among the new breed, most voluntary exits from the House have come in attempts to move to the Senate. As with Paul Simon, the decision is phrased in "up or out" terms, although Simon at fifty-six was relatively old for such a decision. Still, the rewards can be great. In Simon's case, aside from the possibility of influencing policy, a Senate seat allowed him to make a run at the presidency.

In general, the exit of ambition reflects a combination of frustration and adventure. Toby Moffett concluded:

> When I took that very sober look at where I was going in the House, I concluded that I wasn't going to be chairman of the Commerce Committee until I was 80. . . . I thought there was a better opportunity to talk about the issues that I care about and bring them onto the national stage in the Senate.[7]

In retrospect, the House looked a good deal better to Moffett, but as a sitting legislator, the "up" was worth the risk of the "out."

Ironically, running for the presidency is a less risky proposition than running for the Senate. Most senators do not have to surrender their seats to run, and House members have frequently kept their names on the legislative ballot as they made their long-shot bids. Of the three most serious recent House-based presidential candidates—Morris Udall, Richard Gephardt, and Jack Kemp—only Kemp decided not to seek reelection as a congressman.

The pace and frustration of legislative life has produced a spate of retirements, but in the Senate, not the House. Almost 20 percent of the senators up for reelection in 1988 have announced their retirement, including Budget Committee Chair Lawton Chiles at the relatively youthful age of fifty-seven. Aside from mounting a presidential candidacy, there is no "up or out" possibility in the Senate. House members may convince themselves of the benefits of the six-year term and the potential for influence, but senators know what they face. As Chiles noted, "I wasn't looking forward to another six years in the Senate. . . . it was time to serve out the 18 years and let someone with the enthusiasm and zeal take over."[8]

VOICE: PLAYING THE GAME

Discussing his boss, class of '74 member Phil Sharp, a long-time aide noted that by the mid-1980s,

> he's become an old-timer [at age forty-two!], especially on Energy and Commerce, where there's been so much turnover. And he's sought a position in the whip organization. He's a player, but not necessarily a leader. . . . he wants to be in the room when the decisions are made.

Underlying almost all the House reforms of the 1970s was a single broad principle—to give most, if not all, legislators a real voice in the proceedings. Although some Republicans would disagree strenuously, there is no shortage of avenues for expression within the House. In the Senate, the problem is one of too many voices, talking for too long, about too many issues. In today's Congress, legislators can make their points.

Beyond mere articulation of issue positions, however, legislators who know the issues, work hard, and exhibit patience can be heard, if not always listened to. The legislative process has increasingly become a long series of conversations and negotiations, some taking place on the floor, some in dozens of different committee, caucus, and task force arenas, and some in the news media.

Having a voice does not mean having power. As one mid-seniority Democrat puts it, "For all practical purposes, power doesn't keep people here. They come, they realize they don't have it."[9] What they do have, however, is a voice, both figuratively and literally. As time passes and reputations are built and positions won, legislators' voices often change, becoming more authoritative. Listening to a George Miller, for example, one hears youthful enthusiasm and emerging power, blended together. This is always the case in the changing of the guard, but it is especially striking with the class of '74, a core of young veterans who will have their legislative say well into the twenty-first century.

For many legislators, meaningful participation—being in the room when key decisions are made—is enough. But for the Congress as a whole, a set of voices is not adequate. Rather, there must be bonds that tie the individual to the institution.

LOYALTY: "WARTS AND ALL"

Policy entrepreneurs. Free-lance artists. Independent operators. Idea merchants. Central to almost all characterizations of a new political style is a sense of independence. Congressmen and senators can depend on their own enterprises for reelection, for legislative initiatives, for publicity, for a sense of certainty in their uncertain lives. At the same time, the Congress as a whole is an object of scorn, both in the nation and increasingly on Capitol Hill.[10] With democratization and increased participation has come a Congress that has raised its members' expectations that they can make a difference, while simultaneously making it more difficult for them to do so.

What is lacking is a sense of loyalty or patriotism toward the Congress and its chambers. In the past such loyalty has rested upon tradition and a willingness to wait one's turn, for a decade or two or even three. Interviewed in 1980, the class of '74 expressed virtually no strong sense of institutional loyalty. This was a folkway that seemed to be moribund. By 1987, however, these middle management members seemed more sanguine about the House and the Congress as a whole. They and their colleagues had shaped the contemporary institution, and, if not totally pleased, they had generally made their peace with congressional process and structure.

By the late 1980s, it is true, the heavily Democratic class of '74 is well ensconced within the committee and party leadership structures. Freshmen, Republicans, and senators would have less positive assessments. In any event, loyalty to the Congress as an institution today can only be built upon continued high levels of participation for all involved. Activist entrepreneurs and full-blown enterprises have become the norm; fostering loyalty and a sense of institutional patriotism is thus a collective problem that neither individual members or their leaders can easily solve. As Senator David Pryor (D-Ark.) notes, "Individually, [the senators] all gripe about [life in the Senate]. But collectively, I'm not sure what they'll do. All of a sudden some of them become fearful that some right of ours will be diminished."[11] At the same time, no one asks for perfection. The Congress will remain a sloppy, inefficient place, even in the best of times, and loyalty cannot be totally contingent upon performance. Pryor continues, "There are easier ways to make a living. But when you love it, you love it and take warts and all."[12]

New Politicians: The Road from Here

It is January 3, 2005, and Speaker of the House Tony Coelho is swearing in the 108th Congress. Looking over the chamber, he observes various veteran committee chairs taking their oaths. The still-contentious David Obey heads Appropriations, Tom Downey chairs Ways and Means, Butler Derrick leads the Rules panel, George Miller remains in charge of the Interior Committee, Steve Solarz heads Foreign Affairs, and of course Henry Waxman wields the gavel for Energy and Commerce. In addition, Les Aspin retains his position at the helm of Armed

Services. Such a scene is not farfetched at all. None of this group would be over sixty-seven years old, relatively young for the legislative world.

This kind of extrapolation is a game subject to the vagaries of political life, yet it illustrates the potential importance of a series of decisions that began in the early 1970s and would continue over the course of a generation's span of public service. Not only will Watergate continue to have a major (if indirect) effect on policy making thirty years after the event, but the new politicians of the seventies will have made indelible impacts on both policies and political institutions. After all, persistence is a key trait for issue activists.

As policy entrepreneurs, these politicians have demonstrated that ideas do have consequences. Perhaps more important, they exhibit how politics can affect the ways in which ideas are played out. As policy entrepreneurs who are comfortable both on television and behind closed doors, the Downeys, Waxmans, Wirths, and Millers of the Watergate group will continue to participate, to play the game, and to exert influence well beyond any single congressional generation in the twentieth century. All this is separate from the substantial odds favoring the election of one president or more from the great pool of newcomers who entered national life during the 1974–82 period of great congressional turnover.

At the same time, these politicians can leave a legacy of failure, if their entrepreneurial styles do not generate more productive deliberations on crucial issues (for example, deficits) and overcome institutional failures (the individualistic Senate). In an emerging decision-making system that requires great energy and a fair amount of cooperation, an exhausted or selfish or dispirited set of top-level entrepreneurs would be unable to cope with the demands of policy making within the very set of complex relationships that they had molded during their early years in Congress.

NOTES

List of interviews with Members of Congress and Capitol Hill journalists (all in Washington, D.C., except as noted)

From the Class of '74:

Jerome Ambro (D-N.Y.), August 9, 1976; October 23, 1984.
Max Baucus (D-Mont.), August 5, 1976.
Berkley Bedell (D-Iowa), August 4, 1976; February 22, 1987.
Michael Blouin (D-Iowa), August 5, 1976.
William Brodhead (D-Mich.), July 30, 1976.
Norman D'Amours (D-N.H.), July 7, 1976.
Butler Derrick (D-S.C.), August 2, 1976; June 14, 1984.
Christopher Dodd (D-Conn.), August 6, 1976; March 10, 1984.
Tom Downey (D-N.Y.), September 16, 1984.
Robert Edgar (D-Pa.), March 10–11, 1984, Delaware County, Pa.
Joseph Fisher (D-Va.), February 3, 1987.
Floyd Fithian (D-Ind.), December 7, 1984; January 30, 1987.
James Florio (D-N.J.), December 6, 1984.
Mark Hannaford (D-Calif.), February 25, 1984.
William Hefner (D-N.C.), May 7, 1984.
William Hughes (D-N.J.), July 28, 1976.
Andy Jacobs (D-Ind.), July 24, 1976.
Martha Keys (D-Kans.), October 30, 1984.
Elliott Levitas (D-Ga.), August 3, 1976; May 16, 1984.
Matt McHugh (D-N.Y.), March 22–23, 1984.
Andrew Maguire (D-N.J.), July 28, 1976.
George Miller (D-Calif.), February 26, 1987.
Norman Mineta (D-Calif.), July 21, 1976; February 4, 1987.
Steven Neal (D-N.C.), March 30, 1984.
Jerry Patterson (D-Calif.), July 29, 1976.
Edward Pattison (D-N.Y.), August 8, 1976; January 7, 1985.
Richard Ottinger (D-N.Y.), July 25, 1976.

Fred Richmond (D-N.Y.), August 7, 1976.
Martin Russo (D-Ill.), February 26, 1987.
James Santini (D-Nev.), August 2, 1976.
Phil Sharp (D-Ind.), August 4, 1976; June 20, 1984.
Paul Simon (D-Ill.), August 3, 1976; June 27, 1984.
Henry Waxman (D-Calif.), February 24, 1987.
Tim Wirth (D-Colo.), July 28, 1976.

Members of Congress, Not from the Class of '74:

Richard Bolling (D-Mo.), March 12, 1982, Kansas City, Mo.
Thomas Foley (D-Wash.), March 5, 1982.

Capitol Hill Journalists:

Richard Cohen, *National Journal,* February 5, 1987.
Diane Granat, *Congressional Quarterly Weekly Report,* March 22, 1984.
Cokie Roberts, National Public Radio, February 3, 1987.
Martin Tolchin, *New York Times,* January 27, 1987.

Chapter 1. Politics and Politicians in a New Era

1. "Washington Talk," *New York Times,* August 8, 1986, p. A18.

2. Alan Ehrenhalt, ed., *Politics in America: The 100th Congress* (Washington, D.C.: CQ Press, 1987), pp. 1279, 231.

3. Christopher J. Matthews, "The Old Breed Strikes Back," *New Republic,* March 2, 1987, p. 21.

4. Diane Granat, "Whatever Happened to the Watergate Babies?" *Congressional Quarterly Weekly Report,* March 3, 1984, pp. 498–505.

5. See Richard E. Cohen, "A 'Watergate Baby' Turns to Peacemaking," *National Journal,* March 28, 1987, p. 774.

6. See Eric Uslaner and M. Margaret Conway, "The Responsible Congressional Electorate: Watergate, the Economy, and Vote Choice in 1974," *American Political Science Review* 79 (September 1985): 788–803.

7. Martin Tolchin, "Young Democrats on Rise in House," *New York Times,* November 4, 1981, p. A24.

8. Thomas P. O'Neill, *Man of the House* (New York: Random House, 1987), p. 284.

9. See Thomas Edsall, *The New Politics of Inequality* (New York: W. W. Norton, 1984); and Kevin P. Phillips, *Post-Conservative America: People, Politics, and Ideology in a Time of Crisis* (New York: Random House, 1982), chap. 5.

10. Quoted in Kirk Victor, "New Kids on the Block," *National Journal,* October 31, 1987, p. 2727.

11. See Burdett A. Loomis, "The Congressional Office as Small (?) Business," *Publius* 9 (Summer 1979): 55; see also Steven H. Schiff and Steven S. Smith,

"Generational Change and the Allocation of Staff in the U.S. Congress," *Legislative Studies Quarterly* 8 (August 1983): 465.

12. Granat, "Whatever Happened?" p. 503.

13. Ibid., p. 498.

14. David Broder, "Democratic Illusion on Old Guard Seems Ready to Shatter," *Lawrence* (Kans.) *Journal-World,* March 24, 1985, p. A4.

15. See Robert Salisbury and Kenneth Shepsle, "U.S. Congressman as Enterprise," *Legislative Studies Quarterly* 6 (November 1981): 559–76.

16. John Kingdon, *Agendas, Alternatives, and Public Policies* (Boston: Little, Brown, 1984), p. 192; see also Robert Eyestone, *From Social Issues to Public Policy* (New York: John Wiley & Sons, 1978), p. 89.

17. Paul Simon, *The Tongue-Tied American* (New York: Continuum, 1980), p. 178.

18. Kingdon, *Agendas, Alternatives,* p. 90.

19. Barbara Sinclair, "Senate Norms, Senate Styles, and Senate Influence," paper presented at the annual meeting of the American Political Science Association, Washington, D.C., August 28–31, 1986, p. 29.

20. Salisbury and Shepsle, "U.S. Congressman as Enterprise," 559.

21. Ibid., 560.

22. Peter Bragdon, "In 'Permanent Campaign' Era, Members' Funds Find Many Uses," *Congressional Quarterly Weekly Report,* September 12, 1987, p. 2187.

23. Common Cause, "Almost Half of U.S. Representatives Received 50% or More of Campaign Funds from PACs," news release, Washington, D.C., April 7, 1985, chart VII.

24. Howard Kurtz, "Congress Is a Convenient Place to Stockpile Campaign Aides," *Washington Post National Weekly Edition,* July 13, 1987, p. 12.

25. Jacob Epstein, *Ambition: The Secret Passion* (New York: E. P. Dutton, 1980), p. 1.

26. Ibid., p. 3.

27. See Joseph Schlesinger, *Ambition and Politics* (Chicago: Rand McNally, 1966).

28. David T. Canon and David J. Sousa, "Realigning Elections and Political Career Structures in the U.S. Congress," paper presented at the annual meeting of the American Political Science Association, Chicago, September 3–6, 1987.

29. Robert L. Peabody, Norman J. Ornstein, and David W. Rohde, "The United States Senate as a Presidential Incubator: Many Are Called but Few Are Chosen," *Political Science Quarterly* 91 (Summer 1976): 237–58.

30. See Heinz Eulau and Paul Karps, "The Puzzle of Representation: Specifying the Components of Responsiveness," *Legislative Studies Quarterly* 2 (August 1977): 233–54.

31. See generally James L. Sundquist, *The Decline and Resurgence of Congress* (Washington, D.C.: Brookings Institution, 1981).

32. Seymour Martin Lipset and William Schneider, *The Confidence Gap* (New York: Free Press, 1983), pp. 45–50.

33. See Leroy Rieselbach, *Congressional Reform* (Washington, D.C.: CQ Press, 1986).

34. See David Brady, "Congressional Party Realignment and Transformations of Public Policy in Three Realignment Eras," *American Journal of Political Science* 26 (May 1982): 333–60, among other works by Brady.

35. Eric Uslaner, "Policy Entrepreneurs and Amateur Democrats in the House of Representatives: Toward a More Party-Oriented Congress?" in *Congressional*

Reform, ed. Leroy Rieselbach (Lexington, Mass.: Lexington Books, 1978), pp. 105–16.

36. See Sundquist, *Decline and Resurgence,* p. 2, and Louis Fisher, *The Politics of Shared Power* (Washington, D.C.: CQ Press, 1987).

37. Sundquist, *Decline and Resurgence,* p. 6.

38. Richard F. Fenno, Jr., *Home Style* (Boston: Little, Brown, 1978), pp. 164–68.

39. Phillips, *Post-Conservative America,* p. 75.

40. See, among others, Jack L. Walker, "The Origins and Maintenance of Interest Groups in America," *American Political Science Review* 77 (June 1983): 390–406; Kay Lehman Schlozman and John T. Tierney, *Organized Interests and American Democracy* (New York: Harper & Row, 1986), chaps. 4, 7.

41. Quoted in Charles Clapp, *The Congressman: His Work As He Sees It* (Washington, D.C.: Brookings Institution, 1963), p. 221.

42. See Harrison W. Fox, Jr., and Susan Webb Hammond, *Congressional Staffs: The Invisible Force in American Lawmaking* (New York: Free Press, 1977), chap. 2.

43. Donald Matthews, *U.S. Senators and Their World* (New York: John Wiley & Sons, 1960), p. 82.

44. Charles S. Bullock III, "Congress in the Sunshine," in *Congressional Reform* (1978), ed. Rieselbach, pp. 209–22.

45. David Broder, *Changing of the Guard: Power and Leadership in America* (New York: Simon & Schuster, 1980).

46. Burdett A. Loomis, "The 'Me Decade' and the Changing Context of House Leadership," in *Understanding Congressional Leadership,* ed. Frank Mackaman (Washington, D.C.: CQ Press, 1982), p. 161; on comity, see Eric M. Uslaner, "The Decline of Comity in Congress," paper presented at the annual meeting of the Midwest Political Science Association, Chicago, April 9–11, 1987.

47. Richard F. Fenno, Jr., *Congressmen in Committees* (Boston: Little, Brown, 1973), pp. 1–14.

Chapter 2. The Class of 1974: The First Hundred Days and Beyond

1. Charles Tidmarch, "The Second Time Around: Freshman Democratic House Members' 1976 Reelection Experiences," paper presented at the annual meeting of the American Political Science Association, Washington, D.C., September 1–4, 1977, p. 2.

2. Ned Pattison, unpublished manuscript (n.p., 1979), chap. 2, pp. 3–4.

3. William P. Schaefer, "The Career Development and Maturation of the Watergate Class," paper presented at the annual meeting of the American Political Science Association, Washington, D.C., September 1–4, 1983, p. 9.

4. Pattison manuscript, chap. 2, p. 2a.

5. *1975 CQ Almanac* (Washington, D.C.: Congressional Quarterly Inc., 1975), pp. 26–33.

6. Pattison manuscript, chap. 14, p. 3.

7. Ibid., chap. 16, p. 3.

8. See, for example, Barbara Hinckley, "Seniority 1975: Old Theories Confront New Facts," *British Journal of Political Science* 6 (October 1976): 397–98.

9. *1975 CQ Almanac,* p. 32.

10. Editorial, *Wall Street Journal,* July 19, 1976, p. 21.

11. Toby Moffett, "System Absorbs 'Watergate Babies,'" *Central Connecticut Times,* June 1, 1983, p. 9.

12. Matt Pinkus and Bruce F. Freed, "Freshmen in the House: A Sobering Six Months," *Congressional Quarterly Weekly Report,* August 2, 1975, p. 1674.

13. Three of these appointees were, in Congressman Andy Jacobs's words, "retreads"—having previously served in the House and returned in 1974.

14. David E. Rosenbaum, ". . . Especially, the Startling New Man from Texas," *New York Times,* May 2, 1976, sec. 4, p. 2.

15. Nevertheless, Krueger later discovered that his aggressive entrepreneurial style had created some problems. In the 95th Congress, the House leadership bypassed Krueger in selecting members for coveted seats on the ad hoc Select Committee on Energy. Political scientist Bruce Oppenheimer, a veteran observer of energy politics, points out that the Democratic leaders concluded that Congressman Charles Wilson (another Texan) "would be more open to compromise and leadership influence." See Bruce I. Oppenheimer, "Congress and the New Obstructionism: Developing an Energy Program," in *Congress Reconsidered,* ed. Lawrence Dodd and Bruce Oppenheimer, 2nd ed. (Washington, D.C.: CQ Press, 1981), p. 295.

16. Rosenbaum, "Startling New Man," p. 2.

17. See Christopher J. Deering, "The New Apprenticeship: Strategies of Effectiveness for New Members of the House," paper presented at the annual meeting of the American Political Science Association, Washington, D.C., August 30–September 2, 1984; and Steven Smith, "Going to the Floor: Changing Patterns of Participation in the U.S. House of Representatives, 1955–1986," discussion paper, Brookings Institution, Washington, D.C., September 1987.

18. Observation of the traditional apprenticeship norm was already declining; see Herbert B. Asher, "The Learning of Legislative Norms," *American Political Science Review* 67 (June 1973): 499–513.

19. Deering, "New Apprenticeship," p. 16.

20. Burdett Loomis and Jeff Fishel, "New Members in a Changing Congress: Norms, Actions, and Satisfaction," *Congressional Studies* 8 (Spring 1981): 91.

21. Ibid.

22. See Barbara Sinclair, *Majority Leadership in the U.S. House* (Baltimore: Johns Hopkins University Press, 1983), p. 29.

23. Diane Granat, "Whatever Happened to the Watergate Babies?" *Congressional Quarterly Weekly Report,* March 3, 1984, p. 502.

24. Ibid.

25. Interest in this living arrangement has led to a proposed television series based on a similar, fictional situation.

26. See Ross Baker, *Friend and Foe in the U.S. Senate* (New York: Free Press, 1980).

27. Granat, "Whatever Happened?" p. 501.

28. Eric M. Uslaner, "The Decline of Comity in Congress," paper presented at the annual meeting of the Midwest Political Science Association, Chicago, April 9–11, 1987, pp. 17–19.

29. See Thomas P. O'Neill, *Man of the House* (New York: Random House, 1987), chap. 12; Sinclair, *Majority Leadership;* Burdett A. Loomis, "Congressional Careers and Party Leadership in the House of Representatives," *American Journal of Political Science* 28 (February 1984): 180–201; and Kent Entin, "Reform, Leaders, and Leadership Networks in the House of Representatives," paper presented at the annual meeting of the American Political Science Association, Washington, D.C., August 28–31, 1986.

30. Quoted in Jacqueline Calmes and Rob Gurwitt, "Profiles in Power: Leaders Without Portfolio," *Congressional Quarterly Weekly Report,* January 3, 1987, p. 14.

31. Quoted in Jonathan Fuerbringer, "Guerrilla Warfare and the Budget," *New York Times,* February 27, 1987, p. A24.

32. Common Cause, "Almost Half of U.S. Representatives Received 50% or More of Campaign Funds from PACs," news release, Washington, D.C., April 7, 1987, chart VII.

CHAPTER 3. Issues: The Currency of Political Life

1. See Christopher J. Deering, "The New Apprenticeship: Strategies of Effectiveness for New Members of the House," paper presented at the annual meeting of the American Political Science Association, Washington, D.C., August 30–September 2, 1984; more generally, see Thomas E. Mann and Norman J. Ornstein, eds., *The New Congress* (Washington, D.C.: American Enterprise Institute, 1981), and Steven S. Smith, "New Patterns of Decision-Making in Congress," in *The New Directions in American Politics,* ed. John E. Chubb and Paul E. Peterson (Washington, D.C.: Brookings Institution, 1985), pp. 203–34.

2. Nelson W. Polsby, "Goodbye to the 'Inner Club,'" *Washington Monthly,* August 1969, pp. 30–34; see also Michael Foley, *The New Senate* (New Haven: Yale University Press, 1980).

3. Lawrence C. Dodd, "A Theory of Congressional Cycles: Solving the Puzzle of Change," in *Congress and Policy Change,* ed. Gerald C. Wright, Jr., Leroy N. Rieselbach, and Lawrence C. Dodd (New York: Agathon Press, 1986), pp. 3–44.

4. See Barbara Hinckley, *The Seniority System in Congress* (Bloomington: Indiana University Press, 1971); and William S. White, *Citadel: The Story of the U.S. Senate* (New York: Harper & Row, 1956).

5. Richard F. Fenno, Jr., "The Freshman Congressman: His View of the House," in *Congressional Behavior,* ed. Nelson Polsby (New York: Random House, 1971), p. 130.

6. Quoted in Tom Watson, "State Delegations: Power's Payoffs and Pitfalls," *Congressional Quarterly Weekly Report,* January 3, 1987, p. 27.

7. See Richard Bolling, *House Out of Order* (New York: E. P. Dutton, 1965), and his *Power in the House* (New York: E. P. Dutton, 1968).

8. See Joseph Clark, *The Senate Establishment* (New York: Hill & Wang, 1963), and his *Congress: The Sapless Branch* (New York: Harper & Row, 1965).

9. A total of eleven, ranging from a biography of Lincoln to a discussion of Catholic-Protestant marriages. Simon's prolific writings have been frequently noted in discussions of his 1988 presidential candidacy.

10. Paul Tsongas, *The Road from Here* (New York: Alfred A. Knopf, 1982).

11. The most noteworthy is John F. Kennedy's *Profiles in Courage* (New York: Harper & Row, 1956).

12. See Steven E. Schier, "Thinking About the Macroeconomy: The House and Senate Budget Committees," paper presented at the annual meeting of the American Political Science Association, New Orleans, August 29–September 1, 1985.

13. David Stockman, *The Triumph of Politics* (New York: Avon, 1987), p. 61.

14. Quoted in Jacqueline Calmes and Rob Gurwitt, "Profiles in Power: Leaders Without Portfolio," *Congressional Quarterly Weekly Report,* January 3, 1987,

p. 11. The authors cite a *Wall Street Journal* story as the source of the quotation—a telling progression in itself.

15. Dale Russakoff, "Bill Bradley Takes His Shot," *Washington Post Magazine,* March 1, 1987, p. 13.

16. David Schribman, "Paul Simon of Illinois Makes a Mark in Senate by Turning Its Customs to His Own Advantage," *Wall Street Journal,* August 1, 1985, p. 40.

17. Calmes and Gurwitt, "Profiles in Power," p. 12.

18. Ibid., p. 14.

19. Nadine Cohadas, "Press Coverage: It's What You Do That Counts," *Congressional Quarterly Weekly Report,* January 3, 1987, p. 30.

20. John Manley, "Wilbur D. Mills: A Study of Congressional Influence," *American Political Science Review* 63 (June 1969): 442–64.

21. Alan Ehrenhalt, ed., *Politics in America, 1986* (Washington, D.C.: CQ Press, 1985), p. 240.

22. Barbara Sinclair, "Senate Norms, Senate Styles, and Senate Influence," paper presented at the annual meeting of the American Political Science Association, Washington, D.C., August 28–31, 1986, p. 16.

23. Ibid.

24. Transcript of interview conducted by Paul Duke for public television station WETA, Washington, D.C., 1984.

25. Mark Kirchmeier, "Good News Bad News," *California Magazine,* January 1987, pp. 49–53.

26. See Jeffrey H. Birnbaum and Alan S. Murray, *Showdown at Gucci Gulch* (New York: Random House, 1987), pp. 129–31.

27. Alan Ehrenhalt, ed., *Politics in America: The 100th Congress* (Washington, D.C.: CQ Press, 1987), pp. 420–21.

28. Ibid., p. 1116.

29. See Ross Baker, "The Bittersweet Courtship of Congressional Democrats and Industrial Policy," paper presented at the annual meeting of the Midwest Political Science Association, Chicago, April 10–12, 1986; W. Thomas Kephart and Roger H. Davidson, "Congress Explores Industrial Policy," paper presented at the annual meeting of the Midwest Political Science Association, Chicago, April 10–12, 1986.

30. Baker, "Bittersweet Courtship," p. 36.

31. John Kingdon, *Agendas, Alternatives, and Public Policies* (Boston: Little, Brown, 1984), p. 190.

32. Randall Rothenberg, *The Neoliberals: Creating the New American Politics* (New York: Simon & Schuster, 1984), p. 22.

33. Ibid., p. 23.

34. TRB, "The Hazards of Duke," *New Republic,* April 4, 1988, p. 41.

35. Rothenberg, *Neoliberals,* pp. 47–48 (emphasis added).

36. Jonathan Yardley, "The Politics and Power Plays of the 'Neoliberals,' " *Washington Post Book World,* July 1, 1984, p. 3.

37. Quoted in Dorothy Collins, "Simon Running on Traditional Values," *Chicago Tribune,* April 9, 1987, p. A4.

38. Ross Baker, "What's in It for Me?" paper presented at the annual meeting of the American Political Science Association, New Orleans, August 29–September 1, 1985, p. 24.

39. Richard Cohen, "Having It Both Ways," *National Journal,* October 31, 1987, p. 2721.

40. E. J. Dionne, "The Hart Legacy: He Broke Democrats' Link with Politics of New Deal," *New York Times,* May 12, 1987, p. A12.

41. Quoted in Edward Walsh, "Once More, With Hart," *Washington Post National Weekly Edition,* February 9, 1987, p. 13.

CHAPTER 4. Entrepreneurs and the Public Eye

1. See Jacqueline Calmes and Rob Gurwitt, "Profiles in Power: Leaders Without Portfolio," *Congressional Quarterly Weekly Report,* January 3, 1987, p. 17.

2. Gregg Easterbrook, "What's Wrong with Congress?" *The Atlantic,* December 1984, p. 64.

3. Ralph K. Huitt, "The Outsider in the Senate," *American Political Science Review* 55 (September 1961): 566–75.

4. Nelson W. Polsby, "Two Strategies of Influence: Choosing a Majority Leader, 1962," in *New Perspectives on the House of Representatives,* ed. Robert L. Peabody and Nelson W. Polsby, 2nd ed. (Chicago: Rand McNally, 1969), pp. 324–54.

5. Stephen Hess, *The Ultimate Insiders: U.S. Senators in the National Media* (Washington, D.C.: Brookings Institution, 1986), pp. 7–8.

6. Alan Ehrenhalt, "Media, Power Shifts Dominate O'Neill's House," *Congressional Quarterly Weekly Report,* September 13, 1986, p. 2137.

7. Michael J. Robinson, "Three Faces of Congressional Media," in *The New Congress,* ed. Thomas E. Mann and Norman J. Ornstein (Washington, D.C.: American Enterprise Institute, 1981), p. 94.

8. Ibid., p. 58.

9. Quoted in Nadine Cohadas, "Press Coverage: It's What You Do That Counts," *Congressional Quarterly Weekly Report,* January 3, 1987, p. 28.

10. Quoted in ibid.

11. See Hess, *Ultimate Insiders,* and Joe S. Foote and David J. Weber, "Network Evening News Visibility of Congressmen and Senators," paper presented at the annual meeting of the Association for Education in Journalism and Mass Communication, Gainesville, Fla., August 1984.

12. Hess, *Ultimate Insiders,* p. 6.

13. Ibid., p. 103.

14. Foote and Weber, "Network Evening News," tables 2, 4.

15. Timothy Cook, "Marketing the Members: The Ascent of the Congressional Press Secretary," paper presented at the annual meeting of the Midwest Political Science Association, Chicago, April 18–20, 1985, p. 6.

16. Easterbrook, "What's Wrong with Congress?" is an archetypal example.

17. Susan H. Miller, "Reporters and Congressmen: Living in Symbiosis," *Journalism Quarterly* 55 (1977): 667–73.

18. Hess, *Ultimate Insiders,* p. 45.

19. Quoted in Cohadas, "Press Coverage," p. 32.

20. Cook, "Marketing the Members," p. 6; Steven Hess, "A Note on Senate Press Secretaries and Media Strategies," discussion paper, Brookings Institution, Washington, D.C., April 1987.

21. Quoted in Cook, "Marketing the Members," p. 6.

22. Timothy Cook, "Determinants of Media Strategies in the House: Democrats in the 98th Congress," paper presented at the annual meeting of the American Political Science Association, Washington, D.C., August 28–31, 1986,

p. 11; see also Susan H. Miller, "News Coverage of Congress: The Search for the Ultimate Spokesman," *Journalism Quarterly* 54 (1976): 459–65.

23. Quoted in Bob Benenson, "Savvy 'Stars' Making Local TV a Potent Tool," *Congressional Quarterly Weekly Report,* July 18, 1987, p. 1552.

24. See Robinson, "Three Faces," and Norman Ornstein, "The Open Congress Meets the President," in *Both Ends of the Avenue,* ed. Anthony King (Washington, D.C.: American Enterprise Institute, 1983), pp. 200–202.

25. Hess, *Ultimate Insiders,* chap. 2.

26. Marjorie Randon Hershey, *Running for Office* (Chatham, N.J.: Chatham House, 1984), p. 41. See also Marjorie Randon Hershey, "Campaign Learning, Congressional Behavior, and Policy Change," in *Congress and Policy Change,* ed. Gerald C. Wright, Jr., Leroy N. Rieselbach, and Lawrence C. Dodd (New York: Agathon Press, 1986), pp. 148–72.

27. Ned Pattison, unpublished manuscript (n.p., 1979), chap. 13, p. 1.

28. In July 1975 the Congressional Research Service listed sixty-seven national articles on the class in its "Bibliography of Articles on House Freshman Members in 94th Congress" (Washington, D.C.: Congressional Research Service, 1975).

29. Michael Malbin, "A Year Older and Wiser, Freshmen Reassess Their Role," *National Journal,* February 14, 1976, p. 189.

30. Michele Ingrassia, "Politics: They're Taking Charge," *Newsday,* June 4, 1986, p. 5.

31. Ben Bradlee, Jr., "Can Toby Moffett Pick Up the Pieces?" *Boston Sunday Globe,* July 20, 1986, p. C2.

32. In 1976–78 Moffett received an average of eight citations per year in the *New York Times* index; as a subcommittee chair in 1979–81, he received an average of eighteen.

33. Elizabeth Drew, "Letter from Washington," *New Yorker,* July 7, 1986, p. 74.

34. Quoted in Katherin W. Evans, "The News Maker: A Capitol Hill Pro Reveals His Secrets," *Washington Journalism Review,* June 1981, p. 28.

35. Quoted in ibid.

36. Christopher J. Matthews, "The Old Breed Strikes Back," *New Republic,* March 2, 1987, p. 21.

37. See James Miller, *Running in Place: Inside the Senate* (New York: Simon & Schuster, 1986), pp. 128–31, 191.

38. Quoted in Christopher Madison, "Solarz's Brash Style Tempers His Quest for Influence in the Foreign Policy Arena," *National Journal,* October 26, 1985, p. 2414.

39. Paul West, "Competing for Coverage in Congress," *Washington Journalism Review,* June 1986, pp. 39–40.

40. Madison, "Solarz's Brash Style," p. 2414.

41. Ibid., p. 2417.

42. West, "Competing for Coverage," pp. 37–40.

43. Quoted in Ehrenhalt, "Media, Power Shifts," p. 2135.

44. Quoted in Evans, "News Maker," p. 32.

45. Benjamin I. Page, Robert Y. Shapiro, and Glenn R. Dempsey, "What Moves Public Opinion?" *American Political Science Review* 81 (March 1987): 23–44; Hess, *Ultimate Insiders,* chap. 7.

46. Cook, "Marketing the Members," p. 17.

47. Ehrenhalt, "Media, Power Shifts," p. 2134.

48. See James Payne et al., *The Motivations of Politicians* (Chicago: Nelson-Hall, 1984).
49. Cook, "Marketing the Members," pp. 15–16.
50. Evans, "News Maker," p. 33.

Chapter 5. Levels of the Game

1. Quoted in "Washington Talk," *New York Times,* December 2, 1987, p. B10.
2. Alan Ehrenhalt, "The Hunt for Power in Jim Wright's House," *Congressional Quarterly Weekly Report,* March 21, 1987, p. 543.
3. Michael Foley, *The New Senate* (New Haven: Yale University Press, 1980), p. 258.
4. Quoted in John F. Bibby, ed., *Congress off the Record* (Washington, D.C.: American Enterprise Institute, 1983), p. 51.
5. See Barbara Sinclair, "The Transformation of the U.S. Senate—Institutional Consequences of Behavioral Change," paper presented at the annual meeting of the Midwest Political Science Association, Chicago, April 9–11, 1987, p. 1.
6. Quoted in Andy Plattner, "The Lure of the Senate," *Congressional Quarterly Weekly Report,* May 25, 1985, p. 991.
7. Jack Walker, "Setting the Agenda in the U.S. Senate," *British Journal of Political Science* 7 (October 1977): 431.
8. See David Kozak, "House-Senate Differences: A Test Among Interview Data," paper presented at the annual meeting of the American Political Science Association, Washington, D.C., August 30–September 2, 1984; see also Norman Ornstein, "The New House and the New Senate," in *The New Congress,* ed. Thomas Mann and Norman Ornstein (Washington, D.C.: American Enterprise Institute, 1981), pp. 363–84.
9. Sinclair, "Transformation of the Senate," p. 25; Roger Davidson, "Senate Leaders: Janitors fcr an Untidy Chamber?" in *Congress Reconsidered,* ed. Lawrence Dodd and Bruce Oppenheimer, 3rd ed. (Washington, D.C.: CQ Press, 1985), pp. 225–52.
10. James Miller, *Running in Place* (New York: Simon & Schuster, 1986), p. 192.
11. Quoted in John Hyde, "Harkin Stumps with Message of Farm Crisis," *Des Moines Register,* July 13, 1986, p. A1.
12. Steve Smith has argued recently that senators, somewhat more than House members, use their committees as a base; see Smith, "Informed Leadership in the Senate: Opportunities, Resources, Motivations," paper presented for the Project on Congressional Leadership of the Everett McKinley Dirksen Congressional Center and the Congressional Research Service, Washington, D.C., September 30, 1987.
13. Barbara Sinclair, "Senate Norms, Senate Styles, and Senate Influence," paper presented at the annual meeting of the American Political Science Association, Washington, D.C., August 28–31, 1986, p. 18.
14. Linda Greenhouse, "Parental Leave Bill Debated in Senate," *New York Times,* February 2, 1987, p. A11. Dodd received consistent coverage on this issue throughout 1987.
15. Miller, *Running in Place,* p. 65.
16. John Kingdon, *Agendas, Alternatives, and Public Policies* (Boston: Little, Brown, 1984), p. 190.

17. Quoted in Margot Hornblower, "An Angry Man's Education on Getting Along Without Going Along," *Washington Post,* July 6, 1982, p. A6.

18. Quoted in Frank Musica, "Next Issue—The Nation's Water Infrastructure," *Civil Engineering,* May 1983, p. 104.

19. Julia Malone, "One Man's Crusade to Cure Congress of Pork-Barrel Practices," *Christian Science Monitor,* October 11, 1983, p. 3.

20. Hornblower, "Angry Man's Education," p. A6.

21. Stephen Gettinger, "House Narrowly Votes to Cut Funding for 31 Water Projects," *Congressional Quarterly Weekly Report,* June 8, 1985, pp. 1124–25.

22. Margery Lesser Elfin, "The Survivability of the Class of 1974," paper presented at the annual meeting of the American Political Science Association, Chicago, September 3–6, 1987, p. 19.

23. "Congressman Criticizes Funds for Bowling Alley," *New York Times,* September 17, 1985, p. A13.

24. Ibid.

25. Quoted in Bibby, ed., *Congress off the Record,* p. 50.

26. See Eric Uslaner, "The Decline of Comity in Congress," paper presented at the annual meeting of the Midwest Political Science Association, Chicago, April 9–11, 1987.

27. In an interview, Congressman Levitas noted with pleasure that he had "two law review articles coming out on the implications of the [Supreme Court's] *Chada* decision."

28. Quoted in Richard E. Cohen and Burt Solomon, "Congress's Rising Stars," *National Journal,* January 24, 1987, p. 181.

29. Ibid.

30. Richard E. Cohen, "On the Run with Richard Gephardt—A Day in the Life of a House Member," *National Journal,* October 8, 1983, pp. 2059–63.

31. Adapted from ibid.

32. Charles O. Jones, *The United States Congress: People, Place and Policy* (Homewood, Ill.: Dorsey Press, 1982), pp. 31–32.

33. See Barbara Sinclair, *Majority Party Leadership in the U.S. House of Representatives* (Baltimore: Johns Hopkins University Press, 1983); Burdett Loomis, "Congressional Careers and Party Leadership in the Contemporary House of Representatives," *American Journal of Political Science* 28 (February 1984): 180–201.

34. Jeffrey H. Birnbaum and Alan Murray, "Triumph of Tax Law Provides New Impetus on Other Tough Issues," *Wall Street Journal,* April 15, 1987, p. 1.

35. See Steve Smith, "Going to the Floor: Changing Patterns of Participation in the U.S. House of Representatives, 1955–1986," discussion paper, Brookings Institution, Washington, D.C., September 1987.

36. Stanley Bach, "Representatives and Committees on the Floor: Amendments to Appropriations Bills in the House of Representatives, 1963–1982," paper presented at the annual meeting of the American Political Science Association, New Orleans, August 29–September 1, 1985, p. 26.

37. Roger Davidson and Walter Oleszek, "From Monopoly to Interaction: Changing Patterns in Committee Management of Legislation in the House," paper presented at the annual meeting of the Midwest Political Science Association, Chicago, April 9–11, 1987.

38. Steve Smith, "Revolution in the House: Why Don't We Do It on the Floor?" paper presented at the annual meeting of the American Political Science Association, Washington, D.C., August 28–31, 1986, p. 43.

39. See Sinclair, *Majority Party Leadership,* chap. 2; Kenneth Entin, "Reform,

Leaders, and Leadership Networks in the House of Representatives," paper presented at the annual meeting of the American Political Science Association, Washington, D.C., August 28–31, 1986, pp. 17–19.

40. Cohen and Solomon, "Congress's Rising Stars," p. 186.

41. See the discussion of the housemates in Jeffrey Birnbaum and Alan Murray, *Showdown at Gucci Gulch* (New York: Random House, 1987), p. 130. As they note, such living arrangements recall an earlier day of shared roominghouses and even the "boardinghouse coalitions" of the first Congresses; see James Sterling Young, *The Washington Community, 1800–1828* (New York: Harcourt Brace Jovanovich, 1966).

42. Robert Pear, "Immigration Bill: How 'Corpse' Came Back to Life," *New York Times,* October 13, 1986, p. A17.

43. Ibid.

44. Quoted in Alan Ehrenhalt, "Media, Power Shifts Dominate O'Neill's House," *Congressional Quarterly Weekly Report,* September 13, 1986, p. 2133.

CHAPTER 6. The Congressional Enterprise: Offices and Caucuses

1. Terry Sullivan, *Procedural Structure* (New York: Praeger, 1984), chap. 7; James L. Sundquist, *The Decline and Resurgence of Congress* (Washington, D.C.: Brookings Institution, 1981), chap. 13.

2. See Susan Webb Hammond, Daniel P. Mulholland, and Arthur G. Stevens, Jr., "Congressional Caucuses and Agenda Setting," *Western Political Quarterly* 38 (December 1985): 583–605; and other works by Hammond. See also Samuel Kernell, *Going Public* (Washington, D.C.: CQ Press, 1986), pp. 26–32.

3. Much of the interview material reported in this chapter came from work originally done for the Congressional Management Project. Some results have been published in Burdett A. Loomis et al., *Setting Course: A Congressional Management Guide,* 1st and 2nd eds. (Washington, D.C.: American University and Congressional Management Foundation, 1984, 1986).

4. Richard E. Cohen and Burt Solomon, "Congress's Rising Stars," *National Journal,* January 24, 1987, pp. 176–89.

5. Norman J. Ornstein, Thomas E. Mann, and Michael J. Malbin, *Vital Statistics on Congress, 1987–1988* (Washington, D.C.: Congressional Quarterly, Inc., 1987), p. 153.

6. See U.S. Congress, *Final Report of the Commission on Administrative Review,* Volume 2: *Survey Materials* (Washington, D.C.: U.S. Government Printing Office, 1977).

7. Loomis et al., *Setting Course,* 2nd ed., p. 199. More generally, see Steven Frantzich, *Computers in Congress* (Beverly Hills, Calif.: Sage, 1982).

8. See Loomis et al., *Setting Course,* 2nd ed.

9. Leon E. Wynter, "It Takes a Heap of Data to Make a House a Home," *Wall Street Journal,* March 5, 1986, p. 1.

10. Ibid.

11. Ira Chaleff, *1987 Job Description, Salary and Staff Benefits Survey* (Washington, D.C.: Congressional Management Foundation, 1987), p. 5.

12. See Richard F. Fenno, Jr., *Home Style* (Boston: Little, Brown, 1978), pp. 136–70, on the significance of explanations.

13. Loomis et al., *Setting Course,* 1st ed., pp. 88–89.

14. Harrison W. Fox, Jr., and Susan Webb Hammond, *Congressional Staffs: The Invisible Force in American Lawmaking* (New York: Free Press, 1977), p. 179; Burdett A. Loomis, "The Congressional Office as Small (?) Business," *Publius* 9 (Summer 1979): 50.

15. Loomis et al., *Setting Course,* 1st ed., p. 80.

16. For example, see T. R. Reid, *Congressional Odyssey* (San Francisco: Freeman, 1980).

17. Michael Malbin, *Unelected Representatives: Congressional Staff and the Future of Representative Government* (New York: Basic Books, 1980), p. 93.

18. Robert Caro, *The Path to Power* (New York: Alfred A. Knopf, 1982), pp. 225–27; Fox and Hammond, *Congressional Staffs,* p. 4.

19. Chaleff, *1987 Survey,* p. 6.

20. See Timothy Cook, "Marketing the Members: The Ascent of the Congressional Press Secretary," paper presented at the annual meeting of the Midwest Political Science Association, Chicago, April 18–20, 1985; for the Senate, see Steven Hess, "A Note on Senate Press Secretaries and Media Strategies," discussion paper, Brookings Institution, Washington, D.C., April 1987.

21. Quoted in David Broder, *Changing of the Guard* (New York: Simon & Schuster, 1980), pp. 348–49.

22. Ornstein, Mann, and Malbin, *Vital Statistics,* pp. 144–45.

23. Quoted in "House Members Use District Office in Increasing Number, Many Different Ways," *Staff,* Summer 1975, p. 8. (*Staff* was a periodical published by the House of Representatives in the 1970s.)

24. John D. McCartney, "Congressional District Offices: Their Staff and Function," paper presented at the annual meeting of the American Political Science Association, Washington, D.C., August 31–September 3, 1979, p. 4.

25. See John R. Johannes, *To Serve the People: Congress and Constituency Service* (Lincoln: University of Nebraska Press, 1984).

26. Fox and Hammond, *Congressional Staffs,* p. 91.

27. Johannes, *To Serve the People,* p. 179.

28. See Morris Fiorina, *Congress: Keystone of the Washington Establishment* (New Haven: Yale University Press, 1977).

29. Laurily K. Epstein and Kathleen A. Francovic, "The Representative as Ward Boss," unpublished manuscript (n.p., n.d.), p. 3.

30. Robert Salisbury and Kenneth Shepsle, "U.S. Congressman as Enterprise," *Legislative Studies Quarterly* 6 (November 1981): 560.

31. Kernell, *Going Public,* pp. 26–32.

32. David Schribman, "Coalitions Are Skirting the Committee System and Changing Ideas About Clout on Capitol Hill," *Wall Street Journal,* March 11, 1985, p. 56.

33. Eric Uslaner, "Shale Barrel Politics: Energy Policy and Institutional Decentralization in the Congress," unpublished manuscript, University of Maryland, College Park, Md., n.d.

34. Susan Webb Hammond, "Congressional Caucuses and Policymaking," paper presented at the annual meeting of the American Political Science Association, New Orleans, August 29–September 1, 1985, p. 5.

35. Ibid., pp. 13–16.

36. Thomas P. O'Neill, *Man of the House* (New York: Random House, 1987), p. 285.

37. Margot Hornblower, "An Angry Man's Education on Getting Along Without Going Along," *Washington Post,* July 6, 1982, p. A6.
38. Schribman, "Coalitions Skirting Committee System," p. 56.
39. Ibid.
40. Alan Ehrenhalt, "Liberal Activists: Democratic Foot Soldiers," *Congressional Quarterly Weekly Report,* July 19, 1986, p. 1667.

Chapter 7. Enterprise, Position, and Influence

1. "Heroin and Cowardice," editorial, *New Republic,* February 25, 1985, p. 5.
2. Richard E. Neustadt, *Presidential Power,* rev. ed. (New York: John Wiley & Sons, 1977), p. 28.
3. See Steven Smith and Christopher Deering, *Committees in Congress* (Washington, D.C.: CQ Press, 1984), pp. 50–54, 89–119.
4. Gregg Easterbrook, "What's Wrong with Congress?" *The Atlantic,* December 1984, pp. 58–60, represents an archetypal case.
5. Smith and Deering, *Committees in Congress,* p. 198.
6. Burdett A. Loomis, "Congressional Careers and Party Leadership in the Contemporary House of Representatives," *American Journal of Political Science* 28 (February 1984): 180–201; Kenneth Entin, "Reform, Leaders, and Leadership Networks in the House of Representatives," paper presented at the annual meeting of the American Political Science Association, Washington, D.C., August 28–31, 1986.
7. Charles Tidmarch, "Making Subcommittees Work: The Case of the House Committee on Energy and Commerce," paper presented at the annual meeting of the Midwest Political Science Association, Chicago, April 10–12, 1986, pp. 7–10.
8. Jacqueline Calmes and Rob Gurwitt, "Profiles in Power: Leaders Without Portfolio," *Congressional Quarterly Weekly Report,* January 3, 1987, p. 18.
9. Tidmarch, "Making Subcommittees Work," pp. 11–14.
10. Dave Anderson, "Boxing's 'Accountability,'" *New York Times,* March 20, 1983, sec. 5, p. 3.
11. Paul Starobin, "Energy, Commerce Shake Up May Boost Rail Law Revisions," *Congressional Quarterly Weekly Report,* February 14, 1987, p. 292.
12. Ibid.
13. Christopher Deering and Steven Smith, "Subcommittees in Congress," in *Congress Reconsidered,* ed. Lawrence Dodd and Bruce Oppenheimer, 3rd ed. (Washington, D.C.: CQ Press, 1985), p. 206.
14. Ibid., p. 207.
15. Quoted in David E. Price, "Congressional Committees in the Policy Process," in *Congress Reconsidered,* ed. Dodd and Oppenheimer, p. 182.
16. Quoted in Dale Tate, "An Unrepentant Boll Weevil Bolts Party," *Congressional Quarterly Weekly Report,* January 5, 1983, p. 5.
17. Quoted in Jeffrey Birnbaum, "Congress Pokes Again at Perennial Problem, the Budgetary System," *Wall Street Journal,* February 27, 1987, p. 1.
18. These fifteen include Democrats Brodhead, Derrick (twice), Downey, Fisher, Hefner, Miller, Mineta, Oberstar, Russo, Simon, Solarz, and Wirth, and Republicans Goodling, Gradison, and Moore.
19. See John Ellwood, "The Great Exception: The Congressional Budget Process in an Age of Decentralization," in *Congress Reconsidered,* ed. Dodd and

Oppenheimer, pp. 315–42; see also Lance LeLoup, *Budgetary Politics,* 3rd ed. (Brunswick, Ohio: King's Court Press, 1986), chap. 6.

20. Talk at the Brookings Institution, Washington, D.C., February 12, 1985.

21. Steven Schier, "Thinking About the Macroeconomy: The House and Senate Budget Committees in the 1980s," paper presented at the annual meeting of the American Political Science Association, New Orleans, August 29–September 1, 1985, p. 15.

22. Martin Tolchin, "Democratic 'Gang of Five' Reflect New Party Priorities," *New York Times,* June 1, 1980, sec. 4, p. 2. Congressman William Brodhead, a class of '74 member, represented the fifth member of the "gang."

23. Ibid.

24. Witness then–Majority Leader Jim Wright's chagrin at sponsoring the successful Budget Committee candidacy of fellow Texan Phil Gramm in 1981. See Dennis Farney, "Jim Wright, Activist and Yet Reflective, Strives to Rally Democrats," *Wall Street Journal,* July 7, 1981, p. 1; see also Ross K. Baker, "Party and Institutional Sanctions in the U.S. House: The Case of Congressman Gramm," *Legislative Studies Quarterly* 10 (August 1985): 318.

25. Quoted in Alan Ehrenhalt, "Media, Power Shifts Dominate O'Neill's House," *Congressional Quarterly Weekly Report,* September 13, 1986, p. 2137.

26. Michael Munger, "Allocation of Desirable Committee Assignments: Extended Queues vs. Committee Expansion," unpublished manuscript, Austin, Tex., September 1986, p. 11.

27. Schier, "Thinking About the Macroeconomy," p. 11.

28. Quoted in Birnbaum, "Congress Pokes Again," p. 1.

29. Schier, "Thinking About the Macroeconomy," p. 11.

30. Barbara Sinclair, *Majority Leadership in the U.S. House of Representatives* (Baltimore: Johns Hopkins University Press, 1983), p. 29; Thomas P. O'Neill, *Man of the House* (New York: Random House, 1987), pp. 286–88.

31. Quoted in Entin, "Reform, Leaders, and Leadership Networks," p. 21.

32. Barbara Sinclair, "The Speaker's Task Force in the Post-Reform House of Representatives," *American Political Science Review* 75 (June 1981): 397–410.

33. James C. Garand and Kathleen M. Clayton, "Socialization to Partisanship in the U.S. House: The Speaker's Task Force," *Legislative Studies Quarterly* 11 (August 1986): 409–28.

34. Sinclair, *Majority Leadership,* pp. 139–40.

35. Entin, "Reform, Leaders, and Leadership Networks," p. 21; Sinclair, *Majority Leadership,* pp. 139–40.

36. Alan Ehrenhalt, "Influence on the Hill: Having It and Using It," *Congressional Quarterly Weekly Report,* January 3, 1987, p. 3.

37. Quoted in Steven V. Roberts, "Watching the Pendulum of Powers of Congress," *New York Times,* October 23, 1986, p. A24.

Chapter 8. Rust Never Sleeps: The Congressional Enterprise as Campaign

1. Burt Solomon, "When Fat Cats Cry," *National Journal,* February 21, 1987, p. 419.

2. Ibid.

3. Robert Salisbury and Kenneth Shepsle, "The U.S. Congressman as Enterprise," *Legislative Studies Quarterly* 6 (November 1981): 560–62.

4. Gary Jacobson, "The Marginals Never Vanished: Incumbency and Competition in Elections to the U.S. House of Representatives, 1952–1982," *American Journal of Political Science* 31 (February 1987): 126–41. The 1984 and 1986 elections were very pro-incumbent, however.

5. See Thomas Mann, *Unsafe at any Margin* (Washington, D.C.: American Enterprise Institute, 1978).

6. See Jacobson, "Marginals Never Vanished"; but see also John A. Ferejohn, "On the Decline of Competition in Congressional Elections," *American Political Science Review* 71 (March 1977): 166–76; Melissa P. Collie, "Incumbency, Electoral Safety, and Turnover in the House of Representatives, 1952–1976," *American Political Science Review* 75 (March 1981): 119–31.

7. Jacobson, "Marginals Never Vanished," 129–31.

8. For the beginnings here, see David Mayhew, *Congress: The Electoral Connection* (New Haven: Yale University Press, 1974), and his "Congressional Elections: The Case of the Vanishing Marginals," *Polity* 6 (1974): 295–317. More generally, see Lyn Ragsdale, "Legislative Elections and Legislative Responsiveness," in *Handbook of Legislative Research,* ed. Gerhard Loewenberg, Samuel C. Patterson, and Malcolm E. Jewell (Cambridge, Mass.: Harvard University Press, 1985), pp. 57–96.

9. See Morris Fiorina, *Congress: Keystone of the Washington Establishment* (New Haven: Yale University Press, 1977); Keith Kreibel and John R. Wright, "The Incumbency Effect in Congressional Elections: A Test of Two Hypotheses," *American Journal of Political Science* 27 (February 1983): 140–57.

10. See Edie Goldenberg and Michael Traugott, *Campaigning for Congress* (Washington, D.C.: CQ Press, 1984), chap. 7; Gary Jacobson, *Money in Congressional Elections* (New Haven: Yale University Press, 1980); Thomas A. Kazee, "The Deterrent Effect of Incumbency on Recruiting Challengers in U.S. House Elections," *Legislative Studies Quarterly* 8 (August 1983): 469–80.

11. See Jon R. Bond, Cary Covington, and Richard Fleisher, "Explaining Challenger Quality in Congressional Elections," *Journal of Politics* 47 (May 1985): 510–30.

12. Dom Bonafede, "Ideological and Tactical Differences Spice Wirth v. Buechner House Race," *National Journal,* July 17, 1982, p. 1599.

13. Burdett A. Loomis et al., *Setting Course: A Congressional Management Guide,* 2nd ed. (Washington, D.C.: American University and Congressional Management Foundation, 1986), pp. 86–87.

14. Mayhew, *Electoral Connection,* p. 49; Burdett Loomis, "The Congressional Office as Small (?) Business," *Publius* 9 (Summer 1979): 53.

15. Norman J. Ornstein, Thomas E. Mann, and Michael J. Malbin, *Vital Statistics on Congress, 1987–1988* (Washington, D.C.: Congressional Quarterly Inc., 1987), p. 144.

16. Quoted in John McCartney, "Congressional District Offices: Their Staff and Functions," paper presented at the annual meeting of the American Political Science Association, Washington, D.C., August 31–September 3, 1979, p. 48.

17. Ibid.

18. Norman Ornstein, *Vital Statistics on Congress, 1984–1985 Edition* (Washington, D.C.: American Enterprise Institute, 1984), p. 69; Common Cause, "14 Senators Elected in 1986 Are PAC Millionaires," news release, Washington, D.C., February 13, 1987, p. 3.

19. Data from Common Cause news releases: "Almost Half of U.S. Representatives Received 50% or More of Campaign Funds from PACs," Washington,

D.C., April 7, 1987; "14 Senators Elected"; and "House Incumbents Get Nearly 40% More PAC Money in 1983," Washington, D.C., March 20, 1984.

20. "Inside Washington," *National Journal,* February 28, 1987, p. 465.

21. Common Cause, "Almost Half of U.S. Representatives," chart VIII.

22. Common Cause, "House Incumbents Get 44¢ of Every Campaign Dollar from PACs in 1984 Election," news release, Washington, D.C., April 12, 1985, pp. 5–6.

23. Common Cause, "House Incumbents Get 44¢," chart VII.

24. Common Cause, "Almost Half of U.S. Representatives," p. 4.

25. See Kevin Chaffee, "Money Under the Mattress: What Congressmen Don't Spend," *Washington Monthly,* September 1984, pp. 32–38.

26. Kenneth Noble, "Some in House Using Excess Election Cash for Expensive Living," *New York Times,* April 3, 1983, p. A1; Chaffee, "Money Under the Mattress," pp. 34–35.

27. Peter Bragdon, "In 'Permanent Campaign' Era, Members' Funds Find Many Uses," *Congressional Quarterly Weekly Report,* September 12, 1987, p. 2187.

28. See Bill Hogan, Diane Kiesel, and Alan Green, "The Senate's Secret Slush Funds," *New Republic,* June 20, 1983, pp. 13–20.

29. Letter from Congressman William Boner, *Common Cause Magazine,* February/March 1986, p. 4.

30. Common Cause, "House Incumbents Get 44¢," chart VII.

31. Common Cause, "Almost Half of U.S. Representatives," chart VII.

32. Ibid., p. 6.

33. Chaffee, "Money Under the Mattress," p. 37.

34. Quoted in Thomas Edsall, "More Than Enough is Not Enough," *Washington Post National Weekly Edition,* February 9, 1986, p. 16.

35. Steven V. Roberts, "Another New Twist to the Games the PAC Men Play," *New York Times,* August 12, 1986, p. A24.

36. Cited in "Personal PACs," *New York Times,* September 9, 1987, p. A16.

37. Common Cause, "Almost Half of U.S. Representatives," chart VII.

38. Jacqueline Calmes and Rob Gurwitt, "Profiles in Power: Leaders Without Portfolio," *Congressional Quarterly Weekly Report,* January 3, 1987, p. 18.

39. See Barbara G. Salmore and Stephen A. Salmore, "Back to Basics: Party as Legislative Caucus," paper presented at the annual meeting of the Midwest Political Science Association, April 9–11, 1987, p. 35.

40. Sidney Blumenthal, *The Permanent Campaign* (New York: Touchstone, 1982), p. 23.

41. Bragdon, " 'Permanent Campaign' Era," p. 2187.

42. See Margery Lesser Elfin, "The Survivability of the Class of 1974," paper presented at the annual meeting of the American Political Science Association, Chicago, September 3–6, 1987; Charles Tidmarch, "The Second Time Around: Freshman Democratic House Members' 1976 Reelection Experiences," paper presented at the annual meeting of the American Political Science Association, Washington, D.C., September 1–4, 1977; and Stephen Brown, Beth Fuchs, and John Hoadley, "Congressional Perquisites and Vanishing Marginals: The Case of the Class of '74," paper presented at the annual meeting of the American Political Science Association, Washington, D.C., August 31–September 3, 1979.

43. Steven V. Roberts, "The Life of a Watergate Baby," *New York Times,* May 13, 1986, p. A24.

44. Alan Ehrenhalt, "Liberal Activists: Democratic Foot Soldiers," *Congressional Quarterly Weekly Report,* July 19, 1986, p. 1667.

45. Common Cause, "Almost Half of U.S. Representatives," House appendix; Common Cause, "House Incumbents Get 44¢," House appendix.

46. Gary Jacobson, *The Politics of Congressional Elections* (Boston: Little, Brown, 1987), pp. 76–77.

47. Glenn Parker, "Is There a Political Life-Cycle in the House?" paper presented at the annual meeting of the American Political Science Association, Washington, D.C., August 28–31, 1986.

48. Goldenberg and Traugott, *Campaigning for Congress,* p. 22.

49. Mayhew, *Electoral Connection,* p. 84.

50. See Larry Light, "Crack 'Outreach' Programs No Longer Ensure Reelection," *Congressional Quarterly Weekly Report,* February 14, 1981, pp. 316–18.

51. Ibid., p. 316.

52. Ibid.

53. Ibid., p. 318.

54. Michael Barone, Grant Ujifusa, and Douglas Matthews, *The Almanac of American Politics 1980* (New York: E. P. Dutton, 1979), p. 584.

55. Alan Ehrenhalt, ed., *Politics in America 1982* (Washington, D.C.: CQ Press, 1981), p. 1251.

56. Ibid., p. 1038.

57. Loomis et al., *Setting Course,* p. 35.

58. Tom Watson, "Machines: Something Old, Something New," *Congressional Quarterly Weekly Report,* August 17, 1985, p. 1619.

59. See, for example, Robert Salisbury, "An Exchange Theory of Interest Groups," *Midwest Journal of Political Science* 13 (February 1969): 1–32.

60. See Gary Jacobson, "Money in the 1980 and 1982 Congressional Elections," in *Money and Politics in the United States* (Chatham, N.J.: Chatham House, 1984), pp. 38–69.

CHAPTER 9. Ambition: A New Era, a Timeless Drive

1. Michael J. Malbin, "What Did the Framers Want Congress to Be—And Who Cares?" paper presented at the annual meeting of the American Political Science Association, Denver, September 2–5, 1982, p. 4.

2. Ibid.

3. Ibid., p. 39.

4. See Nelson Polsby, "The Institutionalization of the House of Representatives," *American Political Science Review* 62 (March 1968): 144–68.

5. Norman Ornstein, "The Open Congress Meets the President," in *Both Ends of the Avenue,* ed. Thomas Mann and Norman Ornstein (Washington, D.C.: American Enterprise Institute, 1983), pp. 29–30.

6. Ross Baker, "What's in It for Me?" paper presented at the annual meeting of the American Political Science Association, New Orleans, August 29–September 1, 1985, pp. 27, 31.

7. Joseph Schlesinger, *Ambition and Politics* (Chicago: Rand McNally, 1966), pp. 20–24.

8. See Paul Brace, "Progressive Ambition in the House: A Probabilistic Approach," *Journal of Politics* 46 (May 1984): 556–71; David T. Canon and David J. Sousa, "Realigning Elections and Political Career Structures in the U.S. Congress," paper presented at the annual meeting of the American Political Science Association, Chicago, September 3–6, 1987, pp. 13–14; David W. Rohde, "Risk

Bearing and Progressive Ambition: The Case of Members of the House of Representatives," *American Journal of Political Science* 23 (February 1979): 1–26.

9. Robert L. Peabody, Norman J. Ornstein, and David W. Rohde, "The United States Senate as Presidential Incubator: Many Are Called but Few Are Chosen," *Political Science Quarterly* 91 (Summer 1976): 237–58.

10. Richard F. Fenno, Jr., "If, as Ralph Nader Says, Congress Is 'The Broken Branch,' How Come We Love Our Congressmen So Much?" in *Congress in Change,* ed. Norman Ornstein (New York: Praeger, 1975), p. 287.

11. Michael Barone and Grant Ujifusa, eds., *The Almanac of American Politics 1984* (Washington, D.C.: National Journal, 1983), p. 1277.

12. Baker, "What's in It for Me?" p. 24.

13. Jeffrey H. Birnbaum and Alan S. Murray, *Showdown at Gucci Gulch* (New York: Random House, 1987), p. 110.

14. David Broder, "Gephardt Must Protect Credibility," *Lawrence* (Kans.) *Journal-World,* April 27, 1987, p. A4.

15. Linda Wertheimer, on National Public Radio's "Morning Edition," March 28, 1988.

16. Jacqueline Calmes, citing political scientist Robert Peabody, in "The Hill Leaders: Their Places on the Ladder," *Congressional Quarterly Weekly Report,* January 3, 1987, p. 6.

17. Robert A. Caro, *The Path to Power* (New York: Alfred A. Knopf, 1982), chap. 31.

18. See Burdett Loomis, "On Knife's Edge: Politicians and the Life Cycle," *PS* 17 (Summer 1984): 536–42; Ward Just, *The Congressman Who Loved Flaubert* (New York: E. P. Dutton, 1973), p. 14; Daniel J. Levinson, *The Seasons of a Man's Life* (New York: Ballantine, 1981); Paul Hain, "Age, Ambitions, and Political Careers: The Middle-aged Crisis," *Western Political Quarterly* 27 (1984): 265–74.

19. Quoted in John Hyde, "Iowa's Junior Senator Flexes His Muscles on New Playing Field," *Des Moines Register,* July 21, 1985, p. A1.

20. Quoted in Andy Plattner, "The Lure of the Senate: Influence and Prestige," *Congressional Quarterly Weekly Report,* May 25, 1985, p. 991.

21. Transcript of interview conducted by Paul Duke for public television station WETA, Washington, D.C., 1984.

22. Quoted in Plattner, "Lure of the Senate," p. 992.

23. See David C. Kozak, "House-Senate Differences: A Test Among Interview Data," paper presented at the annual meeting of the American Political Science Association, Washington, D.C., August 30–September 2, 1984.

24. John Hibbing, "Voluntary Retirement from the U.S. House: The Costs of Congressional Service," *Legislative Studies Quarterly* 7 (February 1982): 57–74; Joseph Cooper and William West, "The Congressional Career in the 1970's," in *Congress Reconsidered,* ed. Lawrence Dodd and Bruce Oppenheimer, 2nd ed. (Washington, D.C.: CQ Press, 1981), pp. 83–106.

25. Aaron Wildavsky, "The Past and Future Presidency," *Public Interest,* Fall 1975, pp. 62–63.

26. Hibbing, "Voluntary Retirement," 72.

27. Richard F. Fenno, Jr., *Home Style* (Boston: Little, Brown, 1978), p. 168.

28. Ellen Goodman, "Tsongas: Gaining Real Time," *Washington Post,* January 21, 1984, p. A15.

29. Richard E. Cohen, "On the Run with Richard Gephardt—A Day in the Life of a House Member," *National Journal,* October 8, 1983, pp. 2059–63.

30. Quoted in David Schribman, "Lawmakers Find Life in Congress Can Cause Family Life to Unravel," *Wall Street Journal,* April 29, 1986, p. 1.

31. Transcript of interview conducted by Paul Duke for WETA.

32. Tip O'Neill argues that he "more or less" ended evening sessions in the House, but most members with young children would not support this claim; see Thomas P. O'Neill, *Man of the House* (New York: Random House, 1987), p. 274.

33. Michael Kilian, "Paul Simon—Off to a Running Start," *Chicago Tribune Magazine,* June 8, 1986, p. 11.

34. Quoted in Lawrence Meyer, "Washington Looks Best Through a Rear-View Mirror," *Washington Post,* January 6, 1985, p. C3.

35. Quoted in James A. Barnes, "Partisanship," *National Journal,* November 7, 1987, p. 2825.

Chapter 10. The Substance of a New Style

1. Quoted in Bill Peterson, "Another Midwesterner Trying to Put on Harry Truman's Shoes," *Washington Post National Weekly Edition,* December 7, 1987, p. 15.

2. See Steven S. Smith, "New Patterns of Decisionmaking in Congress," in *The New Direction in American Politics,* ed. John E. Chubb and Paul E. Peterson (Washington, D.C.: Brookings Institution, 1985), pp. 203–34; see also Roger Davidson and Walter Oleszek, *Congress and Its Members,* 2nd ed. (Washington, D.C.: CQ Press, 1985), chap. 6.

3. James Sundquist, *Politics and Policy* (Washington, D.C.: Brookings Institution, 1968), pt. 2.

4. Alan Ehrenhalt, "Early Hill Retirements: The Ebb and Flow," *Congressional Quarterly Weekly Report,* January 1, 1984, p. 71.

5. See Albert O. Hirschman, *Exit, Voice, and Loyalty* (Cambridge, Mass.: Harvard University Press, 1970).

6. Alan Ehrenhalt, "Influence on the Hill," *Congressional Quarterly Weekly Report,* January 1, 1987, p. 3.

7. Quoted in Andy Plattner, "The Lure of the Senate: Prestige and Influence," *Congressional Quarterly Weekly Report,* May 25, 1985, p. 988.

8. Quoted in Jonathan Fuerbringer, "Senator Chiles Is Retiring, Saying His Old Zeal Is Gone," *New York Times,* December 8, 1987, p. A1.

9. Quoted in Alan Ehrenhalt, "Early Hill Retirements," p. 71.

10. See Richard F. Fenno, Jr., *Home Style* (Boston: Little, Brown, 1978); Gregg Easterbrook, "What's Wrong with Congress?" *The Atlantic,* December 1984, pp. 57–84.

11. Fuerbringer, "Senator Chiles," p. A1.

12. Ibid.

INDEX